JAMES BALDWIN

A Critical Evaluation

Also edited by Therman B. O'Daniel

Langston Hughes—Black Genius: A Critical Evaluation

JAMES BALDWIN

A Critical Evaluation

EDITED BY *Therman B. O'Daniel*

for the College Language Association

HOWARD UNIVERSITY PRESS WASHiNGTON, D.C. 1981

Copyright © 1977 by the College Language Association

Second printing 1979
First paperback edition 1981

Printed in the United States of America

Library of Congress Cataloging in Publication Data

O'Daniel, Therman B. 1908–
  James Baldwin, a critical evaluation.

  Bibliography: p.
  1. Baldwin, James, 1924– —Criticism and interpre-
tation. I. College Language Association. II. Title.
PS3552.A45Z84   818′.5′409   74–30006
ISBN (paperback) 0–88258–091–4
ISBN (clothbound) 0–88258–047–7

Grateful acknowledgments are made to the following:

The Johnson Publishing Company, Inc., for permission to reprint the following article from *Black World,* XXI, No. 8 (June, 1972), 28–34, "Thematic Patterns in Baldwin's Essays" by Eugenia Collier.

The College Language Association for permission to reprint the following essays from its official publication,

CLA Journal, VII, No. 2 (December 1963), 133–140, "James Baldwin: The Black and the Red-White-and-Blue" by John V. Hagopian;

CLA Journal, VII, No. 3 (March, 1964), 202–214, "Baldwin and the Problem of Being" by George E. Kent;

CLA Journal, VIII, No. 2 (December, 1964), 132–140, "Baldwin Beside Himself: A Study in Modern Phallicism" by John S. Lash; and

CLA Journal, IX, No. 1 (September, 1965), 12–24, "A Note on *Blues for Mister Charlie,* pp. 20–21, an excerpt from "The Contemporary American Playwright" by Waters E. Turpin.

To Donald B. Gibson for permission to print, "James Baldwin: The Political Anatomy of Space." Copyright © 1975 by Donald B. Gibson.

Indiana State University for permission to reprint the following essays from its journal,

Negro American Literature Forum, III, No. 1 (Spring, 1969), 26–29, "James Baldwin's 'Previous Condition': A Problem of Identification" by Sam Bluefarb; and

Negro American Literature Forum, IV, No. 2 (July, 1970), 56–60, " 'Sonny's Blues': James Baldwin's Image of Black Community" by John M. Reilly.

Atlanta University for permission to reprint the following essay from *Phylon,* XXV, No. 3, Third Quarter (Fall, 1964), 288–296, "The Phrase Unbearably Repeated" by Eugenia W. Collier.

To the memory of my aunt—
 Mrs. Margaret Williams Hines
 and
To my brother and his wife—
 Robert and Louise O'Daniel

Preface

J ames Baldwin: A Critical Evaluation is the second in a series of comprehensive studies of major twentieth-century Afro-American authors issued by the College Language Association. Like the earlier book on Langston Hughes, most of the essays—seventeen of the twenty-three, were written by members of the Association, who, like the other six contributing authors, are all serious students of James Baldwin and his works. Like the first book, also, this one contains a few essays—eight of the twenty–three—which appeared earlier in well-known publications: four in the *CLA Journal;* two in *Negro American Literature Forum;* and one each in *Phylon* and *Black World;* but the remaining fifteen pieces—nearly two–thirds of the total—were either written specifically for this collection, or, as in two instances, were selected for inclusion in it from recently completed and unpublished research.

Furthermore, this book, rightfully, may be called a comprehensive study because the essays in it have been carefully selected to cover and evaluate all major products of Baldwin's writing career. In them we see this well-publicized contemporary American author as novelist, essayist, playwright, short story writer, scenarist, and even as a skilled professional in the currently popular genre known as *rapping*. Thus, studious attention is given to Baldwin's *Go Tell It on the Mountain,* as well as to certain short stories that predate this novel, and to all of his principal works including the recent *Tell Me How Long the Train's Been Gone* and *If Beale Street Could Talk.*

As editor, I thank the College Language Association, publisher of the *CLA Journal;* and the publishers of *Negro American Literature Forum, Phylon,* and *Black World* for granting me permission to use the copyrighted material herein reprinted.

I am happy to thank the following contributing authors, individually, for granting me permission to reprint their essays: Professors John V. Hagopian, George E. Kent, John S. Lash, Jean F. Turpin, and the late Waters E. Turpin, whose essays first appeared in the *CLA Journal;* Professors Sam Bluefarb and John M. Reilly, who first published their studies in *Negro American Literature Forum;* and Professor Eugenia W. Collier for her two articles, one published in *Phylon* and the other in *Black World*. Also, I thank Professors Shirley S. Allen, A. Russell Brooks (for two contributions), William Edward Farrison, Nick Aaron Ford, Donald B. Gibson, Hobart Jarrett, Harry L. Jones, Arthenia Bates Millican, Carlton W. Molette, Jacqueline E. Orsagh, Patsy Brewington Perry, Darwin T. Turner, and Kenneth J. Zahorski, whose essays are here printed for the first time by their kind permission.

Again I am indebted to Professor William Edward Farrison, not only for contributing one of the important essays, but for many valuable suggestions while the book was in progress; to the library staff of Morgan State University for prompt and courteous assistance in many ways and on many occasions when it was needed; and to Phil W. Petrie, executive editor, Howard University Press, who was always available with expert advice and friendly suggestions.

Lastly, I thank my wife, Lillian, for her patience, her enthusiastic interest in my work, and her words of encouragement.

1975   Therman B. O'Daniel

Contents

Baldwin as

_____ Novelist

James Baldwin: The Political Anatomy Of Space[1]

Donald B. Gibson

"The only space which means anything to me," I said,
"is the space between myself and other people."

—LEO PROUDHAMMER in *Tell Me How Long the Train's Been Gone*

Through the course of his career James Baldwin has come closer to engagement in political affairs than most American writers. He has not, as have some European writers, actually engaged in affairs of state: American writers almost never do. Yet he has written a good deal of social commentary in which he has indicated support of certain political ideals and disdain for others. On at least one notable occasion he met with the Attorney General, then Robert Kennedy, with intention of participating in discussion relating to the solution of the racial problem.[2] He has as well given many speeches about race in which he has advocated certain political positions and denigrated others. The expression of attitudes of a political character has not been limited to his essays, speeches, and public dialogues. His novels have also been a vehicle for the expression of his thinking, his values, his general social orientation. They are indeed a clear record of the development of his thought about social matters, as clear a record as any available.

His outspokenness, his unwillingness to bite his tongue when speaking out on racial matters, the seriousness of his tone, and his tendency to speak in apocalyptic terms have all probably gone to convince many that Baldwin is a political radical. This is by no means the case. Essentially a moralist, Baldwin has continually spoken about racism as a moral problem and has rarely related it, until very recently, to social forces of other kinds.[3] He is primarily an institutionalist who has been critical of the society almost exclusively in regard to moral affairs. He has only recently begun to speak at all about the relation of racism to other social phenomena, having assigned it in his mind to the realm of morality. In this regard he has distinguished himself from black nationalists and socialists, who have tended to see the problem and its solution far more in economic and cultural terms than he. He has remained for the most part traditional in his orientation.[4] His fiction traces modifications in his basic outlook, significant modifications, but not *essential* changes. His progress from a roundly conservative outlook to one considerably less so is recorded in his fiction from *Go Tell It on the Mountain* to *Tell Me How Long the Train's Been Gone.*

Go Tell It on the Mountain is not only Baldwin's most coherent and unified novel, it is as well an apt testament of Baldwin's basic sense of the way things are. An autobiographical novel, it describes the life of a young boy, John Grimes, from his early years to his adolescence, its focus being on his status within the family and his relation to his father, Gabriel. John is the innocent victim of his father, a religious man steeped in hatred and narrowness, who is self-righteous, sadistic and inordinately authoritarian. While John is powerless to deal with his father except to acquiesce to his demands, he finally reaches adolescence, at which time he rebels in the only way psychically available to him, through successfully competing with his father within the church. The novel describes the progress of John's maturation and the background out of which his life situation proceeds.

The terms in which the story is told suggest something of the scope of the action. Whereas the actual events are somewhat commonplace ones not uncharacteristic of the lives of poor people, it is clear that those events are invested with significance far beyond their actuality. The novel is intended to be cosmic in scope, the interaction, in ordinary terms, between conflicting ultimates. John is the force of love; Gabriel of evil. The plot affirms the victory of love over evil and the denouement of historical necessity. That Baldwin has been known to think in terms of historical necessity is not strange to readers even generally familiar with his work. His reference, for example, to the idea of cosmic vengeance suggested at the end of "Down at the Cross: Letter from a Region in My Mind" is a case in point.

> If we do not now dare everything, the fulfillment of that prophecy, re-created from the Bible in song by a slave, is upon us: *God gave Noah the rainbow sign, No more water, the fire next time!*[5]

This is not intended to be hyperbolic, rhetoric merely. It reflects what seems to be Baldwin's basic belief that there exist outside the natural world forces to which man is accountable and that his lack of accountability will evoke punishment. The above quotation appeared originally in 1962, but Baldwin has said similar things in more recent times. In his recorded conversation with Margaret Mead, *A Rap on Race,* he reiterates the notion of retributive justice in stating that slavery is a crime that demands atonement as does all sin. The context in which he puts this, "Maybe I am an Old New England, Old Testament prophet . . . " and slavery "is the crime which is spoken of in the Bible," makes it clear that he is not speaking in sociological terms.[6] Though Baldwin does not explicitly speak here of vengeance being visited upon the perpetrator of crime, the implication is clear enough. Crime or sin affects the course of events in nature. The commission of evil so influences history as to determine that its course will run in such a way as to bring about retribution. This is all reflected in the plot of *Go Tell It on the Mountain.* The pasts of the individuals described there have all been directed toward the time on the threshing floor during which John's problem is worked out, and the terms in which the problem is worked out suggest the operation of forces existing beyond the province of the natural.

The cosmic scope of the novel is reflected in its style and in the large-scale religious framework within which the story is conceived and executed. The quality of the style, its biblical intonations, its authority, all are rooted in Christian tradition. The rhetoric of the novel, its parallel constructions and repetitions of words and phrases, its frequently archaic character and high seriousness all point toward the author's sense of a level of reality beyond the natural. Such passages as the following are common throughout the novel and they serve, in their style alone, to indicate something of the author's sense of the great weight brought to bear on the events of the novel by the tradition to which it refers.

> And he began to shout for help, seeing before him the lash, the fire, and the depthless water, seeing his head bowed down forever, he John, the lowest among these lowly. And he looked for his mother, but her eyes were fixed on this dark army—she was claimed by this army. And his father would not help him, his father did not see him, and Roy lay dead.[7]

> But he could never go through this darkness, through this fire and this wrath. He never could go through. His strength was finished, and he could not move. He belonged to the darkness—the darkness from which he had thought to flee had claimed him. And he moaned again, weeping, and lifted up his hands. (P. 275)

These typical passages reveal through their style, especially their tone, the writer's attitude toward the cosmic context in which the events of the story transpire. It would be one thing if the religiosity of the novel were confined to the outlooks of the characters themselves. If that were the case, then we should expect to find distance indicated between the perspectives of the author and characters. As it is, however, the supernatural dimension of the novel is never questioned. There is no disparity between the author's view and his characters' views in this regard. This observation is significant because it bears directly on the plot of the novel and on the novel's ultimate philosophical (perhaps better, *theological*) meaning.

The resolution of the plot comes about when John achieves his salvation on the threshing floor. What is resolved? All the fears, anxieties, tensions of John's life up to that point are washed away. His father is finally seen by John in "proper" perspective. He has, that is, changed his relation to Gabriel and will no longer be dominated by him. He has divested Gabriel of authority by transference of his allegiance from his earthly to his Heavenly Father. The salient point in the threshing-floor episode is the lack of distance between the author and the main character. Another writer might have seen the dynamics of the scene as indicating the resolution of the relation between father and son, and the particular mode it takes as simply the vehicle through which the transformation occurs. As it is, the author believes as much as the character in the contextual scheme. Hence there is no irony or ambiguity present. John's religious experience is seen not as a subterfuge for dealing with a difficult and not unusual psychic phenomenon—the tension between fathers and sons during adolescence—but rather as in itself true and real. This means, then, that John's experience is a truly Christian one, that the novel is a Christian novel and that it points to what the author conceives to be a sphere of reality beyond the experiential.

The style and plot resolution are only two of the facets of the novel pointing to the writer's commitment to the scheme of Christianity described there. There are as well the title of the novel, its section titles, the epigraphs (to the book, to the sections, and to the interchapters). These are all quotations from the King James Bible or from spirituals or gospel songs. The text is heavily interlarded with similar quotations, with words, phrases, and sentences from the same contexts. Here again the matter of tone is important, because a novel could conceivably be written that would rely heavily upon the Christian tradition yet would view that tradition with varying degrees of skepticism, irony, or ambivalence. But, as noted above in relation to Baldwin's handling of John, no such attitude distinguishing or even qualifying the author's perspective exists.

Baldwin's commitment to a religious scheme accounts for the conservative character of *Go Tell It on the Mountain*. Though such a commitment does not in itself bespeak conservatism (there is the possibility that an individual's other views and values might counterbalance these), such a thoroughgoing, all-pervasive commitment as his does indeed indicate a rather rigid conservatism. The perspective put forth in the book tells us—without qualification—that the chief institution of the society is religion and that all others are subsumed beneath it; human action and interaction are to be seen against the background of Christian values, and the significance of human action derives from this context. This view is conservative because of its implied definition of man's nature and his relation to society. It suggests that authority does and should reside in that particular institution and that man's nature is such that it needs to be contained, defined, and restrained within its framework. It suggests further that man's relation to his society ought to be determined by his attempt to mold himself to the imperatives dictated by the institution.

These implications are borne out by the novel. Their corollaries are part and parcel of its plot, characterization, and theme. They indeed are the basic premises from which the novel is written. Consequently it is not surprising to find the brief foreword of the Grosset and Dunlap edition of the novel hailing it as a "milestone in the development of American literature" because it is "the first novel about Negroes to be written from a non-racial point of view." The point of view is indeed "non-racial" because Baldwin's premises are such that they minimize the importance of the impingement upon the lives of his characters of social or racial realities. There is no indication in the book that the nature of the lives of its characters is largely determined by poverty and racial oppression in general. I do not intend to imply that Baldwin *must* have written a book about characters whose lives are entirely the result of the impingement on them of social circumstance. But I do mean to say that to exclude that factor to the extent Baldwin does in this novel constitutes a distortion.

The omission from the novel of the realities of race is responsible for the emphasis on individual responsibility in Baldwin's judgment of his characters. Each of the characters seems to be who or what he is because he has willed himself to be or because of some flaw in his personality. Admittedly, the fate of Richard—his arrest, incarceration, and suicide—points to racial injustice and to the social dimension. But even so, the emphasis is on the fate of that particular individual and on his relation with Elizabeth and not on Richard's life and death as in any way representative of, or not unlike, the lives and deaths of many other black people. And in any case the focus of the novel is on a private, personal matter, and the resolution of the plot again reflects the basic premises from which it is written in that the resolution takes place within the psyche of a particular individual. "The Threshing Floor," the apogee of the plot line, describes the change that takes place in John's character and is the most subjective episode within the novel. Consonant with the lack of emphasis on the social dimension, the action of the novel moves toward the subjective and private, away from external reality. Again this reflects Baldwin's conviction in this novel that true reality exists elsewhere than in the facts of man's social experience. From this perspective, any accolades that the book has received for being written from a nonracial point of view seem something other, indeed, than literary judgments.

The step from *Go Tell It on the Mountain* to *Giovanni's Room,* Baldwin's second novel, is not a very long one if we are aware that some of the basic assumptions of the first novel are operative in the second. The scope of the action of *Giovanni's Room* is smaller in not being cosmic. That dimension is missing. But, like the first novel, the second is focused on the subjective inner experience of a single individual, a focus far more limited and intense because of the technical point of view, the events being circumscribed by their filtration through a single consciousness. The implication is, as in the previous novel, that the unique experience of the specific individual is *per se* of great consequence, greater consequence indeed than his experience as a member of a social group on any but the smallest scale. Again, as in the earlier novel, the social framework in which the action takes place is of minimal significance and at most in this novel adds local color. The central character of *Giovanni's Room,* David, has a social identity—he is an American in Paris—but that national identity is so broad and general as to be less meaningful than the author probably thinks. He, as are the other characters, is far more individualized than representative of national origin.

It is here, in Baldwin's conservative assumptions about the character and significance of individual experience, that one should look for the reasons for his choosing to write about characters who are white or who are, more precisely, not black.[8] If one feels, as Baldwin does at the time of this novel, that the inner experience of the unique individual is of greater import than experience deriving from or dependent upon race or socio-economic class, then it stands to reason that a black writer should write "raceless" novels. The key to the question of race in *Giovanni's Room,* in other words, is not to be sought in race psychology (identification with the aggressor, Baldwin's wish to be white) but in the author's politics, a conservative politics whose nature leads him to take the least *ostensibly* political road and to withdraw into the "normality" and tensionlessness of the *status quo.*

The treatment of homosexuality in the novel, however, *seems* radical. It appears radical because of its seeming relation to received social standards of conduct and morality regarding homosexuality. The novel's standards, simply, seem contradictory to commonly accepted norms in Western society.

How, then, does one reconcile the apparent radicalism of the book with the conservatism of its basic assumptions?

The fact of the matter is that Baldwin's attitude toward homosexuality is decidedly critical. Whereas there is a great deal in the novel which stands to sympathize with homosexuality, the overwhelming evidence is negative in character, not positive or supportive. On the one hand the initial descriptions of the actual physical relationship between David and Giovanni are created in such a way as to indicate complete sympathy on the part of the author with their legitimacy and beauty. We are led to believe that the general relation between Giovanni and David is a true-love relation on a par with true heterosexual relations. Their love for each other, we are told, goes beyond the physical. They are contrasted with lesser homosexuals who seek only physical gratification. So much for the positive side.

On the other hand the resolution of the plot of the novel itself stems from Baldwin's analysis of the nature and character of homosexuality—at least as its nature and character are exhibited through David. The murder responsible for sending Giovanni to the guillotine comes about because David has abandoned him. He abandons him out of his preference for a heterosexual relationship and because, as he implies in his question to Giovanni, ("What kind of life can two men have together, anyway?"),[9] the possibilities contained in an extended homosexual relationship are quite limited. "What," David asks again, "do you think can happen between us?" (P. 209) Though David does indeed feel morally responsible for Giovanni's fate, his response in leaving Giovanni comes about because of the claims of an older, prior sense of morality, the same sense of morality, operative in his first homosexual affair, which causes him to flee from his friend Joey. In both cases David is acutely aware of moral imperatives stemming from his sense of masculine identity.

The distinction between David and Giovanni and other homosexuals in the book is a distinction stemming from the masculinity of both and the imputed resulting character. The novel makes clear the author's disgust with fairies, with males who assume feminine guise of dress or manner, and with males who are not at least bisexual. (Both David and Giovanni are.) David's commitment to Hella—and his resulting abandonment of Giovanni's little, dirty, disorderly room—is again a function of the claims of character. Hence the plot's resolution stems from the character of the central figure, and his character itself constitutes a judgment of homosexuality.

Other elements of the plot constitute rather clear negative judgments of homosexuality. The episode where David briefly encounters a sailor walking along a boulevard is a case in point.

> I was staring at him, though I did not know it, and wishing I were
> he. He seemed—somehow—younger than I had ever been, and
> blonder and more beautiful, and he wore his masculinity as unequiv-
> ocally as he wore his skin. (P. 133)

The sailor passes and, seeing a certain look in David's eyes, gives him in return "a look contemptuously lewd and knowing."

> I knew that what the sailor had seen in my unguarded eyes was envy
> and desire: I had seen it often in Jacques' eyes and my reaction and
> the sailor's had been the same. But if I were still able to feel affec-
> tion and if he had seen it in my eyes, it would not have helped, for
> affection, for the boys I was doomed to look at, was vastly more
> frightening than lust. (P. 135)

His escapades after he leaves Hella and goes to Nice, where he picks up a
sailor, are hardly a glorification of homosexuality but are rather a description of its sordidness, a revelation of the depths to which he has sunk, and a
harbinger of his future life. The fact of his leaving Hella is itself tragic in
that it suggests his inability to sustain *any* human relationship, hetero- or homosexual. All in all, the book is about decent behavior and is heavily
weighted—understanding and sympathetic as the author might be—against
homosexuality; although his treatment is subtle, it is as vividly negative as
any religious sermon might be. Hence the *apparently* radical morality of the
novel turns out to be not radical at all but far more disdainful of homosexuality than the most bleeding heart liberal view might be.[10]

Another Country reveals a liberalizing of Baldwin's attitudes but by no
means an abdication of basically conservative values. The context of the
novel is social, not cosmological; it focuses on problems related to racial interaction; it contains far more social protest than any of the preceding novels;
its morality is less stringent, though no less imperative, than heretofore. At
the same time, however, its assumptions about the basic nature of the social
problems it confronts give rise to a societal analysis essentially conservative
in character. It assumes that large-scale social problems, such as racial oppression and its resulting social manifestations, are the result of limitations
within the psyches of individuals rather than of the dynamics of contending
social forces. Hence, the responsibility for social problems lies with the individual, be he oppressed or oppressor, victimizer or victim.[11] In the terms of
the novel, this means that black people are shown oppressing whites as well
as conversely, and there is no clear distinction to be made between the one
act of oppression and the other. In *Another Country* race does not matter in
the sense that every individual has the capacity, regardless of color, to be vic-

tim or victimizer. Equal-opportunity suffering indeed! I do not wish to argue the problem of the responsibility of the victim in his victimization. I would contend, however, that equating the two roles as a general premise serves more to justify oppressors, whether groups or individuals, than to condemn them.

The problem exists in the novel because of Baldwin's assumptions about individual responsibility. More particularly, Baldwin believes that the injustices committed by groups against other groups, and individuals against other individuals, come about because individuals do not know themselves, cannot be honest with themselves or others, and do not possess, therefore, the capacity to love. The idea of love is central to Baldwin's thinking and lies at the heart of his system of values.[12] We noted its role in *Go Tell It on the Mountain*; its role in *Giovanni's Room* is likewise central. *Another Country* can be analyzed in terms of what it says about love, given the relations that Baldwin sees between love and the rest of life, given the politics involved when love is seen as more basic to societal life than factors having to do with the dynamics of complex, industrial society.

The key to understanding *Another Country* lies in the antithetical relation in which its two chief characters, Rufus and Eric, stand. Rufus is black and a Northerner. He is incapable of sustaining relations of any kind with other people because he neither understands nor accepts himself. His desperate plight is precipitated when his desire for self-destruction is projected outward onto Leona, his mistress, whom he drives into insanity before himself committing suicide. Prior to his suicide he has exiled himself from family and friends, and we see him at the nadir of his life—hungry, filthy, homeless, and alone. Seeing no possibility of changing the essential quality of his life, he climbs atop the George Washington Bridge and, piteously addressing God, "Ain't I your baby, too?" leaps to his death. His first sexual experience with Leona is described in such a way as to define their developing relationship, to indicate his character and something of the influence of race on his personality, to present the racial basis of his sado-masochistic relation to her and others.

> He wanted her to remember him the longest day she lived. And, shortly, nothing could have stopped him, not the white God himself nor a lynch mob arriving on wings. Under his breath he cursed the milk-white bitch and groaned and rode his weapon between her thighs. She began to cry. *I told you,* he moaned, *I'd give you something to cry about,* and at once, he felt himself strangling, about to explode or die. A moan and a curse tore through him while he beat

her with all the strength he had and felt the venom shoot out of him, enough for a hundred black-white babies.[13]

Thereafter, their relationship, strained by his self-annihilating impulse and his simultaneous desire to punish the white race through her, advances toward its bitter, destructive end, an end ostensibly avoidable had he the capacity to understand and accept himself and hence to love and be loved.

Eric is in most ways diametrically opposite Rufus. If we compare the first chapter of Book One with the first chapter of Book Two, the former dealing with Rufus and the latter with Eric, the point is patently clear. The structure of the book and the content of the parallel sections require that we make the comparison between the two chief characters. Whereas Rufus is in hell, Eric is in paradise. We need only compare Rufus' state throughout the first chapter of the book with Eric's as we first meet him, sitting in a garden overlooking the sea. His situation is idyllic, his place of residence as well as his relation with his lover, Yves. Despite the peculiarity of the relation, Yves being another male, it stands, as described, in contrast with Rufus' supreme isolation. Throughout the scene we are led to believe that the relation exists with its particular quality because Eric is honest, open, and self-accepting. His personality is such that people, male and female, are drawn to him, and he feels no tension between himself and the rest of the world. His sexual preferences produce for him no shame or guilt. On the contrary his bisexuality seems to allow him to avoid the normal conflict between the sexes. Other characters in the book experience difficulty because of the conflicts they discover between themselves and others of the opposite sex, men or women; Eric, whose character leads him away from distinctions among people as regards sexual identity, has no tensions emanating from that source.

In that the attitudes Baldwin expresses about homosexuality (or more accurately bisexuality) in this novel are completely positive attitudes, the novel is in regard to that subject radical, radical because Baldwin's judgments stand in total opposition to accepted norms of behavior. There is some suggestion that the bisexual male is for Baldwin the apogee of human development. That is, if we ask *why* Eric is created in the novel as the most understanding, best adjusted character, it would seem that the novel would answer that Eric simply does not observe the usual distinctions and categories of sex and race (in Baldwin's thinking) observed by others. He is therefore freer. Baldwin's stance here, however, implies some standard of judgment extraordinarily personal and private as well as sexist in nature. But, nonetheless, it is consistent with the subjectivity of the love theme in the novel. Since bisexuality is hardly a matter of free choice among men—it not representing a cultural norm—its presentation as a viable alternative to generally existing modes of social behavior is hardly realistic. On the other hand, if Baldwin meant to suggest by his bisexual male characters an attitude less rigidly bound by standard categories of social differentiation, then he would have done well to show us a male who might possess the good qualities of an Eric without imposing the necessity of his being in fact bisexual. The implication that Rufus' life might have been saved had Vivaldo made some sexual gesture toward him (Baldwin would say a "loving" gesture) simply suggests an option not generally available in this culture and one therefore expressive of Baldwin's utterly private sense of values and little else.

The novel's theme of love is again pertinent here.[14] The assumption that the chief problem among the characters in the novel (and in the world) is the incapacity to love, generated by whatever psychic condition keeps them out of touch with their basic selves, leads to a basic contradiction in the novel. On the one hand the novel contains more social protest than any of Baldwin's novels heretofore. Rufus and Leona constantly encounter racist reaction to their being on the street together and living together. So do Ida and Vivaldo. The novel on many occasions shows policemen at the ready to enforce the uncodified laws regarding proper relations between the black and white sexes. Hence there is a real and actual social dimension to racial relations shown in the book. We see even that the interaction between Rufus and Leona is determined by social attitudes that they act out. Yet, the novel, in implying that the imperative to love is the responsibility of the individual, contradicts itself in that its assessment of the root of the problem of racial relations allows the author to blame his characters regardless of race and to ignore many considerations of race. What, for example, does a black writer mean when he shows the best-adjusted character in his novel to be white and the worst black? What does he mean when he is unable or unwilling to show a single good relationship, homosexual or heterosexual, between two black people? What does he mean when he requires a black woman, Ida, to confess her infidelity to white Vivaldo but does not require her white lover to confess his infidelity to her? At worst these considerations could suggest a writer who has a great deal of spite for himself and his race. At best, and I choose to favor this explanation, they show that his basic assumption involving the primacy of love minimizes racial considerations. The hero is he who has the capacity to love; the villain is he who has not the capacity. Though whites seem favored in its possession, not all whites in the novel have it—Richard, for example—and at least one black character, Ida, is on her way to achieving it.

Another Country demonstrates the limitations of Baldwin's greatest strength as a writer of fiction and non-fiction, his ability to express the innermost, deepest longings of his psyche. He comes closer to putting himself on the printed page than most contemporary novelists and than any contemporary essayist. The problem, however, consists in the fact that his analysis of his own personal needs is indistinguishable in his mind from his analysis of the world and its society. Admittedly, the subjectivism of his work has decreased with the passage of time, but even at his most objective, in *Another Country,* in the novels thus far considered his basic presuppositions remain highly subjective reflections of personal need and desire. Hence the accuracy and relevance of his social analysis can be of but limited scope. His most recent novel to date, *Tell Me How Long the Train's Been Gone,* further bears out this assessment despite the fact that it is still more politically liberal than *Another Country*—more liberal yet ultimately conservative in that the author's initial social assumptions remain constant.

Tell Me How Long the Train's Been Gone is Baldwin's most directly political novel in that the issues regarding the question of the relation of men to society and to each other are more dramatically and explicitly posed than in any of the preceding fiction. In this novel Bladwin pushes his liberalism to its extreme limit, stating finally his great sympathy for radicalism (for the radicalism of black youth during the sixties) but ultimately rejecting it for himself and claiming a spot on the political spectrum to the left of center but far inward from the limit. A measure of the degree of Baldwin's political shift may be established by comparing this most recent novel to the earliest, *Go Tell It on the Mountain,* in terms of their expression of attitudes toward religion, their relative evaluation of the significance of private and public experience, and, as a corollary, their sense of the relation of the fate of the individual to social dynamics.

The conception of religion revealed in *Tell Me How Long the Train's Been Gone* seems essentially atheistic, though Baldwin's earlier Christian commitment remains, however obversely stated and redefined. It goes without saying that the central character of the novel, Leo Proudhammer, is the character most nearly representative of the perspective of the author, so much so, the tone indicates, that there is no disparity between Leo's thoughts and values and James Baldwin's. Nowhere in the book is there the slightest suggestion of disjunction between their outlooks. Obviously Leo is *not* Baldwin himself—Baldwin has not, of course, achieved success as an actor—but the biographical parallels are so many as to suggest some degree of autobiography here. Hence we may infer that Leo's rather consistent attitudes toward God, the church, and toward his brother after Caleb becomes a minister—especially given the tone in which these attitudes are expressed—are not inconsistent with the author's own attitudes at the time the novel was written. Leo says, "I cursed God from the bottom of my heart, the very bottom of my balls. I called Him the greatest coward in the universe because He did not dare to show Himself and fight me like a man."[15] And later, during the course of sexual interplay between him and his brother, he says further, "I'll love you, Caleb, I'll love you forever, and in the sight of the Father and the Son and the fucking Holy Ghost and all the filthy hosts, and in the sight of all the world, and I'll sing hallelujahs to my love for you in hell." (P. 211) Leo is quite young at this time and one might read his bitter diatribe as a kind of obverse confession of faith, a reading suggested by an impression, an insight which Leo has much later, when, as a young man, he again has bitter thoughts about God.

> A faint breeze struck, but did not cool my Ethiopian brow. Ethiopia's hands: to what god indeed, out of this despairing place, was I to stretch these hands? But I also felt, incorrigible, hoping to be reconciled, and yet unable to accept the terms of any conceivable reconciliation, that any god daring to presume that I would stretch out my hands to him would be struck by these hands with all my puny, despairing power; would be forced to confront, in these, my hands, the monstrous blood-guiltiness of God. No. I had had quite enough of God—more than enough, more than enough, the horror filled my nostrils, I gagged on the blood-drenched name; and yet was forced to see that this horror, precisely, accomplished His reality and undid my unbelief. (P. 98)

We may, then, infer the writer's belief when he later curses God in the presence of Caleb, by this time a minister.

> "That God you talk about, that miserable white cock-sucker—look at His handiwork, look! . . . I curse your God, Caleb, I curse Him, from the bottom of my heart I *curse* Him. And now let Him strike me down. Like you just tried to do." (P. 425)

The disparity between the denotation of the words and their actual meaning puts Leo in the paradoxical position of the apparent atheist whose disbelief is so strong that it means the contrary. Who or what, after all, is there for the atheist to curse? No such attitude exists in the first novel, nor could it have existed as an expression of the view of the writer himself. If the strongly negative exhortations against God are indeed to be taken as testaments of faith, still the point remains that no such ambiguous assertions on the part of the author are in the earlier novel. Hence his position has shifted but not changed; his commitment to the institution is in any case a far lesser one.

Nonetheless, the implication is, especially given the conception indicated above of the role of God in men's affairs, that for Leo (and for Baldwin) the universe is essentially God-centered, however difficult that idea has become for the older Baldwin.

The relative value that Baldwin, through the course of the novel, places on inner experience as opposed to outer, public experience is, as said before, a measure of the relative value that he places on social existence. One way of interpreting Baldwin's novels is in these terms. From the earliest novel to the latest we can trace a clear and definite shift of emphasis on Baldwin's part from interest in the "inner space" to consideration of the role of the "public space" in determining the nature, character, and quality of human experience.[16] *Tell Me How Long the Train's Been Gone* does not focus exclusively on the public space—there is, in fact, a tension in the novel between the complex of values associated with the one emphasis and those associated with the other. Just as the whole body of his novels may profitably be analyzed in these terms, so may this particular novel.

It is indeed interesting and more than happenstance that Leo Proudhammer, who so closely resembles Baldwin, should be an actor and not a writer. A writer may practice his craft in privacy and his work may be presented without the requirement of his presence. An actor, however, usually must be present in order to practice his craft. The actor's role is the more public one and usually at a lesser remove from his audience. Leo Proudhammer does not like to be around people, and hence there is a certain tension between the requirements of his vocation and his personal feelings. At the time of his first meeting with Black Christopher, Leo says to him, "The only space which means anything to me is the space between myself and other people. May it never diminish." (P. 448) The tension suggested here between the desire for privacy and the necessity of public involvement—a tension inherent in the character and vocation of Leo—is a reflection of the basic theme of the novel. The biography of Leo as described in the novel is a history of his achievement and a description of his rejection of those around him. He rejects his brother, Caleb, to whom he has been inordinately close, his father, and his mother. Though he does not totally reject Barbara and Christopher, the people ostensibly closest to him, he maintains a certain distance from both, through his acknowledgment to each that he is emotionally and sexually committed to the other. After his heart attack, he goes away to Europe alone, thus maintaining his isolation.

His commitments to Barbara and to Christopher are of a somewhat differing order, the antagonism between his two lovers mirroring forth this most significant inner conflict. His commitment to Barbara is to racelessness

(whiteness),[17] to art, to privacy, to respectability, to fame, to wealth and social status, to prestige, to high culture, to individualism, to sexual orthodoxy,
to *status quo* politics, to the privileges reserved by society to the wealthy and
successful. His early dream of being an actor has meant not only leading a
life different from that of his family but rejecting that life entirely along with
all the suffering and humiliation attendant upon it. Barbara represents for
him all that his early life was *not*. She is the "princess" (as she is actually
called), and he the "prince" (as he is once referred to) who has won her, who
has transformed a fairy-tale reality into actuality.

His commitment to Black Christopher, on the other hand, is to specific racial identity, to revolutionary politics, to social involvement, to sexual aber-
ration, to repudiation of the value of wealth and social status, to identification with the underprivileged, to reconciliation with his family and with his
personal and racial pasts. He knows that the world does not in some sense
honor the distinctions he makes; that from certain perspectives he and Christopher are indistinguishable. Yet they are truly not bound by a common racial identity, for socioeconomic class creates between them a significant distinction. Christopher himself recognizes this: "But, naturally, a whole lot of
black cats think you [Leo] might be one of them, and, in a way, you know,
you stand to lose just as much as white people stand to lose." (P. 480)

The whole novel, with its unprecedented emphasis (in Baldwin's work) on
its main character as a social person, is in a sense a justification of the value
underlying the resolution of the plot. The forces responsible for Leo's success
have been those very forces that have sought to destroy him. There is ample
apology for the necessity of escaping the circumstances of Leo's youth and
young manhood. Yet the problem lies heavy on his soul, so heavy, in fact,
that he has a "heart" attack, not from overwork, but from the impingement
on his psyche of the problem made clear in a conversation with Christopher
near the end of the novel.

> "If you don't want me to keep going under the feet of horses,"
> Christopher said, now with his dreadful distinctness, his muffled ur-
> gency, "and I know that you love me and you don't want no blood on
> my hands—dig—but if you don't want me to keep going under the
> feet of horses, then I think you got to agree that we need us some
> guns. Right?"
>
> "Yes," I said. "I see that." He parked the car. I looked out over
> the water. There was a terrible weight on my heart—for a moment I
> was afraid that I was about to collapse again. I watched his black,
> proud profile. "But we're outnumbered, you know."

> He laughed and turned off the motor. ". . . So were the early
> Christians." (P. 483)

The resolution of the plot has Leo leaving the country alone, the intended
implication being that he makes no choice, that he leaves the dilemma lying.
That, however, is not in fact the case, for he returns and resumes his career
and the complex of values associated with it. A choice is made by default and
Leo (and Baldwin) opts for the one value cluster over the other.

For the first time the novelist has come to see that love, the personal feelings for each other, is not enough. His response, to flee, is likewise not
enough, for the problem waits to greet him at Ellis Island every time he returns to America. His problem has no solution, however, in the framework of
his politics. He is American to the core and a liberal Democrat. He believes
in his success and, with whatever discomfort and difficulty, ultimately accepts it. Only with difficulty has he been able to accept wealth, status, prestige, but he has nonetheless accepted them, and he has done so because he
feels in his heart of hearts that he has earned them. Just as God is held responsible for the ill fate of individuals, so must He smile at the fortunate.
Baldwin sees himself as one of the chosen, and therefore confronts the system with a morally based rhetoric but does not question its basic operations.
He wants certain things to change, but only certain things. He wants attitudes to change, but he has been unwilling, except very recently and then
only very tentatively, to question much further. Perhaps further questioning,
about the uses of power in the society, for example, would unsettle too many
things that have been thus far settled for him.

Baldwin and the Problem of Being

George E. Kent

In a *New York Times Book Review* essay, James Baldwin has stated that the effort to become a great novelist "involves attempting to tell as much of the truth as one can bear, and then a little more."[1] It is likely in our time to mean attacking much that Americans tend to hold sacred, in order that reality be confronted and constructively altered. As stated in "Everybody's Protest Novel," it means devotion to the "human being, his freedom and fulfillment; freedom which cannot be legislated, fulfillment which cannot be chartered."[2] Baldwin then wishes to confront and affect the human consciousness and conscience. He rejects the tradition of the protest novel because he feels that it denies life, "the human being . . . his beauty, dread, power," and insists "that it is categorization alone which is real and which cannot be transcended."[3] He tries to write the way jazz musicians sound, to reflect their compassion,[4] and it is noteworthy that Baldwin's tendency in *Go Tell It on the Mountain* and *Another Country* is to focus upon the individual characters' experiences in a way similar to Ralph Ellison's description of Jazz:

> For true jazz is an art of individual assertion within and against the group. Each true jazz moment (as distinct from the uninspired commercial performance) springs from a contest in which each artist challenges all the rest; each solo flight or improvisation, represents . . . a definition of his identity, as member of the collectivity, and as a link in the chain of tradition.[5]

It should be generally observed that Baldwin's writings owe much to Negro folk tradition (the blues, jazz, spirituals, and folk literature), and to the chief experimental practitioners of modernist fiction, with especial emphasis upon Henry James.

The moral vision that emerges is one primarily concerned with man as he relates to good and evil and to society. For there is evil in human nature and evil abroad in the world to be confronted, not through Christianity, whose doctrine tends to be the perverted tool of the ruling classes and groups whose bankruptcy was registered by the slaughter of the Jews during the Third Reich,[6] but through the love and involvement available from those able to eat of the tree of the knowledge of good and evil and live. Within the breast of each individual, then, rages a universe of forces with which he must become acquainted, often through the help of an initiated person, in order to direct them for the positive growth of himself and others. The foregoing achievement is what Baldwin means by *identity*. To achieve it, one must not be hindered by the detritus of society and one must learn to know detritus when one sees it.

Perhaps the question that throws most light upon Baldwin's works is simply, how can one achieve, amid the dislocations and disintegrations of the modern world, true, functional being? For Baldwin, the Western concept of reality, with its naive rationalism, its ignoring of unrational forces that abound within and without man, its reductivist activities, wherein it ignores the uniqueness of the individual and sees reality in terms of its simplifications and categorizations, is simply impoverishing. He who follows it fails to get into his awareness the richness and complexity of experience—he fails to be. And freedom is unattainable, since, paradoxically, freedom is discovery and recognition of limitations, one's own and that of one's society;[7] to deny complexity is to paralyze the ability to get at such knowledge—it is to strangle freedom.

Groping unsteadily amidst the reductivist forces is an America that does not achieve, therefore, its primitive and essential moral identity. For the great vision that motivated the American adventure there has been substituted a quest for spurious glory in mass production and consumption. And yet, " . . . there is so much more than Cadillacs, Frigidaires, and IBM machines. . . . One of the things wrong with this country is this notion that IBM machines *prove* something."[8] Still until America achieves its moral identity, its people, whether white or black, can fulfill nothing.

The struggle for identity, i.e., for functional being, is the major issue of Baldwin's first novel, *Go Tell It on the Mountain*. Attempting to tell part of the story found in the Negro's music, which "Americans are able to admire because a protective sentimentality limits their understanding of it,"[9] Baldwin examines three generations of a Negro family whose life span extends from slavery to the present day. The novel investigates, with warmth and perception, the Negro's possibility of achieving identity through the discipline of Christianity. The style is richly evocative, and one hears echoes of Joyce and Faulkner, the rhythms of the old-time Negro sermon and the King James Bible. Unfolding in a series of major movements, the story proceeds as follows: the first movement introduces the reach of fourteen-year-old John Grimes for identity, a fearful, faltering reach from a boy filled with guilt, hatred, fear, love, amidst the stern, religious frustrations of his elders and the pagan rebelliousness of his brother, Roy; the second presents the tragedy of Florence, unable to overcome, among other things, the concept of the Negro she has internalized from the dominant culture—and therefore on insecure terms with herself and others; the third presents Gabriel Grimes, stepfather of John, blocked from complete fulfillment by his attempts to escape his pagan drives in a fierce, frustrated embrace of Christianity; the fourth presents Elizabeth, mother of John, who after brief fulfillment in illicit love, retreats, frightened and awestricken, into the frustrated and frustrating arms of Gabriel Grimes. The final movement is the questionable flight of John Grimes from the quest for identity into the ostensible safety of religious ecstasy.

Vitally represented through a series of scenes occurring on his fourteenth birthday, reflected through images of poetic intensity, are the conflicts of young John. He stands upon a hill in New York's Central Park and feels "like a giant who might crumble this city with his anger . . . like a tyrant who might crush this city with his heel . . . like a long awaited conqueror at whose feet flowers would be strewn, and before whom multitudes cried, Hosanna!"[10] Or concerning the rewards to be inherited from his preacher father: " . . . a house like his father's, a church like his father's, and a job like his father's, where he would grow old and black with hunger and toil. The way of the cross had given him a belly filled with wind and had bent his mother's back. . . . "[11] Mixed with his vision and perverting it is John's guilt over his sexual drives, the religious concept of the city as evil and the fatal tempter of the soul, and his parents' feeling that the city (New York) is filled with antagonistic whites who will block the worldly aspirations of Negroes. Over such obstacles John peers, enveloped in a solitude that seems well nigh unbreakable.

Part II, containing the stories of the adult members of the family who came to manhood and womanhood at the time of Emancipation, begins powerfully. Passionate scenes reveal the problems with which each character struggles. For Florence, the sister of the minister Gabriel, the central problem is to achieve an identity that excludes the concubinage already offered by her white Southern employer, the general sexual opportunism, or the image of the toil-blasted bearer of children with its attendant heritage—a cabin like her mother's. In addition, Florence is one of a long line of Baldwin's characters who have absorbed from the dominant culture the concept of blackness as low, contemptible, evil. Baldwin has said, "The American image of the Negro lives also in the Negro's heart; and when he has surrendered to this image life has no other possible reality."[12] Controlled by such an image, Florence founders in a mixture of self-hatred, self-righteousness, sadism, and guilt feelings. Married to a ne'er-do-well she succeeds merely in outraging herself and him and in driving him away. She bows to religious ecstasy. Baldwin's point, of course, is that she was unable to achieve a life-affirming love or her potential identity, and that her ecstatic surrender to Christianity as she nears the end of life is a gesture of desperation.

A man of titanic drives, Gabriel is a sufficient metaphor for man in a grim struggle with the forces of the universe; he stops just short of evoking the sense of tragedy, since self-recognition is not clearly confessed. What is available for articulating the self amid these forces, however, is a version of St. Paul's Christianity which assures the self a Pyhrric victory by a repression that carries the mere coloring of a humanistic morality. Since sex, for Baldwin, is obviously a metaphor for the act of breaking one's isolation and, properly experienced, responsibly entering into the complexity of another human being, Gabriel's evasion of it by marrying the sexless Deborah (symbolically enough, mass-raped by Southern whites and sterile) is his flight from dealing with his humanity. Baldwin contrasts him well with the pagan Esther, by whom a temporarily backsliding Gabriel begets a child he does not acknowledge. Esther has a firm concept of her dignity and humanity, and what is life-affirming and what is life-negating, and some of his fellow ministers, too, show that they do not take their fundamentalist concepts to rigid conclusions. Gabriel's response is to retreat more fiercely into religion, marry, after the death of Deborah, the fallen Elizabeth, and harden in his grotesqueness.

Elizabeth is the ethical and moral center of the book. It is through her attachment to her father and reaction against her mother and aunt that she gains the sense of a love that is life-giving. She knows that love's imprisonment is not a "bribe, a threat, an indecent will to power"; it is "mysteriously, a freedom for the soul and spirit . . . water in the dry places."[13] It seems to me, however, that Baldwin's hand falters in his analysis and presentation of her as a young woman. Her important relationship with her father, to the extent that it is at all rendered, is simply that of the conventional petting and "spoiling" afforded by a loose-living man who does not take his fatherhood very seriously. That is to say that the father's free-loving nature binds him to nothing, and, after cautioning Elizabeth (as we learn through a summary) never to let the world see her suffering, he returns to his job of running a house of prostitution. Amidst the religious illusions of the other characters, however, she retains a strong, quiet sense of her integrity, despite a relative commitment to religious passion.

Her fall comes through her common-law husband, Richard, to whom she gives a self-sacrificial, life-creating love. Although the portrayal of Richard as victimized by society and as a man whose being cannot fulfill its hunger is moving, the explanation of his curiosity and hunger seems oversimplified, if not, indeed, dehumanized: ".... that I was going to get to know everything them white bastards knew ... so could no white-son-of-bitch nowhere never make talk me down, and never make feel like I was dirt. . . ."[14] Although the statement well reflects Richard's sensitivity and insecurity under the racial system of America, it hardly explains "his great adoration for things dead."

After the proud young Richard kills himself in reaction to extreme humiliation by the police who have imposed upon his consciousness the image of the low bestial Negro that he has tried to escape, Elizabeth gives birth to the bastard John, whose quest for identity forms the central movement of the book. As the second wife of Gabriel, she emerges as a person of complexity, and is sensitively involved in John's reach for life.

By a series of flashbacks, the author keeps us mindful that the present involves John Grimes' search for identity, the achievement of which is to be understood within the context of the lives of his elders. In the last section of the story, he is in crisis, and with the help of his friend Elisha, in a religious ecstasy, commits himself to the Cross. At various points, Baldwin uses a character by whose views the reality witnessed is to be qualified. In addition to the foreshadowings scattered throughout the story, there is Gabriel to point out that the ecstatic conversion is still to be tested by the long, complex journey of life. So quite without surprise, we encounter in a later short story, "The Death of the Prophet," an apostate Johnny, who returns guiltily from some place of estrangement almost to collapse in the presence of his dying father.

That Baldwin in *Go Tell It on the Mountain* has drawn heavily upon autobiographical experiences is obvious, and those who like the pursuit can make interesting parallells with autobiographical situations reported in the essay collections: *Notes of a Native Son, Nobody Knows My Name,* and *The Fire Next Time.* But, from the artistic point of view, what is more interesting is their transmutation, their representation as organized energies that carry mythic force in their reflection of man attempting to deal with destiny. Much power derives from the confrontation of the ambiguity of life. That ambiguity carries into the various attitudes suggested toward the version of Christianity that his characters relate themselves to. The relatively non-religious characters do not deny the relevance of God but seem to feel as Esther, the spurned mother of Gabriel's illegitimate child, puts it: " ... that [the Lord's] spirit ain't got to work in everybody the same, seems to me."[15] Of the religiously engrossed characters, only Elizabeth achieves a relatively selfless being. However, the religion sustained the slave mother of Gabriel. Even for the twisted, it is a place of refuge, an articulation of the complexity of the mysterious forces of a demanding universe. But finally, the religion only partially illuminates, and the characters must grope in its light and bump against forces within and without that the religion has merely hidden or damned.

With some admitted oversimplifications inescapable in tracing thematic lines, it may be said that in his two succeeding novels Baldwin is preoccupied with sex and love as instruments in the achievement of full being. As a novelist still under forty, he is no doubt creating works important to his total development, but in neither of these novels—*Giovanni's Room* and the best seller *Another Country*—does he seem to create fully his fictional worlds and characters; in short, he does not seem to have found characters who release his very real ability to create.

In an essay "Preservation of Innocence," Baldwin explicitly makes his criticism of popular concepts of sexuality. His chief point is that our rational classifications of sexual characteristics and our efforts to preserve conventional norms tell us little about what it means to be a man or a woman. Our classifications are not definitive, and therefore we panic and set up safeguards that do nothing more than guard against sexual activities between members of the same sex. But such reductive simplicity, he argues, guarantees ignorance merely, or, worse, the probability that the bride and groom will not be able to add to the sum of love or know each other since they do not know themselves. Whatever position one takes regarding the argument, the following statements shed uncomfortable light upon the relationship between the sexes in much of American fiction:

> In the truly awesome attempt of the American to at once preserve his innocence and arrive at man's estate, that mindless monster, the tough guy, has been created and perfected, whose masculinity is found in the most infantile and elementary externals and whose atti-

tude towards women is the wedding of the most abysmal romanticism and the most implacable distrust.[16]

Further complaint of the reductive approach to sexuality is contained in a review of André Gide's *Madeleine,* in which he describes the possibility of communing with another sex as "the door to life and air and freedom from the tyranny of one's own personality. . . ."[17] And he describes our present day as one in which communion between the sexes "has become so sorely threatened that we depend more and more on the strident exploitation of externals, as, for example, the breasts of Hollywood glamor girls and the mindless grunting and swaggering of Hollywood he-men."[18] Despite our claim to knowledge, Baldwin implies, sex is a mystery that each person must find a way to live with.

In the light of the foregoing, it seems to me, Baldwin's intention in the novel *Giovanni's Room* is more easily understood. The main line of the story portrays the way a youth's inherited definitions of sexuality fail him in his attempts to come to terms with his own, and adds to the sum of evil in his relationship with others. The chief character, David, represents the rational Westerner, who has absorbed the simplified, compartmentalized thinking of his background. Falling first into a romantic homosexual experience with a fellow adolescent, Joey, he experiences the escape from isolation and the heightened spiritual awareness that love is supposed to bring. However, "A cavern opened in my mind, black, full of rumor, suggestion . . . I could have cried, cried for shame and terror, cried for not understanding how this could have happened to me, how this could have happened in me."[19] Unresolved oedipal conflicts are hinted, and just when he needs spiritual sustenance from a father, his father, who knows nothing of the son's experience, insists upon retaining the simplified concept of himself as his son's "buddy." In flight from Joey, David repeats the mishap in the army, then takes flight to France to "find himself," but once there tentatively enters into a similar relationship with Giovanni. David expects Giovanni to be but an interval in life, since David has also a girlfriend, Hella, a very rational-minded girl who has gone to Spain to think out whether she is in love. But, moving just one step ahead of the predatory homosexual underworld, Giovanni's life demands David's love as its only hope for transcendence. Irresponsibly, and in a way that denies their complexity as human beings, David disappoints the hopes of Giovanni and disillusions Hella.

What Baldwin registers well is the desperate need for love that brings transcendence. The homosexual's problem is shown to be the threat of being forced into the underworld, where bought love of the body, without transcendence, is simply productive of desperation. The women pictured face a similar problem on a heterosexual level. The world portrayed is nightmarish, but hardly, in any sense, really vital. One of its serious problems, though, is that the reader is not allowed to escape the feeling, in the bad sense, of staginess and theatricality. The characters are in hell all right, but the reader never is, and I do not think that this is so simply because the approach to sex is unconventional. The characters do not root themselves deeply enough to become momentous in fictional terms, nor do they stand with intensity for elemental forces that we are forced to consider an inescapable part of our lives. Despite claims for complexity, the characters are too easily defined with relationship to a thesis.

Before coming to a consideration of *Another Country,* I should point out that Baldwin is the author of several stories of distinction, though there is hardly space for more than a brief mentioning of them. "Previous Condition" is the intense story of a young Negro's attempt to secure his being from its alienated condition within and the forces of prejudice without. It appeared in *Commentary,* October, 1948, as Baldwin's first story. "The Death of the Prophet," *Commentary,* March, 1950, was mentioned in connection with *Go Tell It on the Mountain.* "Come Out the Wilderness," *Mademoiselle,* March, 1958, reprinted in *Best Short Stories from Mademoiselle,* New York, 1961, explores the dilemma of a Negro girl who has been alienated from her original racial environment. "Sonny's Blues," *Partisan Review,* Summer, 1957, reprinted in *Best Short Stories of 1958* and Herbert Gold's *Fiction of the Fifties,* New York, 1959, carries the venture of a Negro boy through narcotics to music, where he finally gains a sense of identity expressed. "This Morning, This Evening, So Soon," *The Atlantic Monthly,* September, 1960, reprinted in Martha Foley, *The Best Short Stories of 1961,* New York, 1961, an issue dedicated to Baldwin, explores the need of a successful young Negro actor to come to terms with his place in history. Each story shows a sure sense of the short-story form, a moment of illumination that has significance for the total life of the character. Baldwin's greatest indebtedness in the short story is to Henry James.

Another Country, New York, 1962, is a serious and ambitious attempt, a fact that should be recognized despite the fact that to make it a serious novel of the first rank would demand severe cutting and some intensive rewriting. The problem is still that of arriving at a definition of one's being which will be adequately sustaining in the face of the evils of life, and to support another's complexity through love. Both heterosexual and homosexual scenes abound, but, as stated in the discussion of *Giovanni's Room,* these are instruments for the exploration of being, the metaphors for self-definition and for responsibly entering the complexity of another. They have, therefore, a serious purpose, and Baldwin is too concerned about whether the sex experience provides a transcending love to make distinctions between the heterosexual and homosexual experience. Most of the men have engaged in a homosexual act, and have from it defined their sex for the future; that is, they decide whether the homosexual experience is or is not for their being, with most deciding in favor of heterosexuality.

The first story is that of Rufus, the Negro musician, who is fighting within himself both the real and the imaginary aspects of the race problem, and therefore cannot communicate with Leona, the Southern poor-white girl whom he picks up with the conscious purpose of sexual exploitation and of getting rid of her before she can "bug" him with her story (i.e., involve him in her complexity as a person). Rufus has suffered real racial persecution, so that even harmless remarks by Leona send him into a rage, and he finally drives her into a nervous breakdown and succumbs to his own frustrations by committing suicide. The horror of their experience is communicated with considerable skill. Rufus' failure in *being* is then re-tested in the lives of other characters who were, in varying degrees, associated with him.

Vivaldo Moore, the Irish-Italian attracted to Rufus' sister at first partly through being a "liberal" and partly because of his sense of having failed her brother, must be made to confront her as a complex human conundrum, capable of ruthless exploitation and high-level prostitution: that is, he must lose his innocence. Cass and Richard Silenski must abandon their oversimplified classifications of each other and achieve a sense of reality in their marriage. Eric, the homosexual, must overthrow his Southern background and come to terms with himself in France. Everybody, indeed, must learn his own name. Thus the lives of successive sets of people must come against the problems of being, love, and involvement.

One trouble with the scheme is that so few of the characters exemplify the complexity contended for them. Rufus, Ida, and Eric are the more adequately developed characters. The rest are not projected far enough beyond the level of nice, erring people. Thus the central problem of the book lacks momentousness. Ralph Ellison has said of the novel that " . . . it operates by amplifying and giving resonance to a specific complex of experience until, through the eloquence of its statement, that specific part of life speaks metaphorically for the whole."[20] It is precisely the foregoing illusion that *Another Country* in its totality is unable to create. The section concerned with the discovery of Rufus' death and the attendance at his funeral is excessive in its reportorial detail, sometimes theatrical, sometimes written at the level of a women's magazine. And the social criticism is inert, for the most part, a part of the chatty reflections of a particular character or of long clinical discussions.

On the other hand, there are some penetrating scenes that reflect the fine talent of Baldwin. In addition to the story of Rufus, I should cite most of the scenes where Ida is present and some of the scenes between Cass Silenski and Eric. In such scenes, the bold use of naturalistic devices—the sex scenes and four-letter words—project meaning well beyond surface communication. What else could so well convey Rufus' horrified retching at his dilemma or the terrible exasperation of Ida and Vivaldo? Still, scenes abound in which naturalistic detail simply thickens the book and the four-letter words provide a spurious emphasis, galvanizing the reader's attention to no end. And yet *Another Country* is a book that has much to say, and, as I have tried to indicate, sometimes does.

It is not too much to assert, then, that Baldwin's novels since *Go Tell It on the Mountain,* though fine in segments, tend to reflect a hiatus in his artistic development. In *Go Tell It on the Mountain,* he was working with a body of understood, crystallized, and only partially rejected religious and racial mythology which, therefore, carried coiled within it the wires of communication. It is not to say that the artist's challenge and task were simple to point out that he had primarily to manipulate the myth, to steep it in deliberate ambiguity in order to reflect its sphinxlike betrayal of those who uncritically absorbed it. The religious interpretation, after all, is within touching distance of the overall idea of Matthew Arnold's famous essay "Herbraism and Hellenism." His autobiographical intimacy with such material required and received artistic skill and distance. Creating against such a background, Baldwin effected a novel that transcended racial and religious categories— became an evoked image of man facing the mysterious universal forces.

On the other hand, the Baldwin of the last two novels confronts the modern consciousness amidst fluxions more talked about than crystallized, and moving at considerable speed: elements of modern man connoting fragmenting certainties eroded at the base, the succor for which has been sought mainly in the vague horizons of the backward look. The workings of sex amidst those fluxions are certainly, in the modern awareness, one major element in the choppy sea of our minds in which definable shapes seem to appear for the purpose of disappearing. To define them artistically would seem to demand extraordinary effort indeed, whether in traditional or experimental terms.

The conclusion, therefore, to which a full reading of Baldwin seems inescapably to lead is that since his first novel he has not evolved the artistic form that will fully release and articulate his obviously complex awareness.

And that to do so may require an abandonment of safety in the use of form equal to that which he has manifested in approach to subject, an act that may concomitantly involve estranging many of the multitude of readers which he has acquired. For an artist of Baldwin's fictional resources, talent, and courage, of his obvious knowledge of evolved fictional techniques, the challenge should hardly be overwhelming.

The Ironic Voice In Baldwin's Go Tell It On The Mountain

_____ Shirley S. Allen

A number of questions raised in critical interpretations of James Baldwin's first novel, _Go Tell It on the Mountain,_ can be answered by studying his use of irony. Such questions include Baldwin's artistic distance from the characters, his attitude toward their religious beliefs, the identity of the ironic voice in Part Three, and the meaning of the novel's denouement. Although there are at least three different kinds of irony in the novel, they are closely related because they result from the narrative technique Baldwin employs, an internal and subjective point of view limited to the thoughts, feelings, and perceptions of the main character. In order to transcend the limitations of this point of view, Baldwin uses irony in the narrator's diction, irony of statement and event in the action, and an ironic voice as a character.

In the major action of the novel, which is the struggle of young John Grimes to leave childhood and achieve maturity with a sense of his own identity, the narrator is limited to John's internal point of view. Although he speaks in the third person, this point of view is strictly maintained, so that even the physical appearance of the hero is described subjectively through comments he hears from others and the images he sees in the mirror.

The point of view is further limited by confinement in time. Although the narrator uses the past tense, he recounts events as they happen, unedited by the perspective of time. We follow John Grimes through the course of his fourteenth birthday as if we were experiencing the events with him. Careful use of adverbs denoting present time, such as "now" and "still," maintain this sense of contemporary action. So does a scrupulous use of tenses, particularly the past-perfect for every event occurring even recently before the moment of the present action and frequent use of "would" to express future time in the past tense. A few sentences taken from the episode of Roy's injury illustrate Baldwin's use of tenses:

> His mother leaned over and looked into Roy's face with a sad, sympathetic murmur. Yet, John felt, she had seen instantly the extent of the danger to Roy's eye and to his life, and was beyond that worry now. Now she was merely marking time, as it were, and preparing herself against the moment when her husband's anger would turn, full force, against her.[1]

The effect of this narrative style is immediacy and directness like the first-person, present tense point of view, but it avoids the literary awkwardness of that form. Although such a narrator is not uncommon in modern fiction, Baldwin's use is remarkable for consistency and suppleness. He also exploits fully the freedom of a third-person narrator to use whatever diction the author chooses without limitation to language characteristic of the protagonist. Baldwin's excellent command of language (improved over his earliest short stories) and his talent for almost poetic expression are used to present the thoughts of a Harlem schoolboy without restriction to his grammar and vocabulary.

In fact, the contrast between the narrator's diction and the dialogue of the characters emphasizes both the universality of their inner conflicts and the particular circumstances of their lives as Negroes in America. Baldwin's ear for language and his skill at representing it in print are nowhere better displayed than in the dialogue of *Go Tell It on the Mountain,* where the dialect is conveyed with such subtlety and economy that the rhythms, accent, and colloquialisms of Harlem speech do not blur the individuality and dignity of the speakers. Contrasted with the dialogue is the educated and highly literate voice of the internal narrator, compelling the reader's understanding and sympathy beyond suggestions of race or class.

The separation between the subjective narrator and the character that is implied by use of the third-person form is also useful in this novel because in Part Two, "The Prayers of the Saints," the narrator enters the minds of three other characters serially, maintaining the same point of view in relation to each as his relation to John in Part One and Part Three. The narrator becomes in thoughts, feelings, and perceptions John's aunt, then his stepfather, then his mother; but his diction remains his own. This device is important for preserving the continuity of the novel, which has few external indications of continuity.

Having set up this type of narrator, with immediate and intimate knowledge of the character, Baldwin partially overcomes his limitation to a single, internal point of view by introducing verbal irony into his diction. Sometimes he merely uses a word with connotations opposite to the values assumed by the character, as when he describes the great preaching mission that Gabriel regards as the most important of his career as "a monster revival meeting" and his more venerable colleagues as "war horses." (PP. 100–101) Sometimes he simply lifts out of its churchly context a word used with religious conviction by the characters, as when he speaks of the saints doing their housecleaning or refers to Praying Mother Washington as "the praying mother." (PP. 49, 208) Several times he describes obviously human motives in terms of divine providence with such naiveté that the statement becomes ironic:

> Tarry service officially began at eight, but it could begin at any time, whenever the Lord moved one of the saints to enter the church and pray. It was seldom, however, that anyone arrived before eight thirty, the Spirit of the Lord being sufficiently tolerant to allow the saints time to do their Saturday-night shopping, clean their houses, and put their children to bed. (P. 49)

He also uses biblical language to describe an action contrary to the spirit of biblical precept and thus reveals hypocrisy in the pious:

> The ministers were being served alone in the upper room of the lodge hall—the less-specialized workers in Christ's vineyard were being fed at a table downstairs. (P. 107)

Although much of the irony is related to the religious views and practices of the characters, some is purely secular:

> Elizabeth found herself in an ugly back room in Harlem in the home of her aunt's relative, a woman whose respectability was immediately evident from the incense she burned in her rooms and the spiritualist séances she held every Saturday night. (P. 162)

The ironic detachment of the narrator is subtly suggested by Baldwin's careful use of the past tense to express a timeless conviction: "For the rebirth of the soul was perpetual; only rebirth every hour could stay the hand of Satan." (P. 113)

Such irony in the narrator's voice runs the risk of leading the reader's sympathy away from the characters and breaking the illusion of intimacy. Indeed, Wallace Graves has charged Baldwin with "literary cuteness" and lack of "moral energy" (honesty) in his treatment of John's mother and natural father, Elizabeth and Richard, because of the narrator's verbal irony in

"Elizabeth's Prayer," where he finds a "shift in technique" from the "highly serious narrator elsewhere in the book."[2] The narrator's irony, however, is not limited to one section of the novel, and it avoids literary cuteness by its subtlety and sparseness. The ironic voice that speaks occasionally through the narrator's diction merely reminds us that there are other points of view from which the ideas and actions might be regarded. Moreover, in many cases the character whose thoughts are being presented may actually share this double view, consciously or unconsciously. A good example is the description of Sister McCandless, seen through John's mind but infused with the narrator's irony:

> There were times—whenever, in fact, the Lord had shown His favor by working through her—when whatever Sister McCandless said sounded like a threat. Tonight she was still very much under the influence of the sermon she had preached the night before. She was an enormous woman, one of the biggest and blackest God had ever made, and He had blessed her with a mighty voice with which to sing and preach. (P. 57)

Similar ambiguity is found in Elizabeth's view of her aunt's threat to move heaven and earth:

> Without, however, so much as looking at Heaven, and without troubling any more of the earth than that part of it which held the court house, she won the day. (P. 155)

Since both John and Elizabeth have serious reservations about the accepted view of the character being described, the irony may reflect their own feelings expressed in the more sophisticated language of the narrator.

The narrator's sophistication and detachment are balanced by his serious tone and poetic intensity of expression in describing important events or psychological perceptions in the lives of his major characters, so that his occasional irony is more like a wry smile than ridicule. The touch of humor in an otherwise passionately serious work relieves tension and gives the complexity of view needed to avoid sentimentality in so closely autobiographical a novel.

Baldwin also uses other kinds of irony to escape from the limitations of the subjective narrator in *Go Tell It on the Mountain.* Most obvious is the dramatic irony made possible by the three long flashbacks, which give the reader information unknown to other characters. For example, when Gabriel is thinking over the events in his life, the reader already knows, because of Florence's revelations, that Gabriel's wife is aware of his infidelity; and therefore the reader finds much irony in his account of scenes between them. Baldwin also uses irony of event to give the reader a corrective viewpoint. So

Gabriel's two chance meetings with his bastard son occur under circumstances that emphasize sexual potency and thus contradict the purely paternal relationship Gabriel assumes.

But the most important and pervasive kind of irony in this novel is developed through the use of biblical texts and Christian doctrine to comment upon the attitudes and actions of the characters. Critics disagree about Baldwin's attitude toward the religious faith he ascribes to the characters in *Go Tell It on the Mountain,* often citing statements from Baldwin's subsequent essays to bolster their arguments.[3] The question is important for understanding the novel, since its main action is the conversion of the hero to that faith and the reader must know whether this resolution is tragic or victorious.[4] Aside from other evidence, unrelated to the subject of irony, which I believe points to the latter interpretation, a cogent argument can be found in Baldwin's use of this religious faith to pronounce judgment on his characters by irony of statement.

For example, Gabriel is ironically judged by his own quotations from the Bible and doctrines of the church. Under the title "Gabriel's Prayer" is an epigraph taken from a Negro spiritual, which asserts, "I ain't no stranger now." This expresses Gabriel's conviction that he is "saved," the fundamental tenet of his religious faith and the basis for his holier-than-thou attitude. If this assumption were allowed to stand uncorrected, the reader would condemn that faith as illusory and deplore John's conversion to it, since Gabriel is revealed as more devilish than saintly. But Baldwin carefully shows the irony of Gabriel's assumption by contrasting it with his own preaching. We learn early in the novel that he has taught his sons that they are in more danger of damnation than African savages precisely because they are not strangers to the gospel. (P. 40) In one of his sermons, he stresses the need for humility and consciousness of sin before God: "When we cease to tremble before him we have turned out of the way." (P. 103) In his thoughts about the tarry service, he remembers that "the rebirth of the soul is perpetual." (P. 113) Gabriel, the preacher and expositor of the faith, thus passes ironic judgment on his own self-righteousness.

Baldwin makes ironic Gabriel's favorite text, which is Isaiah's message to Hezekiah: "Set thine house in order, for thou shalt die and not live"—a quotation Gabriel uses both to terrify his children and to assert his own righteousness. The first mention of this text is ironically placed just after the breakfast scene, which has shown how disordered Gabriel's house is in its family relationships. (P. 32) A second mention during Florence's prayer suggests the further irony that Gabriel is unaware of his own approaching death, or at least of the inevitability of death. (P. 67) But more significantly, the text is used to make ironic Gabriel's unshakeable confidence in the "sign" he believes he received from God. He seizes upon the advent of Elizabeth and her bastard as the sign that God has forgiven him after he has ignored a sign that the reader recognizes as similar to that given Hezekiah the moment after Esther told him of her pregnancy, when the sun stood still and the earth was startled beneath his feet. (P. 129)

In another instance Gabriel's belief that God speaks aloud to men, sometimes through thunder, is turned ironically against his assumption of righteousness. First mentioned early in the novel, (P. 29) this belief becomes important during Deborah's confrontation of Gabriel with his mistreatment of Esther. (PP. 148–149) He justifies his action as God's will: " 'The Lord He held me back,' he said, hearing the thunder, watching the lightning. 'He put out His hand and held me back.' " To make certain that the reader sees the irony, Baldwin has Gabriel repeat his belief about the thunder: " 'Listen. God is talking.' " Gabriel is thus contradicted by the voice of his own God. The final irony on this theme occurs in the conversation between Gabriel and Florence at the end of the novel:

> "I been listening many a nighttime long," said Florence, then, "and He ain't never spoke to me."
> "He ain't never spoke," said Gabriel, "because you ain't never wanted to hear. You just wanted Him to tell you your way was right." (P. 214)

Although Gabriel is the character most often ironically judged by his own religious convictions, Florence and Elizabeth also unwittingly pronounce judgment on themselves. Florence recites the conditions for successful prayer and then fails to meet them in her cry for salvation. (P. 66) Elizabeth tells herself that she is on her way up the steep side of the mountain (P. 185), and then contracts a loveless marriage as "a hiding-place hewn in the side of the mountain." (P. 186)

By using the tenets of their faith for ironic comment upon the characters' actions and attitudes, Baldwin transcends the limitations of his subjective narrator and at the same time establishes as trustworthy the religious faith they profess, even when they misinterpret it. Within the novel the universe works according to the principles of the Hebrew-Christian tradition, and therefore John's conversion is the opening of his eyes to truth—a giant step on his way up the mountain.

In Part Three, "The Threshing Floor," Baldwin introduces an ironic voice that speaks to John during the early stages of his internal struggle. Critics disagree about the identity of this anonymous internal speaker. David Noble asserts that it is the voice of Gabriel, because it expresses Gabriel's wish that John would get up off the threshing floor.[5] In order to accept this identification the reader must see Gabriel as a conscious hypocrite who could encourage John to rebel against his authority to prevent John's salvation, but Baldwin carefully shows Gabriel as an unconscious hypocrite, never capable of overt double-dealing. Other critics have taken the ironic voice as John's own common sense, fighting a losing battle against his weakness for hysterical religion.[6] If the voice is common sense, then John's conversion is a tragedy and his joyful faith an illusion; and this interpretation is contradicted by the tone of the last few pages, by the meaning of the book's title and supporting epigraph, and by the serious attitude toward religious faith implied by Baldwin's use of it for ironic comment. Moreover, John's struggle on the threshing floor is described in terms of birth imagery, and the accomplished delivery sets him free from the womb of childhood. After his conversion he stands up to his father on the equal footing of adulthood, refuting Gabriel's scornful doubts, openly recognizing the enmity between them, and refusing to obey his command. (PP. 207, 220) Obedience to the urging of the ironic voice would have prevented this deliverance and left John in his state of childish rebellion, a prisoner to his longing for parental love and his feeling of sexual guilt.

In terms of the novel, we see the ironic voice as an enemy who presses John to do what Gabriel secretly hopes he will do, what Florence did when she rejected her brother's church and her brother's God. The narrator describes it as malicious: "He wanted to rise—a malicious, ironic voice insisted that he rise—and, at once, to leave this temple and go out into the world." (P. 193) The voice comes from within John, expressing his own wishes, and its main attack is against any belief in this religion, which it attempts to discredit by associating it with "niggers" and by ridiculing the Bible's story of Noah's curse on Ham. (PP. 194, 197) The voice, then, is the voice of unbelief within John, which Baldwin describes as predominant in his state of mind before his conversion. At the beginning of the tarry service he is scornful of the praying women and replies to a kindly, though pious, remark by Sister Price with "a smile that, despite the shy gratitude it was meant to convey, did not escape being ironic, or even malicious." (P. 57) Like Florence, who prays, "Lord, help my unbelief," (P. 67) he is not a believer. His unbelief and hidden scorn are expressed by the ironic voice in the first stages of his struggle on the threshing floor.

The voice also expresses his rebellion against his father, his father's religion, and his father's social status. It labels the tarry service as a practice of "niggers," with the implication that John is above that level, and its spurs him to resist his father's authority:

> Then the ironic voice spoke again, saying: "Get up, John. Get up, boy. Don't let him keep you here. You got everything your daddy got." (P. 196)

This explicit connection of his sexual maturity with his father's enmity brings him to the brink of understanding, but it is not until the ironic voice leaves him that John is able to penetrate the mystery:

> But now he knew, for irony had left him, that he was searching something, hidden in the darkness, that must be found. He would die if it was not found. (P. 199)

When he has rid himself of malice, he is free to search the subconscious depths of his mind until he grasps the true relationship of father and son—the Oedipal situation common to all human experience or, in Baldwin's interpretation, original sin.

Ridding oneself of malice is a necessary condition to salvation. Florence, unable to escape her hatred of Gabriel, founders on this rock, just as Gabriel's pride prevents him from reaching true understanding of the Oedipal situation. When John's malicious irony is swept away, he faces the psychic realities of his subconscious, and then only fear is left—the fear of being an adult, unprotected by parental love and responsible for his own life. Overcoming this fear is the final step—the step Elizabeth has not yet been able to take, and John makes it with Elisha's help. The ironic voice of unbelief, of the devil, of childish rebellion is replaced with the humble voice of faith, of God's angel, of mature self-acceptance, saying, "Yes, go through." (P. 202)

Perhaps Baldwin is suggesting that all irony is in a sense malicious, that human problems cannot be solved by sophisticated detachment or even common sense reasonableness. Certainly the ironic voice of the narrator is lost in the passionate seriousness of John's religious experience, which is the climax and resolution of his conflict.

The Phrase Unbearably Repeated

Eugenia W. Collier

James Baldwin's novel *Another Country* has, as the cliché says, something for everyone—in this instance, something offensive for everyone. Hardly anyone can read this novel without finding one part or another about which this is not true, be it the sordidly graphic descriptions of sex, the detailed treatment of male homosexuality, or the degrading references to race. Set in a junglesque New York, the novel deals with the tangled fortunes (or more accurately, misfortunes) of six characters who can hardly, at first glance at least, be called attractive. Central to the relationships of the other characters is Rufus, the gifted Negro drummer, who commits suicide early in the book but whose ghostly presence is felt throughout like a muffled drumbeat in a sad, sad melody. His sister, his friends, and his near-friends revolve around his memory, caught in his persistent influence, becoming deeply involved in each other's lives and each other's beds. The result is a lurid tale, not always skillfully told, of misplaced sexual passions, a tale seasoned with violence and obscenity.

Yet the book is more than this. It is a brutal book, a violent book; but beneath the violence and brutality there is a terrible tenderness, a hurting compassion. For this is not primarily a book about race or sex. It is a novel about the individual's lonely and futile quest for love. Each of the characters has lost what social workers call his "sense of self," or perhaps has never developed this sense, because of the subtle psychological restrictions imposed by the conform-or-perish demands of contemporary American culture. Each character seeks to complete his incomplete self in the arms of another, but none finds this desperately sought haven because he is a Negro in a white world, or because he is white and loves a Negro, or because he is a man who can love only men, or because he realizes that his marriage is, after all, only another Genêt hall of mirrors. Only Eric, the sensitive actor, comes close to finding the love he seeks, and even he admits that the relationship lacks the security of permanence, for it is a homosexual relationship with a young French boy. The characters remain essentially tragically isolated, seeking peace and certitude in relationships that contemporary mores have made socially unacceptable.

This isolation, this devastating loneliness is the text of Baldwin's sermon in *Another Country*. He develops his theme with the aid of various techniques —descriptions of the cold and often hostile New York landscape, symbols such as the cathedral whose shadow looms like a menacing phallic symbol over the French town, frequent descriptions of physically passionate but spiritually impotent sexual encounters. Of the techniques for underscoring loneliness and the elusiveness of love, the most effective is the use of music. Throughout the book Baldwin plays scorching jazz solos and low-down blues, historically the folk Negro's most expressive means of crying out his pain. By adding a strain of music here and there, Baldwin gives tone and meaning to the deeper emotional aspects of the novel.

The musical idiom gives depth to Baldwin's characterization of Rufus, the person on whom the entire novel hinges. Through Rufus the impenetrable isolation that afflicts the other characters can be seen with three-dimensional clarity. By most standards Rufus is an undesirable. He gets drunk, takes dope, allows himself to be supported by his mistress, hurts his friends, uses vile language, and indulges in a virtually amoral sex life. He is largely responsible for the complete destruction of Leona, his Southern-white mistress. There is little about him that would endear him to the reader. Yet if the novel is to make any sense at all except as a series of case studies in licentiousness, there must be more than this to the pivotal character. And there is. Through musical passages Baldwin reveals other dimensions of Rufus' being, and through Rufus he highlights the underlying theme of loneliness and love.

Rufus' interpretation of a saxophone solo not only gives the reader a sense of his isolation but also represents the keynote of the entire book. Early in the novel, Rufus is part of a jazz combo in a night club. He is feeling good, a little high on pot, when the youthful saxophonist is spotlighted. It is apparent that "somewhere along the line he had discovered that he could say it with a saxophone."[1] As Rufus observes:

> He stood there, wide-legged, humping the air, filling his barrel chest, shivering in the rags of his twenty-odd years, and screaming

through the horn *Do you love me? Do you love me? Do you love me?* And again, *Do you love me?* This, anyway, was the question Rufus heard, the same phrase, unbearably, endlessly, and variously repeated, with all the force the boy had. The silence of the listeners became strict with abruptly focused attention, cigarettes were unlit, and drinks stayed on the tables; and in all of the faces, even the most ruined and the most dull, a curious, wary light appeared. They were being assaulted by the saxophonist who perhaps no longer wanted their love and merely hurled his outrage at them with the same contemptuous, pagan pride with which he humped the air. And yet the question was terrible and real; the boy was blowing with his lungs and guts out of his own short past; somewhere in the past, in the gutters or gang fights or gang shags; in the acrid room, on the sperm-stiffened blanket, behind marijuana or the needle, under the smell of piss in the precinct basement, he had received the blow from which he would never recover and this no one wanted to believe. *Do you love me? Do you love me? Do you love me?*[2]

This passage contains the essential message of the entire book. The nameless, hurt young saxophonist could be any of the characters, could perhaps be Everyman, full of a need that he can express only indirectly—"say it with a saxophone." The boy is young, "twenty-odd years," but already he has been irreparably damaged by the bitter necessity to survive alone in an uncaring world. He has received "the blow from which he would never recover." And so he cries out for love, a vague, generalized cry aimed at the faceless crowd within earshot, "unbearably, endlessly, and variously repeated, with all the force the boy had." The cry does not arise from a desire to give—it is not, "I love you"—but from a desperate need to receive. But even before the cry might possibly elicit positive response, the boy's inability to accept love becomes apparent, for the cry becomes an assault, a hostile expression rather than a loving one, as he "hurled his outrage" with "contemptuous, pagan pride."

This is the experience of each of the principal characters. Rufus seeks Leona's love, admits that he loves her and needs her desperately, but destroys them both with his sadism, for he, too, somewhere has received "the blow from which he would never recover." Vivaldo and Ida seek each other, but their love-making is cruel and belligerent; his possessiveness and her determination to succeed at any price as a singer are symptoms of their respective hurts, which make it necessary for them to approach destruction. Cass, bewildered by a world that she cannot understand, finds temporary respite in the arms of homosexual Eric, but she is left eventually with a shattered marriage that offers none of the security she thought she had. Only Eric seems able to attain a partial ability to function. Homosexuality is the blow he has received. He has been nearly destroyed by his attachment to Rufus; yet he has compromised with life through his relationship with the boy Yves and through a painful acceptance of his lot. Essentially, the saxophonist, with his profound need, his inability to communicate except indirectly, and the hurt that prevents him from accepting the love he needs, is the personification of each of the characters in the book.

The response of the audience as perceived by Rufus also typifies the novel. The screaming question of the sax strikes a responsive chord in each person, "even the most ruined and the most dull," indicating that the lonely search for love is universal, at least in this time and this place. Yet the response is not one of receptivity, but rather one of guardedness and suspicion, for in each face "a curious, wary light appeared." Like the boy who cried out for love and then transformed his cry into an outraged assault, the individual in the audience reveals for an instant his own need (listening raptly, forgetting his cigarette and his drink) but quickly throws a guard around his temporarily exposed sensitivity. Throughout the book this hostile-love reaction occurs, not only in the strange bedroom cavortings of the principals, in which there is a mutual seeking and simultaneously a mutual closing out, but also in numerous flash descriptions of people walking hand in hand but not together, of couples on their way to make dismal love in barren furnished rooms, and of youngsters seeking the meaning of life in liquor, narcotics, and forbidden thrills. The audience is startled by the question in the boy's music. It does not want to believe in the boy's pain, or in its own. Not only in the passage but also in the entire book the question is repeated: "Do you love me? Do you love me?" And the answer on all sides is "I can't."

Baldwin's saxophonist occupies a brief paragraph, pinpointing the theme of the book and giving some insight into the character of Rufus, who hears the disturbing question and notes the response it brings. Later in the novel the author plays a blues accompaniment to an entire scene, utilizing the lovely, earthy blues of Bessie Smith as background music. The scene is the emotional climax of Rufus' life; the blues gives it meaning.

The profound suffering revealed in blues music, especially in the music of Bessie Smith, seems to have special significance for Baldwin himself, if one is to believe his essays and if one is to believe that the most moving and effective art is autobiographical. In an essay in *Nobody Knows My Name,* in which he is explaining how he fled to Europe and there discovered his identity as an American, Baldwin mentions that he "suffered a species of breakdown and was carried off to the mountains of Switzerland. There," he continues, "in that absolutely alabaster landscape, armed with two Bessie Smith records and a typewriter, I began to re-create the life that I had first known as a child and from which I had spent so many years in flight." Bessie Smith (he speaks as if it were the woman herself, not merely her recorded voice) helped him "to dig back to the way I myself must have spoken when I was a pickaninny, and to remember the things I had heard and seen and felt. I had buried them very deep."[3] The blues, especially the blues rendered by Bessie Smith, must have had for Baldwin some meaning intricately tied to the basic emotions and the fundamental experiences that make one what he is, the things that are buried deep and that are only half remembered, or not consciously remembered at all, until some little thing like a strain of music releases them. Baldwin does not say which of Bessie Smith's recordings he had, but one could risk an intelligent guess that among the numbers was "Backwater Blues," which he mentions in another essay in the same volume, describing a Richard Wright story as being as "spare and moving an account as that delivered by Bessie Smith in 'Backwater Blues,' "[4] and which he quotes in another, comparing the "diluted" pain and loss in a Kerouac passage with the real pain and loss in the blues.[5] The blues seems to have special meaning for Baldwin; it is involved with his identity as a Negro and his simultaneous identity as an American, and certainly with the personal and indefinable something that makes him an individual.

In *Another Country,* Baldwin uses Bessie Smith blues to heighten the effectiveness of Rufus' time of self-revelation and decision. A shattered Rufus has come out of his exile in the crowded city, seeking temporary shelter with his friend Vivaldo, who is white. Desperately he tries to understand his part in the series of sadistic episodes which has culminated in Leona's mental collapse. Vivaldo, caught in his ambivalent emotions concerning Rufus, wanders to his phonograph and puts on a recording of "James Pete Johnson and Bessie Smith batting out Backwater Blues."[6] The tone of the scene is set thereafter by the influence of the record.

Here Baldwin describes the apartment. The blues form is extremely economical in language and in pattern. Vivaldo's apartment, the backdrop for the scene, is extremely spare, with no frills or fancy ornaments: "Besides Vivaldo's phonograph, there wasn't much else in the apartment. There was a homemade lamp, brick-supported bookshelves, records, a sagging bed, the sprung easy chair, and the straight-backed chair."[7] The blues is starkly realistic, revealing the sordid details of living. Baldwin's description of the apartment does not neglect unattractive details: "The sink was full of dirty dishes, topped by a jaggedly empty and open tin can. A paper sack of garbage leaned against the kitchen table's uncertain legs."[8] The economy and realism of the blues are fitting background for the glimpse of Rufus' surroundings.

The conversation of Rufus and Vivaldo, which started a page or two back, now assumes a deeper emotional tone:

> *There's thousands of people,* Bessie now sang, *ain't got no place to go,* and for the first time Rufus began to hear, in the severely understated monotony of this blues, something which spoke to his troubled mind. The piano bore the singer witness, stoic and ironic. Now that Rufus himself had no place to go—*'cause my house fell down and I can't live there no mo',* sang Bessie—he heard the line and the tone of the singer, and he wondered how others had moved beyond the emptiness and horror which faced him now.[9]

Through the music one senses the desolation of Rufus' situation. He has lost Leona and, worse than that, he has become aware of his own lost selfhood. Like the saxophonist, he has both sought and rejected love. His house has indeed fallen down, and, being penniless and alone, he has no place to go. Worse than the external "noplace" (for he does have Vivaldo and his own parents) is the inner "noplace," the essential emotional refuge having been revealed to him as illusion. Moreover, through the words and cadences of "Backwater Blues" he has sensed that not only he but actually many people "ain't got no place to go." He finds no comfort in this thought.

With Vivaldo, Rufus gropes about for an idea of what to do next, but soon reverts to the questions of his guilt in Leona's destruction and his own aloneness. Yet somehow the two friends cannot communicate; the raw pain that Rufus is enduring has erected a barrier between them. Rufus has an inexplicable desire to hurt Vivaldo. Vivaldo, trying to help, suggests that Rufus try to forget, but Rufus declares silently (he cannot say this to his friend) that one cannot possibly forget a thing that is so much a part of himself. As the recorded voice has said, he "ain't got no place to go."

When "Backwater Blues" ends, Vivaldo flips over the record, and they listen in silence while Bessie sings:

> When my bed get empty, make me feel awful mean and blue,
> My springs is getting rusty, sleeping single like I do.[10]

The conversation now turns to Rufus' sexual confusion. He speaks of his fear of being consumed by a woman and of latent homosexual desires. He finds that Vivaldo, too, has had these desires. He thinks of his quest for fulfillment with Leona and of the tragic failure of that quest. The music provides an effective background for his thoughts; his bed is permanently empty because he lacks the selfhood to relate positively with another person. As a result, he feels "mean and blue." The realization of the emptiness of his bed is destroying him. Finally Rufus begins to cry, muttering, "I don't want to die." The music continues, "far from him, terribly loud," as Vivaldo strokes Rufus' hair in a vain attempt to comfort him, and as Rufus realizes for the first time that his agony will never stop, that forces within him have made his desperate situation inevitable. The music puts it starkly: ". . . Bessie was saying that she wouldn't mind being in jail but she had to stay there so long."[11] Rufus' own personality, the sum of his experiences and his reaction to them, have created a prison from which escape is impossible.

This scene is one of the most crucial and revealing in the book. After weeks of solitary roaming, Rufus has come to his closest friend, where he has sought some meaning in it all. He has looked deeply into himself and has realized that there is no help for him or any way out of the "jail" that his personality has made inevitable. Perhaps it is here that he has decided upon death as the only alternative. Baldwin has made the scene moving and convincing, and at the same time through his use of the blues has avoided mawkishness.

Relieved by his tears, Rufus reminisces about some of his bad times with Leona. Then he and Vivaldo go out for a nightcap at Benno's, where one becomes aware of the loneliness of people in noisy, gay crowds, people who beneath all the chatter "were locked in a silence like the silence of glaciers. Only the juke box spoke, grinding out each evening, all evening long, syncopated, synthetic laments for love."[12] Even in a crowd, Rufus' isolation as well as the isolation of each other person, is accentuated and made more vivid by music. At Benno's Rufus and Vivaldo encounter their friends Cass and Richard. For a moment Rufus achieves a wordless sort of communication with Cass; he realizes that she cares, not because he is male and she female but simply because he is Rufus. He responds temporarily to this human contact, feeling for this moment that he is capable of beginning to set his world straight. However, the feeling does not endure after Cass has left. As she leaves, she and Rufus say, "So long," to each other, and as he sits there with Vivaldo and Vivaldo's former mistress, the "so long" of Bessie Smith's weary blues runs beneath the chatty conversation, pointing up clearly the hopelessness of Rufus' situation:

> Everyone was gone except Jane and Rufus and Vivaldo.
> *I wouldn't mind being in jail but I've got to stay there so long.*
> The seats the others had occupied were like a chasm now between
> Rufus and the white boy and the white girl.
> "Let's have another drink," Vivaldo said.

So long. . . .
"Let me buy," Jane said. "I sold a painting."
"Did you now? For a lot of money?"
"Quite a lot of money. That's why I was in such a stinking mood the last time you saw me—it wasn't going well."
"You were in a stinking mood, all right."
Wouldn't mind being in jail. . . .
"What're you having, Rufus?"
"I'll stick to Scotch, I guess."
But I've got to stay there. . . .
"I'm sorry," she said, "I don't know what makes me such a bitch."
"You drink too much. Let's just have one drink here. Then I'll walk you home."
They both looked quickly at Rufus.
So long. . . .[13]

Baldwin's juxtaposition of the words to a single blues line and the superficial chatter makes Rufus' silent agony stand out in sharp relief. There is an irregular staccato rhythm to this passage, communicating a nervous excitement. The short sentences of the dialogue interspersed with the broken blues line heighten the feeling of confusion and desperation. Rufus is isolated from other people; he cannot make his terrible sense of imprisonment known by any words or any action. The empty chairs of Cass and Richard express physically the emotional separation of himself and his friends. He is reminded that they are white and he Negro, and this is another dimension of the separation. The sexual overtone of the conversation further excludes him. His lonely despair is sharply expressed in the single Bessie Smith line about being in jail for so long. Excusing himself ostensibly to go to the rest room, Rufus walks out of his friends' lives, out of life entirely, for he wanders alone through the city and finally to the river.

The little flashes of blues music have linked the scene in Vivaldo's apartment, where the moment of perception takes place—Rufus' acceptance of his anguish as inevitable and permanent—with the scene at Benno's where, in spite of a glimmer of hope, he takes the first practical steps toward his physical destruction. In these two scenes Baldwin has given form and color to his characterization of Rufus and, with the aid of Bessie Smith, has given some credibility to the image that the other characters have of Rufus after his death.

Baldwin provides another bit of insight into Rufus' inner self through the music his friends remember him by. His favorite hymn, sung at his funeral, is the haunting "I'm a stranger, don't drive me away." And, indeed, Rufus is a stranger, separated from his conventional Harlem parents by his unconventional way of living, separated from both Negroes and whites by his relationship with Leona, separated from Leona by the barriers of race and the psychological quirks that have become his nature. He is a stranger, and he has been driven away. Later, in a smoky night club where she is making her first public appearance as a singer, his sister, Ida, switches from the raucous blues she has rendered, in order to sing a hymn to Rufus' memory. Ceasing her sensuous movements, she stands motionless and sings:

Hear my cry, hear my call,
Take my hand, lest I fall,
Precious Lord![14]

Here one senses a cry for help, which might have been Rufus' cry. The silent cry has been unheeded, and the stranger has been driven away. Rufus' posthumous music rounds out his character and gives it increased depth.

Rufus, then, is not the villain that a superficial glance would make him seem. He cannot be, if the novel is to attain any artistic height at all, for the character of Rufus is basic to the lives of all the other characters. If the book is to have any meaning, that meaning must be apparent in Rufus. It is largely through the medium of music that Baldwin reveals Rufus as a tragic victim of personal and social forces that he cannot control. In Rufus one first senses the lonely and futile quest for love that fills the book behind the flamboyant sex, the racial epithets, the writing on the toilet door. Perhaps it is this, rather than the sensational aspects of the book, that really appeals to the reader and sparks in him a sad recognition: the desperate *Do you love me? Do you love me?* "unbearably, variously, and endlessly repeated" like a persistent theme repeated and repeated in the melancholy wail of a red-hot sax.

Baldwin Beside Himself: A Study in Modern Phallicism

_____ John S. Lash

I

The literary successes of James Baldwin, author of half a dozen important books published over the past decade, have firmly established him as a major young contemporary writer. Baldwin's book of essays, *The Fire Next Time,* is a succinct and brilliant analysis of America's malignant racism, an analysis given urgency and starkness by a bold and creative logic that ruthlessly devastates the old hypotheses and the easy conclusions with which this matter has been encrusted. His latest novel, *Another Country,* is widely praised by college students, popular critics, and lay readers as something of an event in modern American fiction. At his present level of achievement, few would seriously question statements in *Time, Life* and *Library Journal* that Baldwin is "the most gifted young American writer with a black skin."

The phrase "with a black skin" need not be regarded here, as frequently it must be regarded in conventional summaries of Negro accomplishment, with suspicion. Indeed, one of two startlingly, luminously clear facts about Baldwin is that he is objectively, sensitively, even pridefully a Negro. At this, the precise breaking point for so many Negro writers, he succeeds where the self-conscious Harlem literati of the twenties and their indignant literary heirs of the thirties and forties largely failed: he does, to use the words of a young and then-ambitious Langston Hughes, "express the dark-skinned self."

Baldwin may, in point of very fact, well be called "the first American Negro writer," in view of his candid sense of experiential artistry and in view of the slow distillation of the genius of Ralph Ellison. He has comprehended in his works—and particularly in his essays—the irony, the paradox, the bitterness, the sweetness out of which New World experience has spun the web of the Negro life. The test is this, that the Negro who reads Baldwin's lucid prose is uneasily, but compulsively and poignantly and brutally, at home with himself, and finds himself assenting almost fiercely as he reads. This, in turn, means that the white person who reads Baldwin well learns a great deal about *himself* and learns it from a perspective that he does not encounter in ordinary writing. Baldwin is, then, more—much more—than merely a literary or emotional spokesman or a shrewd and deft publicist or even a relentlessly eidetic folk historian. He is that most complex of all American creatures, an American Negro.

II

But an understanding of Baldwin as a full-blooded Negro is only the beginning of an understanding of the author of *Go Tell It on the Mountain, Giovanni's Room,* and *Another Country.* Standing beside the Negro in Baldwin is another man, a surprisingly devout and hopefully persuasive religionist. It must be remembered here that Baldwin is the son of a preacher, and was himself for a time a boy preacher in Harlem. While he tells us that he was impelled to renounce this calling and to denounce Christianity itself for its brutality and its theological degeneracy, it is evident in both the titles and the content of *Go Tell It on the Mountain* and *The Fire Next Time* that he has retained a conscious need for the securities of a value system that can transfigure the self. This value system he apparently thinks he has found is a modern cult of phallicism, the fear and admiration and worship of the male sex organ. In *Giovanni's Room* and in *Another Country,* Baldwin reveals the articles of his current religious faith. He says, in effect, that the search of man for self-realization comes ultimately to a point of genital cognition, that a morality and an ethic gonadic in inception are instinct in the bodily intercourse of man with man, that in the naked moment of sexual confrontation between man and man are to be found truth stripped of hypocrisy and deceit, self-fulfillment beyond the necessity for proof and measurement, peace and security reuniting the male and masculine flesh and spirit.

It may be argued here that the foregoing is merely a rather pretentious description of homosexuality in the idiom of a professional euphemism. After all, the argument might run, Baldwin spent several years in the demimonde of Paris, where conceptions of the roles of sex partners run to the bizarre, the exotic, the unusual. It would be entirely natural that a young and adventurous writer might launch himself into a grand and tragic fling into the erotica of sex, albeit an avant-garde and continental—and therefore wildly exciting —excursion. There is no need to invest such a sowing of authorial "wild oats" with the trappings of a religious commitment.

When one turns to Baldwin's novels, however, there is little support for this interpretation of the matter of phallicism. Baldwin obviously intends his treatment of sex as a serious presentation of fundamental human relationships. Just as *Go Tell It on the Mountain* is often a delicate and evocative experience in religion, so is *Giovanni's Room* often a tender and poetic savoring of a new religion, and *Another Country,* though often obvious and sophomoric, is far removed from the gross shocks of, let us say, *Tropic of Cancer.* It is, in fact, the burden of Baldwin's last two novels to treat homosexuality as a normal or supernormal behavior pattern, so that he sharply differentiates between phallic confrontation and overt effeminacy. In *Giovanni's Room,* for example, he describes through the eyes of David, his hero—or his villain—himself well into an affair with Giovanni, what would ordinarily be called "the sissy":

> There were, of course, *les folles,* always dressed in the most improbable combinations, screaming like parrots the details of their latest love-affairs—their love-affairs always seemed to be hilarious. Occasionally one would swoop in, quite late in the evening, to convey the news that he—but they always called each other "she"— had just spent time with a celebrated movie star—or boxer. Then all the others closed in on this newcomer and they looked like a peacock garden and sounded like a barnyard. I found it difficult to believe that they ever went to bed with anybody for a man who wanted a real woman would certainly have rather had a real one and a man who wanted a man would certainly not want one of *them.* . . . There was a boy who worked all day, it was said, in the post-office, who came out at night wearing makeup and ear-rings and with his heavy blond hair piled high. . . . People said that he was very nice, but I confess that his utter grotesqueness made me uneasy; perhaps in the same way that the sight of monkeys eating their own excrement turns some people's stomachs. They might not mind so much if the monkeys did not resemble—so grotesquely—human beings.

This description embodies the typical attitude that Baldwin takes toward those who would dramatize and advertise their departures from sexual "norms," and toward those who would regard these "freaks" as either symptomatic or typical of the phallicists. For Baldwin, these exhibitionists are the abnormal, the unusual, the deviates. In contrast David himself is virile and earthy and male, and so finds his sexual preference in intercourse with Giovanni rather than with Hella, his female sweetheart. In contrast, Vivaldo Moore, the strong and earnest white male of *Another Country,* who assigns himself to the impossible task of sexual combat with the capacious and vengeful Negro woman Ida Scott, finds his real manhood and his actual virility in the sex act with Eric Jones:

> .... And they lay together in this antique attitude, the hand of each on the sex of the other, and with their limbs entangled, and Eric's breath trembling against Vivaldo's chest. This childish and trustful tremor returned to Vivaldo a sense of his own power. He held Eric very tightly and covered Eric's body with his own, as though he were shielding him from the falling heavens.

One must add here that Eric Jones is the actual hero of *Another Country,* the phallicist to whom men—and one woman—turn in their hours of bafflement and exaltation, the ministering angel, as it were, of the phallic god residual in the flesh of every man. And Eric is never a simpering, limp-wristed poseur.

The men who are Baldwin's nominal heroes—the aforementioned David and Vivaldo, and Rufus Scott, the Negro musician in *Another Country*—are real and practicing men, who have no desire or intention to employ the trappings of conventional maleness as a facade for deviation. True enough, their province is Another Country, but this is represented by Baldwin as an area of traumatic but definitive experience, rather than as an enclave of sexual bohemianism. "I do *not* like bohemia, or bohemians," Baldwin had said earlier, in *Notes of a Native Son.* His men are therefore to be taken as lustful, predatory, and sometimes lascivious, as men sometimes are in their affairs with women. In the cases of Rufus Scott and Vivaldo Moore, it is true, the sex act with women—for Rufus, with white women, for Vivaldo, with Negro women—takes on a perverse racial symbolism, so that frequently what begins as functional copulation gradually becomes misogynic combat, a trial of both parties by sexual ordeal. By and large, however, these men are capable love partners who through long and promiscuous experience with women have developed a casual expertise in sex play. And each of these men turns eventually to the phallic experience for spiritual gratification.

The crux of this phase of Baldwin's conception, then, is that the definitive function of sex in its generative meaning is not to be found in what becomes an animal act with a female, for such an act, compulsive and exhilarating as it may be, is basically incomplete and realistically anticlimactic. Bisexual love in this conception becomes a stage in the development of phallic maturity. It may be the stage at which the superficial, stereotyped male permits his emotional and spiritual growth to be arrested. But its demands on and its corrosions of the human spirit are of such a nature that man and woman are transfixed in the animal position, and their behavior at this stage is essentially animal behavior.

Thus, in *Another Country* Rufus Scott, the Negro musician, and Leona, the Southern white girl who comes to New York in a bewildered search for her soul, are transformed from the human to the animal level at the climax of the sex act: "A moan and a curse tore through him while he beat her with all the strength he had." Thus, David in *Giovanni's Room* comes to say of his passion with Hella: "I sometimes watched her naked body move and wished that it were harder and firmer . . . and when I entered her I began to feel that I would never get out alive." Thus, the affair between Vivaldo Moore and Ida Scott ends in his spiritual surrender to her: "Her long fingers stroked his back, and he began, slowly, with a horrible, strangling sound, to weep, for she was stroking his innocence out of him." The language in which Baldwin describes bisexualism is, or comes to be, the guttural Anglo-Saxon noise of passion, and the climax of this sex act is an orgastic spewing of venom.

Juxtaposed against this conception are the almost transcendent and ineluctable experiences of the phallicists, whose sex acts in Baldwin's novels are veritable acts of love and fulfillment. The fusion of the male with the male is handled with a kind of daintiness that almost, but not quite, becomes delicacy, and there is a disinclination to be specific and gross—one might call it *restraint*—which vaguely conjures up the circumlocutions of *Lolita*. In *Giovanni's Room*, David, guilty and somewhat shrinking but unable to control his situation, says:

> Sometimes when he was not near me, I thought, I will never never let him touch me again. Then, when he touched me, I thought, it doesn't matter, it is only my body, it will soon be over. When it was over I lay in the dark and listened to his breathing and dreamed of the touch of hands, of Giovanni's hands, of anybody's hands, hands which would have the power to crush me and make me whole again.

In *Another Country,* the third section of the book, significantly called by

Baldwin "Toward Bethlehem," includes the reaction of Vivaldo to his passion with Eric:

> Then they lay close together, close, hidden, and protected by the rain. . . . Vivaldo seemed to have fallen through a great hole in time, back to his innocence, he felt clear, washed, and empty, waiting to be filled. He stroked the rough hair at the base of Eric's skull, delighted and amazed by the love he felt.

What is striking about *Giovanni's Room* in comparison with *Another Country* in the matter of phallic ecstasy is the fact that Baldwin assumes the acceptability, if not the respectability, of homosexuality with candor and a certain self-righteousness in the latter work. Having introduced the theme with considerable success in *Giovanni's Room,* he pursues it in *Another Country* with a kind of calm assurance which takes for granted both the honesty and the legitimacy of the phallic experience. This is as it should be if it is conceded that the writer must be granted his hypotheses. What may also be true, however, is that Baldwin senses a more sophisticated audience for his kind of novel, an audience tacitly prepared to suspend any uneasiness or misgiving that homosexuality as a fact of human relations might ordinarily involve. After all, the speech and the mannerisms of Baldwin's men are echoic of the public images of a growing number of theatrical and literary personages who make something of a display of their affection one for the other. It takes little or no effort to call up either the names or the behavior of these real-life people. Thus, Baldwin undoubtedly impresses many of his readers, particularly his adolescent and college audience, that he is writing from the inside of a daring new freedom of sexual choice now frankly enjoyed by a rising generation of "free souls." The reader never enters this province, of course, but he may easily feel that he is catching glimpses of its glamour, and that he is gaining an initiation of sorts into its mystique.

Thus, Baldwin presents these acts of love through indirection and implication. He concentrates on the preliminary love-play, which awakens his men to the exquisite moment of their self-realization. He dwells on the salubrious, emotional, and spiritual effects of phallic experience. He sets forth with some gravity the moral and ethical contexts out of which the phallicists must define their special concepts of virtue and vice. But he veils in ritual mystery the sex experience itself when that experience involves man and man. This does not appear to be a refusal to pander to the appetites of certain readers for lurid detail, since his descriptions of the bisexual act are both lengthy and specific. Moreover, his references to transvestism, sodomy, and other obvious forms of flagellation are uniformly scornful, so that there can be no doubt of the contempt of the phallicists for "perversion." What remains, therefore, is the presentation of an inscrutable sensualism that, we must believe, involves various forms of catharsis and regeneration for the cultist. He is brought to a deeper understanding and a more meaningful comprehension of "the reality of human experience stretched to its limits," to use the words of the publisher's notice on *Another Country.*

It was inevitable, one supposes, that Baldwin should undertake to fuse the two themes, race and sex, which he handled well separately, and that he would submit the problems of American racism to the phallic gods. Historically speaking, at least, the American race problem has always had both overt and subtle sexual involution, and the complications of racial adjustment have frequently knotted themselves into an endless tangle of sexual fears and frustrations. Social historians and psychologists have verified what many novelists have theorized concerning the fact of this involvement of sex in race and the definitive nature of the involvement. There is, indeed, an elaborate and popular mythology that surrounds and beclouds the operation of these two forces in human adjustment. One must presume that a conscientious phallicism of the sort to which Baldwin seems presently committed would necessarily submerge race into sex and would by profession and practice assume the transcendency of the sexual ethic over the racial.

Baldwin must, therefore, show us his racial sinners in the hands of the compassionate phallic gods, gods who must dictate, of course, that racism is so much chaff to be driven away and dissipated by the strong currents of religious seizure. In *Giovanni's Room,* David remembers poignantly his first venture into phallicism, with a certain Joey, a Negro boy whose "body was brown, was sweaty, the most beautiful creation I had ever seen till then." Not realizing at the time how "this could have happened to me, how this could have happened *in* me," David recoils from the experience, but comes much later to know, "I began, perhaps, to be lonely that summer and began, that summer, the flight which has brought me to this darkening window," awaiting the execution of the ardent and petulant Giovanni. *In Another Country,* Eric Jones, then a young boy in the South, found that his passion for a Negro boy made him indifferent, even defiant in his brushes with the folkways of racism. Eventually fleeing from the South, he finds himself once again engrossed in a mature phallic experience, with Rufus Scott, the tragic Negro musician. Scott, in the meantime, has on occasion sought refuge from the whiplashes of the Negro life in New York in sexual indulgences with Vivaldo Moore, his best friend. It is, in fact, their mutual phallic experiences with Rufus which finally enable Eric and Vivaldo to come together "toward Bethlehem" for a darkling glimpse of self-discovery.

On the basis of even a superficial analysis of homosexuality and race, it would appear that a certain camaraderie of cult arbitrates the human relationships of the initiates, so that they are brought together into an adhesion of sorts as a defense against social disapproval. There may also be a compulsive seeking after kind which foreshortens the ordinary dimensions of social distance in such areas as race, class, and family status. It seems clear that those who can summon up the kind of courage or disdain that must always accompany an avowed unorthodoxy would be disposed to minimize that which is irrelevant to their most positive commitment. It follows that the phallicists, in view of both the positive and the negative pressures to which they must be subject, grope through the accidental circumstances of superficial existence to find each other, for they must find each other if they are to find the self.

Ironically, however, the phallic gods have no absolute answers for Baldwin's men, and phallicism itself cannot suffice for Baldwin either in its preachments or in its practices. Baldwin's men can find surpassing delight in their rituals; they can feel exhilaration and satiation in the ceremonies of their profession; they may even find each other and so find a legitimate identity. But they do not find a reconciliation with life itself, except as they abandon themselves to a progressive deterioration toward the furtive and sordid level of twilight existence of which both they and Baldwin are scornful. Thus, David says at last, "I look at my sex, my troubling sex, and wonder how it can be redeemed, how I can save it from the knife. . . . I must believe, I must believe that the heavy grace of God, which has brought me to this place, is all that can carry me out of it." Rufus Scott commits inglorious suicide. Vivaldo Moore, surrendering to Ida Scott, must spend a miserable life with her. Eric Jones, facing reunion with the young, fresh Yves (pronounced, perhaps not without some significance, "Eve") cannot be certain that his young man will not defect from phallicism to the allurements of a bold, egregious New World feminism.

Perhaps Baldwin's actual problem, a problem that he cannot recognize from the close range of experiential writing, is that he has failed to understand the extent of his own rejection of a *religion*—any religion—even though that religion be phallicism. Perhaps his problem is that he cannot see that sex *in any form* is not the ultimate answer to self-fulfillment. Baldwin writes well about sex and he writes well about religion. He can be tender and poetic and expressive on either subject, as he is in *Go Tell It on the Mountain,* as he is in *Giovanni's Room.* But he cannot fuse the two in the phallic orientation which he is presently following, or if he can, he will not realize the marvelous potential which everywhere shines through his great talent.

"One writes of one thing only," he says, "one's own experience. Everything depends on how relentlessly one forces from this experience the last drop, sweet or bitter, it can possibly give." We can hope that Baldwin's yet-to-come experience will enable him, drive him to do what he defines as "the only real concern of the artist, to recreate out of the disorder which is life that order which is art." He has confronted himself as a Negro with searing honesty; he has confronted himself as a phallicist with boldness and candor. What remains is that he shall confront himself as a man.

Baldwin's Female Characters
A Step Forward?

_____ Jacqueline E. Orsagh

By now it is a well-accepted fact that there have been very few, if any, well-developed and believable women characters in English and American literature. Male authors have most often left us with a flat and poorly developed female portrait. Perhaps they have not been able sufficiently to penetrate the female psyche to draw an accurate picture of her, or perhaps they have not cared to. In either case, we have been left with stereotypes.

The treatment of women in literature has reflected a protective, patronizing attitude. Writers have maintained a very strict role definition and have, in most cases, consciously upheld the concept of the double standard. Consequently the equality of men and women is a notion absent from literature. There has often been a certain aura, a certain mystery surrounding the makeup of the female, perhaps stemming from a lack of insight into her character. And this mystery or lack of understanding manifests itself particularly in the literary division of women.

From the earliest folktales and the oldest biblical stories through the literature of Hawthorne, Cooper, Irving, and up to twentieth-century authors including Hemingway and Fitzgerald, writers have divided women into the dark lady and the dove lady: the bad and the good, the prostituted and the pedestaled, the Eve and the Virgin. Women have not been drawn as human, self-fulfilling individuals with the infinite contradictions and conflicts of the human psyche. They have been more easily handled by these authors as stereotypes, which perpetuate preconceived notions.

Female authors have also failed, in large degree, to draw us convincing portraits of self-sufficient women. Austen's women lack "wholeness" in that they are sexless, passionless beings confined to a stiflingly narrow atmosphere and say nothing of profundity. Like their creator, they suffer from the marriage obsession. Alcott's women are perpetually children, and Charlotte Brontë, although she flatters Jane Eyre with possibly the first female childhood in English or American literature, still fails to take Jane out of the "feminine mystique." Jane, always someone's servant, remains patient and enduring, and she lives, she exists, for love.

James Baldwin's literature, however, immediately presents us with female characters who are extraordinarily strong, dynamic, and, even more importantly, interesting. In even his earliest fiction, his women *act*. Florence, Deborah, Esther, and Elizabeth in *Go Tell It on the Mountain* are thinking, passionate, and strong women. In particular, Florence rebels against the injustice and suffocation of sexual role definition and double standard and dramatically leaves the safety of her home for New York, declaring her self-sufficiency: " 'I'm a woman grown,' she said. 'I know what I'm doing.' " (P.77)* Baldwin shows us a glimpse of her adolescence, which makes her unflinching decisiveness, her bitterness toward men, and her religious disbelief believable. We are prepared, also, for Florence's traumatic sexual conflicts. Baldwin has made her too passionate a woman not to be heatedly aroused and, at the same time, too desperately independent and resentful of men to surrender to them. Although at an early stage in his writing, Baldwin has created a female character whose intensity and conflicts we can almost "feel" burn within ourselves:

> And, while he spoke, his hand was on her breast, and his moving lips brushed her neck. And this caused such a war in her as could scarcely be endured. She felt everything in existence between them was part of a mighty plan for her humiliation. She did not want his touch, and yet she did: she burned with longing and froze with rage. (P. 87)

Baldwin's women most obviously differ from other fictitious females in that they *act*. They do not passively wait for Prince Charming and life to embrace them; they act and are not condemned for doing so. Society offers no protection to Baldwin's women; they are realistically thrust into a world hostile to their very existence and the key is survival. This is not true only with his black women; his portrayals transcend race. Leona, Cass, and Barbara exemplify three very different white women to whom the world has been, is, or becomes an antagonistic force to self-fulfillment and meaningful existence. And these women's actions cannot be dismissed along with those of a

---

* All page references in the text of this essay are to the Dell Publishing Company's editions of the works of James Baldwin.

character like Sister Carrie. There is nothing deterministic about Baldwin's females. On the contrary, Juanita, Leona, Cass, Ida, and Barbara appraise and evaluate circumstances, choose, and forge their own paths *in spite of* the pressures of family and society.

Even a minor and relatively non-memorable character such as Jo in *Blues For Mister Charlie* fits into this pattern. She recognizes that her choice to marry Lyle is an attempt to invest her life with meaning. She realizes her intellectual superiority to her husband, and she is aware that she moves in a very limited circle. Yet within this feminine mystique we watch Jo's mind question and sift and we witness her choice and her act. She discovers that Lyle could have loved a black woman with more intensity than he has felt for her, and that such a forceful passion could have led him to kill Old Bill. If Lyle were capable of commiting one murder he could commit another, and Jo startlingly concludes that her husband is a murderer. Before she is to testify, Jo recalls her fears of old-maidenhood and her desperate need for a husband. She realistically surmises that her means of identification and her meaning in life are inextricably tied to her marriage vows. She chooses to protect the life that means so much to her and, of her own volition, perjures herself on the witness stand. The act is a drastic one for a woman so seemingly timid and pallid as Jo.

Baldwin's women are believable: they weep, they laugh, they strike, they bleed. There is no aura of mystery about his female characters—they enjoy sex, they exploit sex, or they fear sex—and Baldwin feels no hesitation in delving into the female psyche concerning sex or anything else. His women are believable and dynamic, especially because they scrutinize life, come to some kind of grips with it, and transcend their old existence in a beautiful but understandable way. Juanita, in a moment of self-realization, declares to Pete that Richard's coming back has forever changed her life. She realizes that she has never really known who she is—she recognizes the whole ignorance of her previous existence. And the knowledge she has gained tells her that life is too complex for her ever to understand herself. The one being who could call himself a man has been cruelly torn from her and she begins to perceive her need for a "flesh and blood" lover. She transcends the Juanita of the first act and, resorting to her gift of creation, passionately hopes that she is, indeed, pregnant. She sees the means of salvation within herself—in the womb that could nourish the life of a man—a man who could begin to save her people:

"I'm not afraid. I hope I'm pregnant—I *hope* I am! One more illegitimate black baby— ... And I am going to raise my baby to be a man. A *man* you dig? Oh, let me be pregnant, let me be pregnant, don't let it all be gone! A man. Juanita. A man. Oh, my God, there are no more . . . Let me be pregnant! Let me be pregnant!" (PP. 125–26)

Before our eyes Juanita enters womanhood in a most profound sense. Few such moments of realization have occurred in literature; fewer moments have involved women.

Just as Jo and Juanita grow and develop to a level of deeper insight, so does a woman like Cass change. In *Another Country* Cass is the sheltered liberal who has come from a "good background" and married the first man with whom she has made love. Baldwin here presents us with a rare phenomenon in his literature—woman as child. Cass is the girl in the fairytale world who tries to heal all the wounds of those around her. Her remarkable intuition and soothing kindness are not necessarily more than the instinctive magnanimity and response of an idealistic child. Baldwin clearly contrasts his naive woman with Ida, his woman of experience, and through the inevitable clash Cass is forced to witness the shattering of her tight and idyllic world:

> She began, dimly and unwillingly, to sense the vast dimensions of Ida's accusation at the same time that her ancient, incipient guilt concerning her life with Richard nosed its way, once more, into the front hall of her mind. (P. 294)

She moves, then, from childlike simplicity and contentment to a sad, but realistic, disillusionment. Yet Cass wears her new-found realistic, if pessimistic, attitude with a dignity, and Baldwin uses her truths not to destroy her but rather to elevate her. Cass' final speeches show her at her most believably dynamic and majestic:

> "I'm beginning to think . . . that growing just means learning more and more about anguish. That poison becomes your diet—you drink a little of it every day . . . You begin to see that you, yourself, innocent, upright you, have contributed and do contribute to the misery of the world. Which will never end because we're what we are . . ." (P. 341)

That Baldwin's female characters are credible and dynamic, and that Baldwin is able and desirous of penetrating their minds, thus explaining moments of profound self-realization, provokes speculation. Why does Baldwin accomplish what scores of writers have not? Why are his women convincing when those of famous writers from past to present are not? Perhaps other authors have not tried to understand the female or perhaps they have felt intimidated by her. In any case, one reason, of course, is Baldwin's blackness and his cultural heritage. Women play a different role in the black community; they cannot afford to "wait," they cannot be passive. Life's suddenness requires instant action. A moment wasted in waiting may mean loss of life. In the matriarchal black community the woman has, by necessity, an *active* role in survival. Thus it is easy for Baldwin, as the product of such a community, to picture woman as strong, dynamic, active, and even dominant. He is not handicapped by the same socialization as the white writer and he does not have to deal with the "white male ego." His blackness, however, cannot alone account for his facility in handling female characters. Black authors such as Wright and Ellison cannot approach Baldwin in this regard; their women, although playing active roles, fail to impress us as dynamic, credible, or fully drawn.

Perhaps Baldwin's success in his female portraits is the result of a genuine attempt on his part to make his women real to us. Perhaps he has assumed one challenge of an artist, to endow all his characters with the persuasive and fully developed attributes of human beings. Perhaps his perception of women is influenced by his bisexuality.

In any case, to do justice to Baldwin's treatment of women, we must scrutinize his more extensive female portraits. Elizabeth and Florence are active, strong, and decisive women, but they are not memorable, and their portraits are relatively brief. Baldwin's women are most carefully and clearly developed in his novels. *Another Country,* for example, presents three memorable, dynamic, and very different women.

The least developed, of course, is the character of Leona. Yet in her Baldwin places the tremendous insight that all his characters, but especially his women, possess and with her he illustrates the conflict always present in racially mixed couples. Rufus looks upon Leona, whom his friend dubs "Little Eva," and he suddenly recalls his days in boot camp in the South, again feeling "the shoe of a white officer against his mouth." (P. 17) One problem with Leona is that Rufus vacillates between regarding her as mere sexual meat and thinking of her as a person. While taking Leona to the party, Rufus' thoughts of her fluctuate within minutes: "And pussy's just pussy as far as I'm concerned. . . ." (P. 17) And then:

> Something touched his imagination for a moment, suggesting that
> Leona was a person and had her story and that all stories were trou-
> ble. (P. 17)

If he can think of her in merely sexual terms, Rufus is spared the threat of an emotional involvement, for at this point in Baldwin's literature, man and woman cannot help but destroy each other. In *Another Country,* the more intense the relationship, the more deadly the result. Only the homosexual lovers can sustain a mutually satisfying and peaceful relationship. For the unstable Rufus, any involvement is dangerous, but a relationship with a white Southern girl who has serious problems herself means, literally, his suicide and, symbolically, his murder of her.

Baldwin depicts Leona as a loving girl who has suffered miserably yet harbors no resentment toward the world. Baldwin forces us to believe in her childlike simplicity, and when Rufus' anger rises at the Italian adolescent's protesting stares, we believe Leona's innocent wisdom:

> "You talking about that boy? He's just bored and lonely, don't know no better . . . Well, that's what's the matter with most people . . . ain't got nobody to be with. That's what makes them so evil."
> (P. 31)

All of Baldwin's women possess amazing insight, but his white women, perhaps because of their relative innocence, possess startling depths of compassion and understanding. After a vicious and unwarranted beating by Rufus, Leona feels no anger or even remorse. On the contrary, her heart goes out to Rufus, again with her childlike wisdom:

> "I love him, I can't help it. No matter what he does to me. He's just lost and he beats me because he can't find nothing else to hit. . . . Rufus ain't going to kill nobody but himself." (P. 55)

Earlier, Leona shows that she clearly understands Rufus when she tells Vivaldo that Rufus does not believe that he is "good enough" for her. Leona's compassion and insight are somehow believable in this simple girl who yearns to crawl into a safe, warm corner of the world and be loved. There is no reason that a "poor white" Southern woman could not possess both great perception and great love, even though the world has lashed out to strike her again and again.

It is interesting to note, however, that in Baldwin's couples the woman always possesses greater personal and worldly insight. More than this, the woman is often more aggressive, more intelligent, and more successful—she is the stronger character. In *Blues for Mister Charlie,* Juanita is clearly the most dynamic, intelligent, clear-sighted, and aggressive character in the drama. Even pallid, timid Jo outshines Lyle in business sense as well as personal insight. In *Another Country,* Leona shows more perspective and love than Rufus, and he becomes wholly dependent on the money she brings home. Cass outsteps Richard in every intellectual and perceptive quality, and Ida dominates Vivaldo with her long-learned knack of managing the world. Thus Baldwin holds to no traditionally defined roles, or, as is more often the case, he inverts those roles. His men—Lyle, Richard, Vivaldo, Rufus, and even Leo—find themselves dependent on and at the mercy of his women. Likewise, Baldwin maintains no double standard in his fiction. Ida, who has made herself "the biggest, coolest, hardest whore around," is applauded rather than condemned for her success in surviving the world and salvaging her self. The only reference in any of Baldwin's material to the double standard or dove lady-dark lady division is found in *Blues For Mister Charlie,* when the pathetic and condemned Lyle, who has exploited every feasible black woman, desires for his wife "the only virgin left in town." (P. 142)

Although what we see of Leona is believable, we see half her portrait through the eyes of Rufus and that portrait is necessarily limited. The characters of Cass and Ida, however, are stronger, more memorable, and we see them through their own eyes. Baldwin allows us, in fact he forces us, to penetrate their minds. Taken together, Cass and Ida are beautifully drawn foils who look upon each other from "opposite sides of a chasm in the mountains, trying to discern each other through the cloud and the fog, but terribly frightened of the precipice at their feet." (P. 294) At opposite ends of the spectrum, Ida and Cass may be understood as Baldwin's representation of the woman of experience and the woman of innocence. Where Ida is initially introduced as an African beauty and later described in terms of a "deep, slow-burning, carnal heat," Cass admits that she has never been "really pretty." Vivaldo recalls that he has never "thought of Cass and Richard as lovers" and we recognize that Cass' portrayal is practically sexless. She moves from what has become a "sexless" relationship with Richard to an involvement with a homosexual. She has known only two men in her life; Ida, of course, has known too many. Baldwin's polarity of whore and virgin make understandable the other attributes of these women. Ida, as black woman, has had to prostitute herself to survive and her outlook, consequently, is a violent and bitter, yet clear-sighted and realistic one. Cass, on the other hand, still exists as a child within the feminine mystique and her outlook is pacifist, idealistic, and lacking in foresight. Both women, for example, look out their taxi window at Central Park, and where one sees "only the trees and the lights and the grass and the twisting road and the shape of the buildings beyond the path," the other looks out resentfully at "one of the world's greatest jungles," knowing from her experience that behind the "damn dainty trees and shit, people are screwing and sucking and fixing and dying." (P. 293) Ida has never allowed herself the luxury of trust, either in herself or in anyone but Rufus. Because she has cruelly used every man she has encountered in order not to be exploited herself, she has become obsessed with the belief that she is and always will be a whore. Her world collapses with the traumatic realization that she actually loves Vivaldo and that the pure and romantic love, so desirable, can never be hers; Vivaldo has come too late:

> "But imagine . . . that he came, *that* man who's *your* man— . . . and there wasn't any place for you to walk out of or into, because he came too late. And no matter when he arrived would have been too late—because too much had happened by the time you were born, let alone by the time you met each other." (P. 294)

Ida, forced to hold her head high in order not to destroy herself with hate, thus develops a "sense of self so profound and so powerful that it does not so much leap barriers as reduce them to atoms." (P. 215) Ida, then, is proud, powerful, and potentially dangerous. Cass, on the other hand, possesses no sense of self. Her whole life has been a deceptive dream and she fails to perceive, until Ida forces her to unwillingly comprehend, her real distance from reality and her own exploitation of Richard.

Ida speculates that although she loves Vivaldo, she will never marry, for "love doesn't have as much to do with it as everybody seems to think." (P. 292) To Cass, Richard and her children have been her whole life, and, in the last analysis, she cannot relinquish them.

Baldwin's polarization of Cass and Ida is not comparable to the simple stereotyping of many authors. Most obviously, the dark lady, Ida, is never condemned or punished for her unladylike behavior. No such judgment of Ida is imposed by the author, nor does he allow his audience one. Only Ida brands Ida whore and Cass is never pedestaled. On the contrary, Cass steps out of the feminine mystique and her only reward is eventual disillusionment. Ida has had several men and she is unhappy with her lot in life. Cass' fidelity to her first love and husband leaves her eventually dissatisfied and she violates her wedding vows and flings herself on Eric. Although depicted as whore, Ida possesses "monarchal beauty" and never, for a moment, is she dispossessed of her dignity or majesty. The woman of sexual experience shows us the "unaccountable Puritan in her" by condemning Cass' lack of foresight and foolishness in her adultery. Ida's sudden morality is understandable if we recall that her struggle for survival, security, and life itself has necessitated an extremely well-calculated behavioral pattern. Cass, on the other hand, cannot comprehend the danger of losing that which she has always so easily possessed.

Neither Cass nor Ida fits a mold, for Baldwin has not made use of stereotypes to facilitate his characterizations. Rather, he has shown us two women who have come from opposite paths in life and thus possess opposite attitudes and personalities; but these women also possess the complex intricacies and ambivalences of all human beings.

Baldwin has also made Cass and Ida believable by furnishing us with an almost infinite number of details about each. When Ida sings her first song for a public audience, we see that the "only sign of her agitation" is "in her hands," which are "tightly, restlessly clasped before her." (PP. 214-15) We learn that she disapproves of surprises and that she sleeps with one hand half covering her face and the other "hidden between her thighs." Of Cass we know that she "rather" likes Puerto Ricans; that she is moved more by one son's "shy, grave charm" than by the other's "direct, more calculating presence"; and that Ida's reddening makes her realize, "for the first time, that a Negro girl could blush."

More importantly, Baldwin brings Cass and Ida to life by allowing us to hear them speak and watch them act and interact. Baldwin bestows several pages of development of thought and insight on his women. We see Ida, for example, in several different, but all very feasible, situations. She spits hatred at Vivaldo when her security or her precariously balanced self-respect is threatened:

> "You meant exactly what I thought you meant . . . Can't none of you white boys help it. Every damn one of your sad-assed white chicks think they got a cunt for peeing through, and they don't piss nothing but the best ginger ale, and if it wasn't for the spooks wouldn't a damn one of you white cock suckers *ever* get laid. That's *right*. You are a fucked-up group of people. You hear me? a *fucked-* up group of people." (P. 237)

But when Vivaldo reacts to her vicious cursing and her shattering of their dishes and the consequent pipe-pounding by the outraged tenants by sliding to the floor and howling in belly laughter, jibing her with, "I'm just a fucked-up group of people," Ida helplessly laughs and lets him pull "her down on top of him." We witness as she checks herself in her sexual passion with Vivaldo and we witness the following morning when he brings her "over the edge" and into "his possession." Indeed the intense love scene between Vivaldo and Ida is so intimate, so human, and so telling of Ida's futile dream to go to bed with someone she *likes*. She desperately wants Vivaldo to know her better and yet she hesitates to be the one to teach him "the score." One moment she independently and determinedly walks out on Vivaldo to earn points for her goal of success by prostituting herself to Ellis, and, at another moment, she clings to Vivaldo "as though she were a child, mutely begging for reassurance and forgiveness."

Baldwin forces us to understand Ida's contradictions by posing her in numerous moods and emotions. We know that Ida is not what she wants to be, but rather what she has had to be, and Vivaldo forces her to realize her hope of what could have been. Vivaldo's whiteness also forces repercussions in Ida's psyche; she has learned to protect herself by hating the white race, and like Rufus, she cannot come to grips with loving a white person:

> "If any *one* white person gets through to you, it kind of destroys your—single-mindedness. They say that love and hate are very close together. Well, that's a fact." (P. 295)

Ida recognizes that her tremendous conflict of emotional forces prohibits her from marrying anyone, least of all white Vivaldo, who knows nothing of what life is like for her. She bitterly informs Cass that marriage "would be the end of him, and the end of" Ida. Forced into an awareness of her own position, Cass realizes her actual relation to Richard:

> She had always seen much farther than Richard, and known much more; she was more skillful, more patient, more cunning, and more single-minded; and he would have had to be a very different, stronger, and more ruthless man, *not* to have married her. (P. 294)

She concludes in a sort of wise epiphany:

> But this was the way it always had been, always would be, between men and women everywhere. Was it? (P. 294)

Indeed both Cass and Ida are stronger, more independent, and more active than their men, and just as the relationship between Leona and Rufus results in her commitment and his suicide, both Cass and Ida will, through that love which so closely holds to hate, destroy their men and, then, themselves. Vivaldo early recognizes "how deadly it must be for Richard . . . to deal with a woman like Cass," (P. 233) and Cass, after her explosive confession to Richard, relates to Eric, in a moment of clarity and self-realization, how she destroyed Richard and scarred herself:

> "And I was happy because I'd succeeded so brilliantly, I thought, in making him what I wanted him to be. And of course he can't understand that it's just that triumph which is intolerable now. I've made myself—less than I might have been—by leading him to water which he doesn't know how to drink. It's not *for* him. But it's too late now." (P. 341)

No male-female relationship can succeed in this novel without seriously damaging the partners, and the woman seems to be the *active* villain in the crime. Only the homosexual relationship remains unscarred. As long as Eric has Yves, he is spared serious entanglement with Cass; but, as Ida points out with characteristic accuracy, if he and Cass continued their affair for five years nothing would remain of either of them, no more than if she and Vivaldo remained together as long. Baldwin's women in *Another Country* are beautifully believable, dynamic, and active, but an ominous tension works beneath every portrait. Is the dominant woman poison to her lover? Is there, can there be a satisfactory male-female love relationship in his literature? In *Another Country*, the answer is no, and Cass' question resounds—*is* this the way it always will be between men and women everywhere? Are women, to Baldwin, always the stronger? Do they always support and bolster their men only, eventually and inevitably, to tear them to shreds?

Baldwin's "final" novel, *Tell Me How Long The Train's Been Gone* (1968), holds his most extensive female portrait and begins to answer Cass' question. At the novel's start, Barbara is a very real and believable character. She is an actress who is paired with Leo Proudhammer as a fellow artist. She revives him after his serious heart attack and we witness what seems to be a beautifully unselfish and mutual love between the artists. Leo, for the first time, recognizes this love without fear and it sheds light on the whole story of his past, the story that becomes Baldwin's novel. The story is that of Leo Proudhammer, but, in part, it is also the story of Barbara, for Baldwin tries desperately to make her real to us. She shares with Leo the spotlight of the dramatic world in which they move and she shares with Leo the action and plot of the novel. She more than influences Leo; she inspires, encourages, and, at times, elevates him. Barbara moves by herself and for herself; but it so happens that this white woman and black man attempt a beautifully proud and free love. And, indeed, they finally do attain what Leo terms their "difficult equanimity."

Barbara, more than any other female character in Baldwin's major fiction, comes close to being a protagonist. And here a male author tries to create a vibrant, powerful, and believable woman and co-star her with his male artist. The symmetry is beautiful. Both have to overcome their backgrounds, opposite and stereotyped though they may be. Where Leo has to shrug off the ghetto with its poverty and misery, Barbara has to shun her Kentucky "class" with its emotional desperateness. She easily overcomes the taught prejudices concerning the black race; Leo, not so easily, overcomes his fear and awe of white flesh. They strive and scrape and fight for survival in the Darwinian atmosphere of the dirty, grimy Village. Slowly and gradually the breaks come—admission into the workshop, execution of a skit for Saul, Leo's becoming a singing waiter (at Barbara's suggestion), and Barbara's being chosen for summer stock. Leo's big move into artistry is spotlighted, where Barbara's is stated as past fact, but this event is so momentous and transcendental to Baldwin that only one such incident may be included and the hero, the protagonist is, beyond doubt, Leo Proudhammer.

As already mentioned, Barbara's first appearance in the novel is one of tenderness and love and credibility. Through Leo's fond memories we see the portrait of a very real young woman, scratching for success among the grit and filth of poverty, struggling to forge a future for herself as an artist. We know that she has come from a wealthy Kentucky family but that, although very young, she is innately too intelligent and too open-minded to live within the stifling atmosphere of bigotry and pretense. We see her first in action at a party to which she has dragged Leo, and at which she stands up marvelously to all the pompous fools present. Already she and Leo are communicating without words, taking cues for their actions from each other. Their rapport stretches beyond word or gesture and they can anticipate the movements and emotions of one another.

Barbara has already proven herself to us as an amazingly independent and self-sufficient young woman. No one can ever get the best of her in an argument and no one seems ever to hurt her. She has grown up exceedingly fast; she has had three affairs and an abortion before the age of twenty, and yet Baldwin shows us no emotional scars. Barbara has no hangups. Indeed the more we know her, the more we see her interact and give and share and be so fair and free and unselfish, the less we tend to believe in her. Her background, by which Baldwin attempts to endow her with depth and, thus, reality, falls flat. We never feel that she is a wealthy Kentucky girl; we feel no background at all; and Baldwin's attempt, near the novel's conclusion, to bring her family to life for us fails miserably. He cannot elevate them above stereotypes.

Where Ida is made real to us through the infinite contradictions in her personality and her obsession with whoredom, Barbara has no conflicts or hangups. She possesses the insight to guess that Leo is bisexual and the humanity for it not to matter. She assures him that she realizes that he will never belong to her, unselfishly and dramatically declaring: "I'm not in your body. I can't live your life. I only want to *share* your life." (P. 211) Barbara possesses too much integrity to gossip and too much magnanimity ever to let Leo know what her relationship with him has cost her. She is *proud* to let Leo be free and she arranges her life so that his "place in it could never be jeopardized." (P. 336) Baldwin attempts to invest their relationship with reality by contriving a suicide attempt by Barbara. The event is recalled by Leo as occurring after their "deadliest, irrevocable fight," but Baldwin fails to describe their fight or even hint at its causes. The fight and suicide remain unconvincing. We never see Barbara scream or burst into a fit of anger; the idea seems preposterous. She never cries, nor does she hope. The flaws in Cass and Ida are what make them believable. The flaw in Barbara is that she has no flaws.

Baldwin presents us with even less background on Barbara than he did with Florence in *Go Tell It on the Mountain*. Barbara does not grow up before our eyes; she is already fully grown. We never see her as a child or as an adolescent. We do not witness her decision to leave home as we do Florence's. All we know of Barbara's childhood is that she walked away from it very early.

In the same way Cass and Ida lose some credibility in that they also, lack an authentic childhood and adolescence. We know that Ida has had to prostitute herself in order to survive and we know that she has encountered psychological and physical horrors that some readers may never comprehend. But Baldwin never shows Ida's first encounter or her first step out of childhood. Ida, like Barbara, is fully matured by the novel's opening pages. Unlike Barbara, however, Ida does undergo traumatic conflicts, and we watch her squirm in anxiety and even pain as she tries to straighten out her life.

In the final analysis, Barbara is Baldwin's greatest failure as a realistic portrait of a woman. She possesses all the qualities of a remarkably brilliant and self-sufficient and generous woman who has managed to arrive at a beautifully mutual and happy love with a man, but her characterization is credible only in fantasy.

What Ida and Cass possess in credibility, they lack in the negativism of their final result. Barbara attains a wonderfully satisfactory relationship with Leo, but she fails to convince us. Ida and Cass convince us of their reality, but they are both causal to the destruction of their lovers and, consequently, of themselves. We are left, then, to choose among Baldwin's women —to choose the credibility of the character or the positivism in it. The unwelcome choice is between Ida and Barbara—between destructiveness and fantasy.

If Baldwin's Train Has Not Gone

_____ William Edward Farrison

James Baldwin began _Tell Me How Long the Train's Been Gone,_ his fourth published novel, in Istanbul, Turkey, late in the summer of 1964. By the end of 1965 he had almost finished it. Late in that year, while he was still working on the novel, he told Dan Georgakas:

> I thought it was going to be a short story when it broke off from a longer work. It starts in the first person with the decay of a Negro actor. His white mistress and ruined older brother are important. In the third part a young Negro terrorist more or less takes over the book.[1]

As the novel was published by Dial Press in 1968, its story is consistent with this brief explanation with two notable exceptions. Caleb Proudhammer, the ruined older brother, is reformed, and no young Negro terrorist takes over any of the three books into which the novel is divided. Between the time of this explanation and publication, assuredly, Baldwin had an opportunity to alter his plan, as he might have thought it wise to do, and presumably the exceptions resulted from authorial alterations in the plan.

The titles of the three books are respectively "The House Nigger," "Is There Anybody There? Said the Traveler," and "Black Christopher." Like the notably long title of the novel itself, each of these titles is accompanied on a flyleaf by a quotation. The first and the last of the four quotations are from Negro spirituals, the second is from a poem of W. H. Auden's, and the third is from a song of Fats Waller's. As captions, the titles of the novel itself and its first two books, together with the accompanying quotations, are of at least questionable appropriateness, for it is difficult to find in the novel convincing reasons for their use. True enough, in Book One, in a Harlem bordello one night, a minor male character says cryptically to the landprop, "The train is in the station, everything's okay"—a statement that reminds one of the Negro spiritual from which the quotation accompanying the title of the volume was taken. But since this statement is without any unmistakably discernible context, it is hardly consequential enough to be considered suggestive of the title of the work as an entity. Also in Book One, one evening Leo Proudhammer, the hero of the story, who is the only Negro at a party in a Manhattan apartment, deliberately but only briefly plays the part of a traditional George, but his act has very little in common with the role of the typical antebellum house Negro. Certainly this brief act is not sufficiently important to justify the title of the first book of the novel. Perhaps the apparent inappropriateness of these titles is also the result of alterations in them or in the original work as a whole. Meanwhile, Black Christopher, who is an exceedingly close friend of Proudhammer's, but who is no terrorist, figures notably in the first book and prominently in the third one, and thus renders the title of that book appropriate—even though the Proudhammer-Black Christopher relationship is not the kind that deserves the approval of normal, healthy-minded people.

Tell Me How Long the Train's Been Gone, an octavo volume of 484 pages, is the longest of Baldwin's novels and also the longest of his books published to date, but it is a prolonged rather than a long story. Reduced to its simplest form, it is the saga in little of Leo Proudhammer (a suggestive if not an heroic-sounding name), a Negro who was born and brought up in unpromising circumstances in Harlem, but who was determined from his youth to become a great actor. The story is told in the first person; this is to say that Proudhammer tells his own story. The time covered in it extends from his birth, in the 1920s, to the 1960s. Proudhammer eventually realizes his ambition but with the loss of his health. This loss, which is presumably the physical counterpart of the decay Baldwin mentioned in his explanation concerning the novel to Georgakas in 1965, is perhaps no less the result of Proudhammer's prodigal living than of his long struggle to achieve success as an actor.

The story, however, is neither simply nor directly told. At the beginning of its first book, Proudhammer, now a famous actor thirty-nine years of age, suffers a heart attack in the midst of his role one evening on a stage in a theater in San Francisco—"by far my favorite town—my favorite American town," says Baldwin in his *No Name in the Street.* Accompanied by Barbara King, the previously mentioned white mistress, who is also a prominent fellow-player, Proudhammer is rushed to a local hospital, where he necessarily remains for some time. At the end of the last book, having recovered from his illness, he leaves the hospital, goes to New York, and thence to Europe to rest as well as to recuperate. Some time afterward, he returns to America, resumes his work as an actor, and finds himself "presently standing in the wings again, waiting for my cue." (P. 484) Between this arrestingly dramatic beginning and this less dramatic end, the story is fraught with a variety of episodes, some brief and some very long and discursive, and many without specific references to sequence in either time or place and often without clear motivation. The story is accordingly developed, not by classical association-ism, as one may suppose at first, but by what may be called errant associa-tion—errant in that the connection between the various episodes is left for the reader to discover or supply for himself.

The quality of coherence in the story is severely strained for the reader by the fact that closely related episodes are separated and recounted in the three books, not in the conventional manner of flashbacks or continuations, but somewhat sporadically and with what amounts to tangential, though often interesting, incidents loosely woven into them. In many instances episodes that appear at first to be flashbacks or continuations prove instead to be reminiscences embedded, sometimes repetitiously, in other reminiscences. This is especially true of the main plot of the novel, namely, the story com-posed of Proudhammer's long struggle to become an actor, the Proudham-mer-Barbara King saternalian *affaire d'amour,* and Proudhammer's even-tual achievement of fame as an actor. For example, in a half-dozen places in the novel, the story of the Proudhammer-Barbara King love affair and of their experience one summer in a New Jersey workshop for actors is partially told without a clear indication of the chronological relationships among these incidents. The experience of the lovers in the workshop was a decisive stage on their way to professionalism as actors, and as such it was too important to be fragmentally recounted. The one thing all of the episodes have in common is Proudhammer's direct or indirect involvement in them. The importance of what happens in them varies in proportion to this involvement. Proudham-mer is thus the genius of unity in the story.

From what Baldwin has written about himself and has said in various in-terviews, it appears that, as is true of *Go Tell It on the Mountain* (1953), his first novel, his own life has been the basis of much of *Tell Me How Long the Train's Been Gone.* This fact is in accordance with what he said in the "Au-tobiographical Notes" in *Notes of a Native Son* (1955), when his ideas about the art of writing were probably still in a formative stage which im-pelled him to do as much rewriting as writing, for he had yet to establish himself as a major author. Said he, with youthful certainty that only increasing practical experience could season with maturity, "One writes out of one thing only—one's own experience. Everything depends on how relentlessly one forces from this experience the last drop, sweet or bitter, it can possibly give. This is the only real concern of the artist, to recreate out of the disorder of life that order which is art."

It should not be assumed, however, that *Tell Me How Long the Train's Been Gone* is anything but a fictionized autobiography. The truth is, rather, that, for the sake of realism, which he sometimes transformed into naturalism, Baldwin doubtless chose for use in his story incidents and situations from his experience and observations and threw over them whatever coloring of imagination he considered necessary to adapt them to the artistic purpose of the story. In doing this he proceeded more or less consistently, if not always restrainedly, with his pronouncement in *Nobody Knows My Name* that "the imagination of a novelist has everything to do with what happens to his material." Although no ghost need come from the grave to tell us this, as Horatio said of a truism in another context, it is, nevertheless, a fact of which criticism should always remain cognizant in its consideration of the possible relationships between life and art in fiction.

Including Leo, four members of the Proudhammer family are involved in various episodes incidental to the main plot. The other three members are the father, the mother, and Caleb, who is Leo's brother and his senior by seven years. The four of them constitute a more or less ordinary Harlem family living below the poverty line. They remind one of four characters in *Go Tell It on the Mountain* partly because of similarities and partly because of differences among them. Those characters are Gabriel Grimes, his wife Elizabeth, and their sons Roy and John. Father Proudhammer is quite different from Grimes, the reactionary religionist, and also from Baldwin's stepfather, who has been repeatedly and ruefully characterized by Baldwin, most recently in *No Name in the Street*. (PP. 3–9) He is a proud, "ruined Barbados peasant, exiled in a Harlem" that he loathes, who has long been at odds with the circumstances surrounding him, and who, having been "beat to his socks," has become "the living example of defeat." The mother differs from Elizabeth Grimes only in minor ways. Caleb has a counterpart in Roy, but he is eventually reformed into a character quite different from Roy. Although Leo and John are radically different, they share to some extent the same kind of sensitivity, which occasionally keeps them from being at home in the world.

Through experiences of the Proudhammers, the reader witnesses some of the circumstances and shocks to which Harlem life is heir. Not the least among these are, or at least were during Baldwin's boyhood, existence in deteriorating, rat-infested apartment houses, conflicts between tenants and landlords, commodity prices inflated above those in other sections of the city, juvenile delinquency, immorality and other kinds of crimes, police tyranny and brutality, and only thinly disguised racism.

While still in his teens, Caleb, whose story is a subplot of the novel, indulges in thievery and fornication. Worse still, he is involved in a robbery for which he serves time on a prison farm. He next spends some time in military service in World War II, in which he is wounded. Afterward, having been converted, he returns to Harlem, marries and begins rearing a family, and becomes an active member and later assistant pastor of the New Dispensation House of God. This is a church similar to the Temple of Fire Baptized, of which Gabriel Grimes was a pillar and eventually a pastor. After becoming a churchman, Caleb becomes more like Grimes and finds less and less rapport with Leo. One reason for the decreasing brotherly feeling between the two of them is that Caleb has achieved a satisfactory mode of life, and Leo has not yet done so, for he is still striving, with no clear vision of success, to become a great actor.

One of the incidents related concerning the Proudhammers is the one in which Leo, when ten years of age, wandered from home one Saturday evening, was lost on a long subway ride, and was found by another passenger, a Negro man, who saw that he safely returned home. This is a minor but most interesting incident and indeed one of the most arriding occurrences in the novel. Whether it contains a "discernible strand" of a long-remembered experience of the author or not, it is a convincingly told and delightful boy's story, in which the boy emerges as a normal, lifelike character. And what is more, it neither has in it nor needs any of the greatly overworked four-letter words—greatly overworked by Baldwin as well as by others—or other Rabelaisian touches to make it interesting. This is imaginative narrative writing at its simplest and best. This incident, by the way, is only tangential to the main plot of *Tell Me How Long the Train's Been Gone,* but it brightly illuminates the adventurous character of the boy who is developed into the hero of the novel, if not a hero in the absolute sense of the word.

The story of the Proudhammer-Barbara King love affair is intricately woven into the story of Proudhammer's eventual rise to fame as an actor. During their summer at the New Jersey workshop for actors, the two of them, each of whom is about twenty years old at the time, fall deeply in love with each other and love extravagantly well if not wisely. But as if in proof anew of the adage that the course of true love never runs smoothly, theirs is an on-again off-again affair for the next seven years. Meanwhile neither of them remains without other lovers very long, and both of them are striving to make their way as actors. At last, with Barbara's help, Proudhammer rises to stardom and fame, with her sharing both. The joy attending his great success, however, is interrupted by his long illness.

Obviously, Proudhammer and Barbara are the most important characters in *Tell Me How Long the Train's Been Gone,* as Baldwin doubtless intended for them to be. To say this, nevertheless, is not to praise them greatly, since they are members of a company of characterizations that are not generally impressive. In spite of the attention they command in the story, neither Proudhammer, after he becomes a man, nor Barbara is a remarkably vital character, except when sexuality is involved. Proudhammer is comparatively less vital and less admirable than Barbara, and her most inspiring quality is her devotion to him even when it would long have been easy for her to find a good reason for giving him up. It is this alone that makes her heroic.

The weakness in the characters of Proudhammer and Barbara is not simply that they are incomparably less than angels. A character need not be angelic to be vital and admirable. Mephistopheles is by no means angelic, but he is indeed admirable as well as vital—admirable especially for his insight, resourcefulness, and sense of humor. These and wholesome vitality, alas, are qualities by which neither Proudhammer nor Barbara is notably distinguished. At least as far as portraying character is concerned, in *Giovanni's Room* (1956) and *Another Country* (1962), his second and third novels, Baldwin did not improve on his achievements in his first novel, nor has he improved on them in his fourth one.

In portraying characters and recounting action, novelists have long followed the practice of philosophizing occasionally and pertinently about life. There is only minimal evidence of this practice in *Tell Me How Long the Train's Been Gone,* probably because Baldwin's interests do not seem inclined toward speculative philosophy, which is ultimately the basis of sound philosophizing. There are in the novel some casual reflections on love, but these are hardly profound enough to merit serious consideration. Perchance the most representative instance of philosophizing found in the novel is in the following remarks, which Proudhammer makes after some self-examination: "One can find oneself in trouble so deep and so bizarre that one *knows* one can never get out of it; and it doesn't help at all, as the years swagger brutally by, to recognize that much of one's trouble is produced by the really unreadable and unpredictable convolutions of one's own character." With special reference to the last clause in these remarks, Proudhammer may well cry *"Mea culpa"* and also be joined by a chorus in the resounding of King Claudius's "O, 'tis true!"

Perhaps the greatest obstruction to profound thought and highly artistic effectiveness in the novel is its extraordinary possession with phallus-consciousness, which is probably both a cause and a consequence of the plethora of sexual acts of various kinds in which the story needlessly abounds. This in turn involves and is involved in the multiplicity of crudely frank words used in the story. There are literally hundreds of uses of them, including all of the familiar four-letter words as well as many others. This profusion of such usage provokes careful consideration of its why and wherefore.

Admittedly, the line between decency and indecency in language has never run perfectly straight. It has often zigzagged, and what has been permissible from time to time has frequently been a matter as much of custom as of morality. But the line has never been completely obliterated—at least not yet. Now, even though in language, as in dress, particularly in feminine dress, and in morality, present-day freedom seems to be approaching infinity, at least three pertinent observations are in order. First, considering the vast synonymy of the present-day English vocabulary and the different levels of usage represented by synonyms, there is no justification for an author to compromise the respectability of what he presumably intends to be good writing by infiltrating it with vulgarity—extreme, crude frankness in language which serves no worthwhile purpose that could not be served as well without it. If his vocabulary suffers from a paucity of terms of different degrees of accuracy and respectability, he can easily improve matters by reading extensively and resorting to standard dictionaries and, for contrast, to dictionaries of substandard usage. Incidentally, it may be noted that in the times of Chaucer and Shakespeare, the English vocabulary was much smaller and much less flexible than it is now, but that those authors and most of their contemporaries managed to express themselves effectively without veering repeatedly to crude extremes of vulgarity.

But is it probable, one wonders, that an established author such as Baldwin would need to resort to vulgar usage for want of a large vocabulary? Or could it be that Baldwin has proceeded on the questionable assumption that he could thus best accord characters and their speech, or could express himself more effectively in vulgar usage than in standard English? Such an assumption would hardly be consistent with his explanation to Georgakas late in 1965 that "I want to get strength within traditional forms, to make elegant sentences do dirty work." This was indeed a very good wish; Baldwin, however, did not take into account that elegant sentences consist not of inelegant but clean words, even when the ideas they convey involve what is dirty. Perhaps Baldwin changed his point of view after his conversation with Georgakas. If he did and if his usage in *Tell Me How Long the Train's Been*

Gone evinces the change, he has left himself ample room in which to change for the better.

The second observation is that extreme, crude frankness in language cannot be justified on the ground of its supposed faithfulness to facts. It is no more accurate or effective than carefully used standard English would be in the same context. Instead of vitalizing and facilitating communication, it is more than likely to attract unfriendly attention to itself and to cause the distraction of interest from the ideas to be conveyed. If an idea cannot be effectively expressed in standard English, it cannot be effectively expressed in vulgar usage; or, what is more, it is probably not worth expressing at all.

The third and perhaps the most important observation pertaining to freedom of usage is as follows: Where decency is concerned, the less external restraint there is on the individual, the more internal restraint he should exercise in the form of self-respect, good taste, and consideration for the feelings of others. If there is an equivalent of valor in the art of writing, the sum total of these three essentials constitutes the discretion that is its better part. One cannot choose but wish that such discretion were more evident than it is in *Tell Me How Long the Train's Been Gone.*

There are, of course, stylistic features of the novel other than Rabelaisian usage which command interest. On one hand, the reader occasionally finds himself in danger of getting lost in exceptionally long paragraphs which do more *to* than *for* the unity and clarity of details. There are in the work a considerable number of paragraphs each of which fills more than two pages. Such paragraphs should have been shortened to make clear distinctions in units of thought and also to provide restful pauses for the reader. In some of the long paragraphs, as well as elsewhere, there occur long, roving sentences whose structure tends to disjoin the ideas they were intended to convey. Such sentences frequently result from awkward word order or from the placement in the middle of them of incidental phrases or clauses, or both, whose relationships to what surrounds them become meaningful only at the ends of these sentences. Such constructions readily identify themselves for the careful reader by drawing attention from what is said to how it is said and thus slowing down the process of reading.

On the other hand, the reader occasionally finds the writing enlivened by rapidly succeeding paratactic constructions that both develop and invigorate ideas. At first, this kind of composition may remind one of the conjunctionless style of *Time, the Weekly Newsmagazine,* but at its best it is more substantial than that, having long been well established in some of the best works in English. It is not, of course, a stylistic device to be adopted impulsively by inexperienced writers who may not realize when they are running unrelated or unequal ideas together. It is a device to be adopted only by those who have learned by writing and rewriting to use it naturally and artistically, as Baldwin generally uses it.

Another felicitous quality of Baldwin's style is his apt and often sparkling wording of phrases and in some instances whole sentences. Exemplary of the former are the previously quoted phrases with which Leo describes his father. Exemplary of the latter are the following two statements with which he refers to two different emotionally tense moments, which he experienced on two different occasions: "I felt a sudden fear, as present as the running of the river (nearby), as nameless and as deep." "There is a fearful splendor in absolute desolation: I had never seen it before this day."

Whatever merits *Tell Me How Long the Train's Been Gone* has, in the light of this critique it is less of an artistic work than one might have expected Baldwin's fourth novel to be, for it is the work of an experienced novelist. There is no complaint that it is not *the* great American novel. It is indeed doubtful that there has yet been or ever will be written *the* great or the greatest novel in any literature. The absolute comparison implied in the idea of such a work is illogical, for unique perfection in the art of writing, as in other arts, is distinguished not by imparity but by disparity, as Thomas De Quincey observed long ago. Still in one way or another, as I have noted in references to Baldwin's first four novels, one novel may be obviously better or worse than another—a fact which one can recognize without dealing in absolutes.

Perhaps during the years that immediately preceded the appearance of *Tell Me How Long the Train's Been Gone,* Baldwin was too busy with civil rights and political activities, as one of his critics seems to have thought, to realize in this work "his full power as a novelist." Since those years, he has apparently been less occupied with nonliterary activities and presumably has had time to improve in many ways as a novelist. It is now six years since his fourth novel was published. The recent appearance of his fifth novel, *If Beale Street Could Talk* (New York, 1974), naturally arouses curiosity as to whether improvements in his art of fiction are evidenced in it. To satisfy this curiosity, a review of this work is in order.

Although its title is arresting, one can search only vainly in the 197 pages of this story for a specifically suggestive reason for that title. True enough, as is said on the book's jacket, the story is one that Beale Street might tell if it could talk; but Lenox Avenue in New York, which Baldwin probably knows much better than he knows Beale Street, could also tell the same story, and so could many, many other streets. It is also said on the book's jacket, but questionably, that the story is "evocative of the Blues." Alas, it is at least doubtful that anyone who knows very much about the motifs of the blues would find much of an evocation of them in this story, even if he searched with Diogenes' lantern in daylight. The truth is that the story is essentially an ordinary tale which Baldwin has enlivened with a new telling and variations, some of which he rendered not altogether convincingly motivated.

If the title of the volume is cryptic, the titles of the two parts into which the story is divided are equally so. These are respectively "Troubled About My Soul" (PP. 1–174) and "Zion" (PP. 175–197). Now two things that no character in the story seems to be really troubled about are anybody's soul and Zion—certainly not the latter in any Christian sense. Since the story can be understood, however, without particular references to the titles, the reader hardly needs to trouble himself very much about them.

The story in *If Beale Street Could Talk* is a simple tale of Tish, who was christened Clementine Rivers, and Fonny, whose real name is Alonzo Hunt. They are members of families who have lived many years in the same neighborhood in Harlem, and who, unlike the Proudhammers, have survived a little above the poverty line. Tish and Fonny have known each other since early childhood and within recent years have found themselves in love with each other without knowing exactly why—indeed, not because either considers the other beautiful. But for the last year they have been doing as much lovemaking as loving; and now in March Tish at age nineteen becomes pregnant by Fonny, who at age twenty-two is a struggling sculptor in Greenwich Village. They have been somewhat casually planning for some time to marry, but their plan has been forestalled, because also in March Fonny was wrongly accused of raping a Puerto Rican woman and has been imprisoned in the Tombs ever since his apprehension, apparently without the privilege of bond. The charge against Fonny has been maneuvered by Bell, a white, dishonest, racist policeman. Law enforcement officers of Bell's kind, it may be noted, are common in Baldwin's stories.

The antecedent action just synopsized and what follows in the story are recounted by Tish herself, some parts in flashbacks which at first may seem disconnected, but whose relationship to the other parts of the story is easily discernible. Fortunately, the story is too brief and too simple—it is not complicated by a subplot—to tax the reader's patience with the kind of errant association found in *Tell Me How Long the Train's Been Gone.*

Following the antecedent action, the span of time in the story begins with Tish's informing her family in June of her three months' pregnancy and their informing Fonny's family of this fact; and it ends one night, presumably in the following November, when Tish is about to give birth to a baby. The action during this span includes Tish's frequent visits to Fonny in the Tombs; a brief and pointless broil between the Rivers and the Hunt families; a weakly motivated and apparently futile trip by Mrs. Rivers (Tish's mother) to Puerto Rico to get from the victim of the rape, who has fled thither, a change in the victim's testimony in Fonny's behalf; apparently successful joint efforts of the families to raise sufficient money for a bond for Fonny, and the suicide of Frank Hunt (Fonny's father). Hunt commits suicide because the dishonesty to which he resorted in the efforts to raise the bond money caused him to lose his job. His loss of his job, however, is hardly convincing motivation for his suicide.

Neither in numbers nor in kinds do the characters in *If Beale Street Could Talk* command the reader's highest regards. None of them are especially admirable for either good or bad qualities, except perhaps a wealth of amorality and the aplomb with which most of them revel in four-letter vulgarities and their derivatives. Tish's and Fonny's parents and sisters figure frequently in the action, but as little more than choruses, and none of them are fully or impressively portrayed. The only two striking characters in the story are Tish and Fonny; and being constantly in the center of the action, Tish is by far the more prominent of the two. They are, of course, the heroine and the hero, respectively, of the story, but this is not to say that either of them is heroic. They seem loyal enough to each other, but not to any socially and morally respectable ideas and ideals, as the truly heroic must be. In fact, poorly educated and unsophisticated as they are, they seem naively incognizant that such ideas and ideals exist.

Tish does not seem aware that her conduct with Fonny has been condemnable. Perhaps there should be no wonder about her obliviousness concerning this fact, however, since her father, upon learning of her illicit pregnancy, says that he is proud of her. (P. 49) Nor does her mother seem to be embarrassed because of it. Whether purposefully or accidentally, in Tish, Baldwin succeeded in creating a notable character distinguished only by minimal intelligence.

Although Fonny is chronologically mature, he is no more alert than Tish and is indeed less credible than she. Like Tish, he also seems naively ignorant that the level on which the two of them have been sharing their lives is far below the established level of respectability. Fonny appears in the story only as Tish sees and understands him; and her point of view and understanding being what they are, he naturally appears from time to time as a shadowy figure hardly suggestive of the Baldwinian exponent of sexuality which he is. Perchance Baldwin developed the character of Fonny as he did to keep it in accord with Tish's want of sufficient acumen to comprehend and portray her lover very well. Possibly for Baldwin artistic consistency thus necessitated artistic restraint which produced what appears at first to be a defect, but which may be, at the worst, a concealed merit. Of such theorizing as this, withal, a modicum is enough if not too much, lest one falls into the error of trying to tell an author what the author intended to do in a given work.

In telling her story, except in one instance, Tish avoided excursions into philosophizing such as are often found in novels, nor did she credit any other character with adventures into speculative thought. In the one exception, she talked only superficially, but characteristically, about the relationship of men and women and their understanding of each other (PP. 58–59). If this instance is typical of the reflective thinking which she could be made to do, Baldwin was wise to have her indulge in no more of it.

As is true of *Tell Me How Long the Train's Been Gone, If Beale Street Could Talk* is deprived of much of its possible value as wholesome reading for many people and of much of its artistic effectiveness by the multiplicity of crudely frank words and their derivatives used in it. Therein, this kind of usage occurs in practically the same proportion in which it is found in the first of these two novels, and still for no apparent good reason. All of the observations previously made in this essay with reference to such usage are equally pertinent with reference to this book.

A less noticeable matter of style in this book than vulgar usage consists of statements in which ideas are awkwardly coordinated, as in "Adrienne looked at him and she started to speak, but she didn't" (P. 66), and in "I got back to my chair and I sat down in it." (P. 195) Such constructions, however, are what might have been expected of Tish, so that they may also be the results of Baldwin's exercise of artistic restraint for the sake of artistic consistency. In contrast to her use of awkward constructions, Tish sometimes expresses her ideas ingeniously and graphically. On one occasion, for example, she says that if any place is worse than New York, "it's got to be so close to hell that you can smell the people frying." (P. 9) On another occasion she refers to the sanctified Mrs. Hunt (Fonny's mother), who, en route to church one Sunday morning, walks "like a queen making great strides into the kingdom." (P. 21)

As I have already observed, *Tell Me How Long the Train's Been Gone* and *If Beale Street Could Talk* have some faults and also some merits in common. The most obvious difference between them is in their length. The latter is less than half as long as the former. There are, however, more important, though perhaps less easily discernible, differences between them. Being an unsophisticated and simply told story, *If Beale Street Could Talk* is not only devoid of tediousness, from which the earlier one is not entirely free, but of the two it also makes much easier reading. In this work, Baldwin did not attempt to plumb to their depths great psychological and social problems, as he attempted to do, but without remarkable success, in his second and third novels and to some extent in his fourth one. Instead he returned to the simple manner of his first novel, which is still his best work of fiction. Presumably, during the last six years, as previously when his interests were not otherwise absorbed, Baldwin has been and still is a devotee of the art of writing. If he is, and if his train which is the art of fiction has not already gone, as no reason appears for assuming that it has, as a novelist he may yet reach the greatest heights of distinction.

Baldwin as

_____ Essayist

The Evolution of James Baldwin as Essayist

Nick Aaron Ford

I

James Baldwin is one of the most talented American essayists since Ralph Waldo Emerson (1803–1882). His first three volumes—*Notes of a Native Son* (1955), *Nobody Knows My Name* (1961), and *The Fire Next Time* (1963)—won a popularity hardly equaled by any other essayist in modern times. His most recent volume, *No Name in the Street* (1972), has neither received nor deserved the attention merited by its predecessors. His four novels, with the exception of *Go Tell It on the Mountain* (1953), his one volume of short stories, and his two published plays are distinctly inferior to his best essays in style and substance. It appears, therefore, that his talents demonstrated thus far lie in the general area of unstructured, instinctive, and emotional utterance often unsupported by rational safeguards. Like his nineteenth-century counterpart, his most valuable contributions are in the realms of pragmatism and prophecy rather than logic and rationality. Like Emerson, too, his major thrust is not to impart abstract or concrete knowledge, but to provoke humane thought and announce eternal truths intended to elevate the consciousness of the reader from animal passion to spiritual or philosophical contemplation.

In this discussion I shall examine Baldwin's four volumes of essays for the purpose of offering critical comments on style, content, and method characteristic of the most representative examples. It is hoped that such an examination will stimulate the kind of further study that the most significant works of Baldwin deserve.

In "Autobiographical Notes," which serves as an introduction to the first volume, the author tells of his birth in Harlem, in 1924, and of his beginning to plot "novels" at about the time he learned to read. His first story, written at the age of twelve, was published in a church newspaper. Later he received a letter of congratulations from Mayor LaGuardia of New York City for one of his pieces of creative writing. Pressured by his semi-illiterate stepfather, who was a storefront preacher, he became an active preacher at the age of fourteen but ended his religious commitment three years later. At twenty-four, after having used up two writing fellowships during the previous three-year period, he left the United States for a nine-year sojourn in France and other European countries, where he discovered what it means to be an American. He confides:

> I know, in any case, that the most crucial time in my own development came when I was forced to recognize that I was a kind of bastard of the West; when I followed the line of my past I did not find myself in Europe but in Africa. And this meant in some subtle way, in a really profound way, I brought to Shakespeare, Bach, Rembrandt, to the stones of Paris, to the cathedral at Chartres, and to the Empire State Building, a special attitude. These were not really my creations, they did not contain my history; I might search in them in vain forever for any reflection of myself. I was an interloper; this was not my heritage. At the same time I had no other heritage which I could possibly hope to use—I had certainly been unfitted for the jungle or the tribe. I would have to appropriate these white centuries, I would have to make them mine—I would have to accept my special attitude, my special place in this scheme—otherwise I would have no place in *any* scheme. What was most difficult was the fact that I was forced to admit something I had always hidden from myself, which the American Negro has had to hide from himself as the price of his public progress; that I hated and feared white people. This did not mean that I loved black people; on the contrary, I despised them, possibly because they failed to produce Rembrandt.[1]

The first two essays in this volume are devoted to literary criticism. "Everybody's Protest Novel" condemns protest fiction as a serious literary activity by castigating the motives and achievements of Harriet Beecher Stowe's *Uncle Tom's Cabin* and the unreality of Richard Wright's *Native Son.* Baldwin denies that such writing can be justified on the basis that it serves "the 'good' of society." He argues that "since literature and sociology are not one and the same, it is impossible to discuss them as if they were."

(P. 18) Evidently it never occurred to him that, like whiskey and water, they could possibly be combined for the improvement of both. In 1955 the thirty-one-year-old author was under the illusion, as many of his fellow blacks were then, that in order to be recognized by the international literary establishment or any legitimate faction thereof he "would have to accept . . . [his] special place in this scheme—otherwise . . . [he] would have no place in *any* scheme." He declares, as if he believes Wright overlooked the fact entirely, " . . . Bigger's tragedy is not that he is cold or black or hungry . . . but that he has accepted a theology that denies him life, that he admits the possibility of his being sub-human and feels constrained, therefore, to battle for his humanity according to those brutal criteria bequeathed him at his birth." (PP. 22–23) This criticism fails to recognize the fact that Bigger's tragedy is in reality twofold; on the lower level it is indeed the fact that he is cold and black and hungry, while on the higher level it is what Baldwin suggests it is. That Bigger does not understand the deeper or higher meaning of his tragedy makes the whole impact of the novel the more poignant.

Baldwin's attempt to prove in this essay that *Uncle Tom's Cabin* made no worthy contribution to the abolition of slavery because "The virtuous rage of Mrs. Stowe is motivated by nothing so temporal as a concern for the relationship of men to one another—or, even, as she would have claimed, by a concern for their relationship to God," (P. 17) is to confuse results with intentions and therefore to succumb to the discredited "intentional fallacy." Enlightened criticism assesses praise or blame on the basis of the pragmatic results of what an author actually achieved rather than on what he or she intended to do. There is ample evidence available to prove that Mrs. Stowe's friends and foes agree that her masterpiece was a powerful force in helping to inflict the mortal wound to the slavery ethic in the United States.

In "Many Thousands Gone" Baldwin concentrates all of his rhetorical power in a massive attack on the validity of Wright's purpose in the creation of *Native Son* with its monster protagonist Bigger Thomas. Although he admits that "the most powerful and celebrated statement we have yet had of what it means to be a Negro in America is unquestionably Richard Wright's *Native Son*," (P. 30) he unfairly contends that at the end of the novel we know no more about the black protagonist than we did at the beginning and, likewise, we know scarcely any more about the social situation in America which is supposed to have created him. On the contrary, the entire novel, including the court scene, is a graphic unraveling of incidents and attitudes that molded Bigger's private and public selves and that characterized the social milieu in which such a monstrous creature was spawned and nourished. It is true, as Baldwin suggests, that an important dimension of black life is omitted, namely, the relationship that Negroes bear to one another and the "depth of involvement and unspoken recognition of shared" (P. 35) community experience, but often rigid isolation is absolutely necessary in the interest of most meaningful diagnosis. In this essay, which seems to be a reinforcement of the previous arguments against the effectiveness of the protest novel, Baldwin unwittingly manufactures arguments for later critics to use against him in his own "protest" novels, *Another Country* (1962) and *Tell Me How Long the Train's Been Gone* (1968), both of which are more violently propagandistic and much less artistic than Wright's *Native Son.*

Further evidence of the author's greater concern for startling rhetoric than for solid fact is his unfortunate hyberbolic statement previously noted in the excerpt quoted above: "This did not mean that I loved black people; on the contrary, I despised them, possibly because they failed to produce Rembrandt." In my opinion Baldwin did not intend for his statement to be taken literally. He was anxious to impress upon the reader's mind the monstrous crime that had been perpretrated against black Americans by the white world in its glorification of European culture and complete denial or denigration of the value of anything that blacks anywhere had ever accomplished. In the given context it seems reasonable to assume that there was no more real hate in Baldwin's heart for fellow blacks than there was doubt in the agonized cry of Jesus on the cross: "My God, my God, why hast thou forsaken me?" But because of Baldwin's failure to distinguish sufficiently fact from fable or rhetoric from rationality Eldridge Cleaver could say in *Soul on Ice,* without fear of contradiction:

> I am not interested in denying anything to Baldwin. I, like the entire nation, owe a great debt to him. But throughout the range of his work, from *Go Tell It on the Mountain,* through *Notes of a Native Son, Nobody Knows My Name, Another Country,* to *The Fire Next Time,* all of which I treasure, there is a decisive quirk in Baldwin's vision which corresponds to his relationship to black people and to masculinity. It was this same quirk, in my opinion, that compelled Baldwin to slander Rufus Scott in *Another Country,* venerate André Gide, repudiate *The White Negro,* and drive the blade of Brutus into the corpse of Richard Wright.[2]

In "The Harlem Ghetto" Baldwin considers analytically the major problems that confront blacks in the largest and most representative ghetto in the United States. He concludes that in searching for a scapegoat upon which to place the blame for all his frustrations—his social ostracism, his economic exploitation, his lack of professional recognition and acceptance— the Harlemite has chosen the Jew. The author argues, "It is not the Jewish tradition by which he has been betrayed but the tradition of his native land. But just as a society must have a scapegoat, so hatred must have a symbol. Georgia has the Negro and Harlem has the Jew." (P. 72) It now seems ironic that since the publication of this essay less than two decades ago, Georgia has elected, with the aid of a considerable number of white votes, the first black congressman from the confederate states, and Baldwin has been condemned by the distinguished black novelist-poet Ishmael Reed as the writer of "Jewish books" whom nobody takes seriously anymore except "Jewish liberals."

With the exception of "Carmen Jones: The Dark Is Light Enough," which is an unfavorable appraisal of a 1955 film by Twentieth Century-Fox with an all-black cast, five of the remaining six essays in *Notes of a Native Son* are commentaries on and interpretations of personal experiences that are covered in a general way by other discussions in later volumes. The sixth essay, however, "Stranger in the Village," deserves comment. The virtually unknown village is located in the mountains of Switzerland four hours from Milan and three hours from Lausanne. The stranger is Baldwin. The six hundred inhabitants are Catholics, and most of the tourists are cripples or semi-cripples who come from other parts of Switzerland to seek relief by bathing in the hot spring water. The essayist's observations and interpretations are made at the end of a prolonged visit. The villagers, who had never seen a Negro before, would often approach the lonely visitor in jocular friendliness and touch his hair with their fingers as though they were afraid of an electric shock and touch his hands as though they expected the color to rub off. Although he admits there was no hint of intentional unkindness, their actions excited within him a feeling that he was considered not quite human. The ambivalence of the situation was most striking when the little children who shouted *Neger!* as he passed glowed with pride whenever he stopped to speak to them.

Baldwin's explanation and interpretation of the interrelations between his historical background and contemporary situation and those of his hosts present the most meaningful understanding of the black-white dilemma that appear in American literature. The following quotations contain the essence of the author's reasoning:

> The idea of white supremacy rests simply on the fact that white men are the creators of civilization (the present civilization, which is the only one that matters; all previous civilizations are simply "contributions" to our own) and are therefore civilization's guardians and defenders.

At the root of the American Negro problem is the necessity of the American white man to find a way of living with the Negro in order to be able to live with himself.

The Cathedral of Chartres, I have said, says something to the people of this village which it cannot say to me; but it is important to understand that this cathedral says something to me which it cannot say to them. Perhaps they are struck by the power of the spires, the glory of the windows . . . and I am terrified by the slippery bottomless well to be found in the crypt, down which heretics were hurled to death, and the obscene, inescapable gargoyles jutting out of the stone and seeming to say that god and the devil can never be divorced.

No road whatever will lead Americans back to the simplicity of this European village where white men still have the luxury of looking on me as a stranger. I am not, really, a stranger any longer for any American alive. One of the things that distinguishes Americans from other people is that no other people has ever been so deeply involved in the lives of black men, and vice versa. (PP. 172–75)

This first volume reveals certain aspects of style and method that have become the hallmarks of Baldwin's essays. One characteristic is the use of the first person. When the narration is completely personal in its application, the pronoun is "I," but when the assertion is intended to represent or be applied to white-American society, the pronoun is "we" or "our." For instance, in "Everybody's Protest Novel" the following statement is intended to apply to white-oriented society: "Society is held together by *our* need; *we* bind it together with legend, myth, coercion, fearing that without it *we* will be hurled into that void, within which, like the earth before the Word was spoken, the foundations of society are hidden" [italics mine]. Another characteristic is its lack of inhibitions in describing what the author considers to be the awful truth. Like the prophets of the Old Testament, he never allows politeness or the fear of offending to interfere with prophecy or eternal truth. A third distinguishing feature is the use of imagery to create a sense of vividness and emotional involvement. A fourth attribute is the employment of personally related examples to illustrate or enhance the meaning of general or universal truths. As we examine later volumes, we will discover that the foregoing characteristics occur with greater frequency and effect.

II

The thirteen essays in *Nobody Knows My Name* were written during the period between 1954 and 1961. Baldwin explains in the introduction that much of the discussion is centered in or revolves around the question of color, a problem that he suggests "operates to hide the graver questions of the self."[3] In the previous volume he sought to justify his preoccupation with matters pertaining to race on the ground that it was "the gate" he had to unlock before he could hope to write about anything else. Evidently, he later found the gate more difficult to unlock than he had anticipated, for only three of these essays eschew the problems of color.

In "The Discovery of What It Means to Be an American" Baldwin declares, concerning his nine years in Europe, that he was compelled to leave America because he felt he could not survive the abnormal strain of the color problem as it existed in his native land. He felt the necessity of a new setting which would enable him to experience relationships that would reveal his kinship with other people of different colors and races rather than those that always emphasized his division, his separation. In short, he wanted to prevent himself "from becoming merely a Negro; or, even, merely a Negro writer." (P. 3) In one sense, at least, his wish was realized, for the book of which this essay is a part appeared on *The New York Times'* best-seller list for many weeks, a success seldom achieved by writing in this genre. Furthermore, Mark Schorer, distinguished scholar-critic, was quoted in *The New York Times Book Review,* December 3, 1961, as saying:

> Were I to find myself in the role of an unofficial or an official ambassador to another country, especially an Asian or an African country, I would carry with me as many copies of James Baldwin's *Nobody Knows My Name* as I could afford. I would do this in part from a motive of pride in the esthetic accomplishments of a countryman, for we have hardly a more accomplished prose stylist in the United States today. But perhaps more important, I would urge this book upon people in other countries to persuade them that we are by no means without our deep cultural scars and conflicts, and by no means without the capacity for the most searching self-criticism.

In another sense Baldwin's sojourn in Europe produced positive effects upon himself, for he declares in this essay, "In my necessity to find the terms on which my experience could be related to that of others, Negroes and whites, writers and non-writers, I proved, to my astonishment, to be as American as any Texas G.I.," (P. 4) although it required two years or more as a visitor in Paris for him to realize that fact. It was not until he had accepted his "role—as distinguished . . . from . . . 'place'—in the extraordinary drama which is America" that he "was released from the illusion that I hated America." (P. 5) It is in this context that he dares to define for *all* American writers what Europe can contribute to them and what they can contribute to the indigenous European, namely, a sense of tragedy for the former and a new sense of life's possibilities for the latter. "In this endeavor to wed the vision of the Old World with that of the New, it is the writer, not the statesman, who is our strongest arm." (P. 12) It seems clear at this point in Baldwin's development that he considers himself to be an *American* writer rather than a *Negro* writer and that his vision must embrace and interpret the universal. Yet in four of the essays that follow—"Fifth Avenue, Uptown: A Letter from Harlem," "East River, Downtown: Postscript to a Letter from Harlem," "A Fly in Buttermilk," and "Nobody Knows My Name: A Letter from the South"—the subject matter is devoted entirely to the evils of segregation, the hypocrisy of whites in their relations with blacks in the North and South, and the indifference of middle-class blacks to the plight of their poorer and weaker brethren. In addressing these evils, he finds it necessary to abandon the pose of universality adopted in his earlier references to the American writer's contribution of "a new sense of life's possibilities" for the European. He apparently discovered that there was greater need for the black writer to expose the unlimited possibilities of exploitation of blacks in America than to contemplate the new sense of life's possibilities for the European.

One of the most meaningful essays, "Princes and Powers," in this volume is Baldwin's interpretive report on the Conference of Negro-African Writers and Artists (Le Congrès des Ecrivains et Artistes Noirs), September 19–22, 1956, in the Sorbonne's Amphithéâtre Descartes, in Paris. The leaders included Richard Wright, who had left the United States in 1946 for permanent residence in France; Alioune Diop, editor of *Présence Africaine;* Léopold Senghor, Senegal; Aimé Césaire, Martinique; and Jacques Alexis and Dr. Price-Mars, Haiti. The five official delegates from the United States were John Davis, Mercer Cook, William Fontaine, Horace Mann Bond, and James Ivy. The purpose of the conference, according to one of the principal organizers, was to afford an opportunity unlike any previous experience for representative black intellectuals from widely divergent areas to meet together under favorable circumstances to define and accept their responsibilities, to assess the riches and the promise of their culture, and to open, in effect, a dialogue with Europe.

Baldwin briefly summarizes each major speech and at the same time interweaves his own critical evaluation of it. One of the highlights was the presentation of Césaire, whose central theme was stated as follows: "Wherever colonization is a fact the indigenous culture begins to rot. And among these ruins, something begins to be born which is not a culture but a kind of sub-culture, a subculture which is condemned to exist on the margin allowed it by European culture!" (P. 34) Baldwin declares that he was stirred in a strange and disagreeable way, for the speaker had very skillfully played on the emotions and hopes of the audience but had not dealt with the most pertinent central question, which was, in Baldwin's opinion, "What *had* this colonial experience made of them [the black colonials] and what were they now to do with it? For they were all, now, whether they liked it or not, related to Europe, stained by European visions and standards, and their relation to themselves, and to each other, and to their past had changed." (P. 36) It was agreed, however, that a culture is not something given to a people but something that they make themselves. Later it was decided to appoint a committee to formulate an acceptable definition of Negro-African culture and to suggest reasons why that culture should be saved.

To Baldwin the question *What is Black-African culture?* cannot be easily or completely answered, but he is satisfied that there is something that all blacks hold in common, even though it may not correctly be defined as *cultural*. This *something* is their precarious and unutterably painful relation to the white world. It is the burning desire to remake the world in their own image, to impose that image on the white world, and to be no longer controlled by the vision of themselves and the world held by other people. The report of the Committee on Culture did little to clarify the main question that it had been appointed to adjudicate, but it did emphasize the fact that there can be no *one* definition of Black-African culture: there are now and will continue to be many such cultures with different characteristics and different emphases. It did, however, insist on the necessity of a continuing effort to compile and evaluate the cultural inventory begun by the committee in relation to the various black cultures that have been systematically misunderstood, underestimated, and sometimes destroyed, and it did enlist the "active aid of writers, artists, theologians, thinkers, scientists, and technicians" in efforts to revive, rehabilitate, and develop these cultures as "the first step toward their integration in the active cultural life of the world." (P. 50)

One of the most significant revelations in Baldwin's report on the address of Léopold Senghor, the poet-statesman from Senegal, is the explanation of the difference between European and African reasoning as illustrated by means of the bloodstream in which all things mingle and flow to and through the heart. He points out "that the difference between the function of the arts in Europe and their function in Africa lay in the fact that, in Africa, the function of the arts is more present and pervasive, is infinitely less special, 'is done by all, for all.' . . . Art itself is taken to be perishable, to be made again each time it disappears or is destroyed. What is clung to is the spirit which makes art possible . . . . European art attempts to imitate nature. African art is concerned with reaching beyond and beneath nature, to contact, and itself become a part of *la force vitale."* (P. 24)

Baldwin's comment on Richard Wright's role in the conference is caustic. He takes exception to the older man's pronouncement that Europe had brought the Enlightenment to Africa and that "what was good for Europe was good for all mankind." He expresses even greater shock at Wright's apparent approval of the dictatorial methods of the new African leaders, who felt it necessary to adopt such tactics temporarily in order to break for their subjects the spell of Western ways of thought and action. (PP. 46–47)

In a three-part discourse entitled "Alas, Poor Richard," the essayist elaborates further on his differences with Wright, who had earlier been an inspiration and adviser to him and many other youthful writers of the period, including Ralph Ellison. With the exception of a few paragraphs concerning his former mentor's sudden death in Paris and the effect of his work upon blacks in America and abroad, he devotes the first section of this essay to a critical review of *Eight Men,* Wright's second book of short stories, published immediately after his death. His personal reaction to the expatriated American's life and death can be summarized as follows: Wright was a great inspiration to him, although he had found it necessary to fight his benefactor occasionally. America, Europe, and Africa had failed his dead friend, but despite this failure the fallen hero had survived long enough to begin to tell the tale of his struggles and achievements. In fact, as he unknowingly approached death he appeared on the threshold of a new beginning. Baldwin's criticism of the eight stories as a group was that they emphasized the fact that Wright's bleak landscape was not merely that of Chicago, as revealed in *Native Son,* or the deep South, as revealed in *Uncle Tom's Children,* but that of his entire world and of the human heart. "Even the most good-natured performance this book contains, good-natured by comparison only, 'Big Black Good Man,' takes place in Copenhagen in the winter, and in the vastly more chilling confines of a Danish hotel-keeper's fears." (P. 186)

Rather than comment on Baldwin's criticism, I submit my own critical summary of the book as it appeared in my annual critical survey of significant books by and about Negroes:

> In each of the eight stories in *Eight Men* Richard Wright presents a situation in which a colored man is a victim of the white man's inhumanity. In half of them the white man or the white man's cause suffers because of this inhumanity. In all of them the reader is made aware that the Negro characters are the sensitive ones, the knowing

ones, the superior ones, that the strong are never right, and that the prejudiced whites are to be pitied as much as the wronged Negroes.[4]

The second section is described by Baldwin as a memoir, and was first published in *Le Preuve* two months after Wright's death. It tells of his great admiration for the deceased, whom he describes as his "ally and my witness, and alas! my father," (P. 191) although he declares in the same paragraph that they were as unlike as any two writers could possibly be. They had met in 1944, two years before Wright left his native America for self-chosen European exile. He admits, however, that the relationship between them was not one of equality, since he was always conscious of a tinge of condescension in the older man's attitude toward him. Finally, the open break came after four years, when he arrived in Paris intent on repudiating his American citizenship, which Wright never did, and wrote for *Zero* magazine "Everybody's Protest Novel" attacking *Native Son* and assigning it to the same "discredited" category as he had assigned Harriet Beecher Stowe's *Uncle Tom's Cabin,* concluding with the pronouncement: "The failure of the protest novel lies in its rejection of life, the human being, the denial of his beauty, dread, power, in its insistence that it is his categorization alone which is real and which cannot be transcended." . . . [5] It is noteworthy that at this time the publication of Baldwin's first novel, *Go Tell It on the Mountain,* which was not in the protest tradition, was four years in the future, and his third and fourth, which contained protest no less acrimonious than that of *Native Son,* were thirteen and nineteen years away. It is conceivable that the twenty-six-year-old essayist was unaware at that time of the necessity for various kinds of protest, as a socially concerned writer struggles to bring to life the compelling vision that his personal and social experiences presage. Recently, as I watched a television colloquy between Baldwin and Nikki Giovanni, the young black poet, I was not surprised to hear the essayist, in reply to a query from his interlocutor, acknowledge that if he were writing "Everybody's Protest Novel" today his point of view would be different.

The third section of "Alas, Poor Richard" is Baldwin's assessment of the effect of Wright's self-imposed exile upon the older writer's life, on his relationships with other black Americans, Africans, and Algerians in Paris, and on his writing career. His commentary might be appropriately entitled "The Decline and Fall of Richard Wright." His major conclusion is: "Richard was able, at last, to live in Paris exactly as he would have lived, had he been a white man, here, in America. . . . Richard paid the price such an illusion of safety demands. The price is a turning away from, an ignorance of, all of the powers of darkness." (PP. 213–14) He accuses his former idol of arrogance and condescension toward American and African blacks, of hypocrisy in pretending to organize a Franco-American Club for the purpose of forcing American businesses in Paris and American government offices to hire American Negroes on a proportional basis, of really not wanting to know the problems of his black countrymen in Paris because "his real impulse toward American Negroes, individually, was to despise them." (P. 212) He fails to point out the continual harassment of Wright by the American Secret Service during his later years, the seeming conspiracy among American and European publishers not to publish new works by Wright during his last years, the unexplainable cooling of the ardor of white friends, and the financial difficulties that plagued the beleaguered expatriate. In sum, this essay seems to support Wright's belief as reported by the essayist earlier: "I know that I liked him [Wright], then, and later, and all the time. But I also know that, later on, he did not believe this." (P. 193)

In "The Male Prison" Baldwin praises André Gide for the manner in which the famous French writer managed his problem of homosexuality in relation to his wife Madeleine, a problem that inhibited in him "all carnal desire" and "meant that some corresponding inhibition in her prevented her from seeking carnal satisfaction elsewhere." (P. 158) Eldridge Cleaver, like Robert Bone, assumes that Baldwin's writings on homosexuality, including all of his novels except the first, are reflections of his own preferences and that these preferences are fair game for critical judgments of his work.... [6] Bone declares:

> One senses that Baldwin in his portrait of Eric [in *Another Country*], has desired above all to be faithful to his own experience. He will neither falsify nor go beyond it. Central to that experience is a rebellion against the prevailing sexual, as well as racial mores. But on either plane of experience, Baldwin faces an emotional dilemma. Like Satan and the fallen angels, it is as painful to persist in his rebellion as to give it up. Total defiance is unthinkable, total reconciliation only less so. These are the poles of Baldwin's psychic life, and the novel vacillates helplessly between them.... [7]

If indeed Baldwin is a victim of the sexual dilemma to which Cleaver and Bone have assigned him, his thoughts on "The Male Prison" as expressed in this essay deserve much better than the shabby treatment by these critics. I recommend the following passage as a typical example of the sympathetic understanding Baldwin has brought to the discussion of this much abused facet of the human condition:

> ... It is one of the facts of life that there are two sexes, which fact

has given the world most of its beauty, cost it not a little of its an-guish, and contains the hope and glory of the world. And it is with this fact, which might better perhaps be called a mystery, that every human being born must find some way to live. For, no matter what demons drive them, men cannot live without women and women cannot live without men. And this is what is most clearly conveyed in the agony of Gide's last journal. However little he was able to un-derstand it, or, more important perhaps, take upon himself the re-sponsibility for it, Madeleine kept open for him a kind of door of hope, of possibility, the possibility of entering into communion with another sex. This door, which is the door to life and air and freedom from the tyranny of one's own personality, *must* be kept open, and none feel this more keenly than those on whom the door is perpetu-ally threatening or has already seemed to close. (P. 161)

I must, however, agree with Cleaver's condemnation of Baldwin's verdict on Norman Mailer's "The White Negro," although for different reasons. In his essay "The Black Boy Looks at the White Boy" Baldwin devotes twenty-five pages to a discussion of his impressions of Mailer, one of the most tal-ented and distinguished contemporary writers, whose major contribution to the literature of black-white relations in America is the essay under exami-nation. In his rather lengthy consideration of Mailer, the essayist chooses to concentrate on several frivolous, self-serving, insipid encounters with his white counterpart, relegating his two-page monologue on the greatly misun-derstood essay largely to commonplace chitchat, of which the following sum-mary is the most meaningful: "I could not, with the best will in the world, make any sense out of *The White Negro* and, in fact, it was hard for me to imagine that this essay had been written by the same man who wrote the novels." (P. 228) Nevertheless, he admits that a black musician talking to him about Mailer—the context seems to imply that Mailer's essay was the subject—said, " 'Man . . . the only trouble with that cat is that he's white.' " (P. 231) Baldwin adds, "What my friend meant was that to become a Negro man, let alone a Negro artist, one had to make oneself up as one went along. . . . Now, this is true for everyone, but, in the case of a Negro, this truth is absolutely naked: if he deludes himself about it, he will die. This is not the way this truth presents itself to white men, who believe the world is theirs and who, albeit unconsciously, expect the world to help them in the achievement of their identity." (P. 232)

In fact, Mailer's thesis, which Baldwin does not choose to explain, is that "in certain cities in America . . . this particular part of a generation was at-tracted to what the Negro had to offer. In such places as Greenwich Village, a ménage à trois was completed—the bohemian and juvenile delinquent came face to face with the Negro, and the hipster was a fact in American life. . . . And in this wedding of the white and black it was the Negro who brought the cultural dowry." . . . [8] The *white* Negro, therefore, is the non-black hipster who has accepted the urban non-middle-class Negro's philosophy of existence, including living in the present, substituting the pleasures of the body for the pleasures of the mind, and voicing in his music the character and quality of existence. Mailer suggests that since the Negro has been living on the margin between totalitarianism and democracy for two centuries, it is natural for him to be the source of Hip—both a special language and a way of life. "Sharing a collective disbelief in the words of men who had too much money and controlled too many things," hipster disbelieves in "the socially monolithic ideas of the single mate, the solid family and respectable love life." . . . [9]

According to Mailer, Hip is a language of energy. The words and/or expressions he chose for discussion are *man, go, put down, make, beat, cool, swing, with it, crazy, dig, hip, flip, creep,* and *square.* As to the future, he believes that the most central fact "is that the organic growth of Hip depends on whether the Negro emerges as a dominating force in American life. Since the Negro knows more about the ugliness and danger of life than the white, it is probable that if the Negro can win his equality, he will possess a potential superiority, a superiority so feared that the fear itself has become the underground drama of domestic politics." . . . [10]

It seems to this writer that Baldwin's appraisal of the basic philosophy expressed in "The White Negro" would have made an infinitely greater contribution to an understanding of Mailer's thought and attitude toward black-white relations than his superficial treatment of the author's personal dealings with him.

III

The Fire Next Time is a book of only two essays, one entitled "My Dungeon Shook" and the other "Down at the Cross: Letter from a Region in My Mind." The first, consisting of seven pages, advises the author's fifteen-year old nephew how to avoid the death his white fellowmen have prepared for him and at the same time to remake America so that he and his would-be executioners will survive together. It is a remarkable exercise in eloquence, hyperbole, sleight-of-hand, romanticism, and naiveté—in other words, a delightful exercise in the creation of what could be the pure poetry Carl Sanburg described in his famous paradox "hyacinth and biscuits." He assures his nephew that, with sufficient stamina, wariness, and love, he can save himself from the diabolical schemes of his white brothers, who intend

> ... that you should perish in the ghetto, perish by never being allowed to go behind the white man's definitions, by never being allowed to spell your proper name. ... But these men are your brothers—your lost younger brothers. And if the word *integration* means anything, this is what it means: that we, with love, shall force our brothers to see themselves as they are, to cease fleeing from reality and begin to change it.[11]

He suggests that there is no reason for Negroes to become like whites, and that there is no basis for the assumption by whites that they must accept Negroes. Rather, Negroes must accept white people in order to save them from self-destruction. Negroes must be their saviors, for "We cannot be free until they are free." (P. 24)

The second essay, consisting of ninety-one pages, provides the background experiences responsible for generating the advice he gave his nephew. It begins with capsule descriptions of his childhood, adolescence, and young adulthood, including the influence on his development of such powerful forces as the Christian religion, dope, prostitution, and other crimes characteristic of the Harlem ghetto, the counterforce of the Black Muslim movement, and the ever-present threat of white power in its varied manifestations. Although at the early age of seventeen he had rejected the Christian church (the storefront variety) and its basic practices, after having been a practicing preacher for more than three years, he admits that its early influences had, in all probability, saved him from the corrupting power of the worst elements of his environment and from a sordid life worse than death. He admits that during his early ministerial experiences "I have never seen anything to equal the fire and excitement that sometimes, without warning, fill a church, causing the church ... to 'rock'. " (P. 47) Nothing that has happened to him since, he confesses "equals the power and the glory" (P. 47) that he sometimes felt when, in the middle of a sermon he knew that he and the church were one. But he was finally convinced that there was no love in the church. Hatred and despair were the constant companions of those who surrendered to the temporary visitations of the Holy Ghost during the services. The admonition to love everybody applied neither to white people nor to blacks whose beliefs were different from theirs. But Baldwin could see no value in salvation that did not permit him to behave with love toward others regardless of their behavior toward him.

Later he discovered in the Black Muslim religion a superiority over Christianity as practiced by the so-called Christian churches. He found that Elijah Muhammad, national leader of the Muslims, "had been able to do what generations of welfare workers and committees and resolutions and reports and housing projects and playgrounds had failed to do: to heal and redeem drunkards and junkies, to convert people who have come out of prison and make men chaste and women virtuous, and to invest both the male and the female with a pride and a serenity that hang about them like an unfailing light." (P. 64–65) In all these things, according to Baldwin, the Christian church has been a spectacular failure. But, despite these successes, the essayist found the Muslims blameworthy in one major respect: their religion forbids the concept of integration among whites and blacks; therefore, he could not accept their doctrine as the best guide to the promotion of acceptable human relations. He made it clear to Elijah Muhammad that he had many white friends and did not object to intermarriage between whites and blacks. He emphasized that if it ever became necessary to die with his friends rather than seek survival at their expense, he would have no choice but to die with the white and the black. He thought to himself as he lectured the Muslim leader: "I love a few people and they love me and some of them are white, and isn't love more important than color?" (P. 85)

It is clear from the tenor of the discussion in both essays that at this period in his life Baldwin is committed to two courses of conduct, *love* and *integration,* for he uses both as fulcrums in each of the two essays. He commits himself, and urges a commitment upon his nephew, to these two modes of conduct despite his admission that in practice neither has been accepted by his white fellowmen. He suggests, in respect to integration, "We, the black and white, deeply need each other here if we are really to become a nation." (P. 111) But he concludes, "To create one nation has proved to be a hideously difficult task; there is certainly no need now to create two, one black and one white. But white men . . . have been advocating exactly this, in effect, for generations." (P. 111) In the conclusion of his letter to his nephew, he links both concepts as the two major poles of his creed: "And if the word *integration* means anything, this is what it means: that we, with love, shall force our brothers to see themselves as they are, to cease fleeing from reality and begin to change it." (PP. 23–24) This is indeed the substance of the gospel of Martin Luther King and the evidence that at this point in his life Baldwin is King's devoted disciple.

In this volume Baldwin offers new definitions for old ideas. He defines love "as a state of being, or a state of grace—not in the infantile American sense of being made happy but in the tough and universal sense of quest and daring and growth." (P. 109) He suggests a new definition of beauty when he says, "And black has *become* a beautiful color—not because it is loved but because it is feared." (P. 91) He pays loving tribute to the "Uncle Toms" of the past who have been maligned and reviled by the new breed of black militants for the necessary compromises they had to make to gain educational advantages for their children. "I have great respect for that unsung army of black men and women who trudged down back lanes and entered back doors," he declares, "saying 'Yes, sir' and 'No, Ma'am' in order to acquire a new roof for the schoolhouse, new books, a chemistry lab, more beds for the dormitories, more dormitories." (P. 114)

This is a beautiful book, a challenging book, a powerful book. It is a profoundly philosophical book. It is the best of Baldwin's writings. But it offers no new solutions to the problem of race relations in America. Indeed, its basic solution is as old as the Holy Bible and as simple as the Sermon on the Mount.

IV

No Name in the Street, Baldwin's fourth book of essays, reveals a sadder but hardly wiser writer than has come to light in the three previous volumes. It is a more hardboiled, pessimistic, disillusioned view of his country and its people. It bids farewell to idealism, to positive and unselfish love, to the belief in integration, and to a viable future for the United States of America. It accepts as a valid prophecy the curse of Job's friend Bildad, who pronounced this doom upon the wicked of his generation: "His remembrance shall perish from the earth and he shall have *No Name in the Street.* He shall be driven from light into darkness, and chased out of the world."

In this book Baldwin has selected for dramatic exposure a *potpourri* of exasperating and tragic incidents of black life in America and abroad and has formulated frightening conclusions based on the reactions of blacks to these incidents. He has rehashed with new insights and emphases experiences in his life from childhood to the present which are responsible for his changing attitudes toward life in general and white Americans in particular. He interweaves in the tapestry of events, moving back and forth in time intimate experiences and associations with Martin Luther King, Medgar Evers, Malcolm X—all charismatic black leaders who were associated because of their forthright determination to secure equal rights for black people—and a young black man named William A. Maynard, Jr., who had served as his bodyguard and chauffeur several years previously and who had been arrested later for a murder he did not commit and who subsequently fled to Hamburg, Germany, while awaiting trial in New York. The Maynard case, including the brutal and inhuman plight of black prisoners in general, is given more space than any other single subject.

Other bitter grievances that influenced Baldwin's repudiation of God, of European culture, which he previously adored, of a belief in the possibility of American justice, and even of the taboo against murder are, among a multitude of others, "the storm of fire and blood which the Black Panthers have been forced to undergo merely for declaring themselves as men," . . . [12] the genocidal treatment of black Algerians by the French, and the determination by the American press and the movie industry to prevent the exposure of worthy achievements of black people. "All of the Western nations have been caught in a lie," he declares, "the lie of their pretended humanism: this means that their history has no moral justification, and that the West has no moral authority." (P. 85) Evidently, he no longer worships at the shrine of the Cathedral at Chartres as he so boldly proclaimed in his first book of essays, *Notes of a Native Son*. In reference to the repudiation of his past attitudes, he says with sarcasm, "It must be remembered that in those great days I was considered to be an 'integrationist'. " (P. 93)

In the closing pages of this volume he summarizes his break with his past in the following dramatic terms:

> . . . whereas white men have killed black men for sport, or out of terror or out of the intolerable excess of terror called hatred, or out of the necessity of affirming their identity as white men, none of these motives appear necessarily to obtain for black men: it is not necessary for a black man to hate a white man, or to have any particular feelings about him at all, in order to realize that he must kill him. Yes, we have come, or are coming to this, and there is no point in flinching before the prospect of this exceedingly cool species of fratricide—which prospect white people, after all, have brought on themselves. (P. 191)

Finally, one of the most sensitive writers in the Western world, in the middle of a brilliant career that has earned him respect and honor at home and abroad, whose early vision was rooted in love and brotherhood and whose faith in the integration of the races was genuine and compulsive, has come to this.

V

A comparative and/or contrasting examination of Baldwin's four volumes of essays in respect to theme, style, and philosophy reveals interesting information. They were published during a span of seventeen years. Some individual essays were written as early as twenty-five years ago and others as late as two years ago. The quarter of a century represented covers the period between the author's twenty-fourth and forty-eighth birthdays, a period in which youthful idealism had to make room for mature realism and possible pragmatism. Certainly *Notes of a Native Son,* containing the first fruits of his authorship, is characterized by exuberance, cockiness, self-assurance, and idealism. The style is fresh and at times eloquent, with the fervor, personal involvement, and conviction of the apostles of the New Testament, which he had learned to emulate in his youthful sermons. On the other hand, *No Name in the Street,* his latest, is sober, somber, pessimistic, and pragmatic. It is steeped in gloom and hopelessness. The New Testament philosophy of forgiveness has given way to the Old Testament's pronouncements of doom. The intermediate volumes fluctuate in style and tone between the two extremes.

In theme, the last two volumes rely heavily upon quotations from the Old Testament to furnish texts for the sermons they preach. *The Fire Next Time* announces the threat "God gave Noah the rainbow sign, No more water the fire next time" but stresses the twin virtues of love and brotherhood as foils for the impending holocaust. *No Name in the Street* flaunts the curse of destruction and holds out no shred of hope for salvation. The only question is how long the imminent catastrophe can be postponed: "There will be bloody holding actions all over the world, for years to come: but the Western party is over, and the white man's sun has set. Period." (P. 197)

In what respect does Baldwin differ from other American essayists? Probably the most unique feature of his style is his tendency to tie in his personal life and experiences with whatever commentary he offers on social and philosophical questions. In other words, his caustic criticisms of local, national, and world conditions result directly or indirectly from his personal experiences. He, therefore, speaks with an authority that most essayists reject as not sufficiently objective. He has accepted as the major theme in all of his writings the horrendous task of exposing with candor and acerbity what it means to be black in a nation and a world dominated by "white" power in social, political, religious, artistic, and ethical matters. He has publicly announced: "We are the generation that must throw everything into the endeavor to remake America into what we say we want it to be. Without this endeavor we will perish. However immoral or subversive this may sound to some, it is the writer who must always remember that morality, if it is to remain or become morality, must be perpetually examined, cracked, changed, made new." [13]

To those who say that a writer who expects to be accepted and respected by his generation must approach his task objectively, taking his subject matter from the past and disguising his criticism by means of metaphor or other types of figurative language, Baldwin replies: "Not everything that is faced can be changed; but nothing can be changed until it is faced."

From a Region in My Mind
The Essays of James Baldwin

_____ Hobart Jarrett

Since I cannot say everything about the subject in one essay, I wish to begin by pronouncing that James Baldwin is a great writer. He is a writer by choice, by talent, by calling. He is a _great_ writer because these persuasions directed him to the essay, the form that shows him at his excellence.

My attention was first seriously called to Mr. Baldwin back in 1962, when an adult, white, male student of mine came in, excited with admiration, to tell me about an essay he had just read, "Letter from a Region in My Mind." It had recently appeared on the newsstands and I had not read it. I soon found that Sol Potegal's admiration was rightly invoked. The essay was tremendous.

The title itself was arresting. Did it mean that its author was holding back, not letting himself say all that was on his mind? In the sophistication that comes from really comprehending hypocrisy and penetrating through it, was he jocularly, in a Mephistophelean way, exposing the grit and sediment in American race relations, which readers of a slick magazine could take? Or was it that he knew he had so much to say that one essay could contain but a peripheral part—enough of a part, however, to boggle and whet the mind and to forewarn readers of matters to come? These questions need not be definitively answered. Every reader of Baldwin knows that the "Region" was intellectually and emotionally stuffed, and that many additional significant, disturbing, irritating matters were to be written about. I read the essay in flight, the shortest I have ever made, so commanding was Baldwin's statement. I have been stimulated, exhilarated, and amazed by his essays ever since.

I must interrupt what I am saying to get this point across—and now. I am obligated to confess that I have somehow never forgiven Mr. Baldwin for inventing such titles as "Letter from a Region in My Mind" and *Nobody Knows My Name*. For I know that, *one* day, I was going to invent them, *Nobody Knows My Name* for my autobiography—Baldwin uses it merely for the title essay of a collection which bears the title—and "Letter from a Region in My Mind" to do the kind of thing Baldwin does with it: to tell of some of the awful, detestable, and terrible matters that really bother me and make me seriously question the efficacy, if not at times the very humanity, of white people. But that's James Baldwin for you. Keep silent forever (while teaching away) and he steals it right from under you.

Baldwin, as I have said, is a great writer. He is so in large part because of the high regard he has for his vocation. He conceives of a writer as one with a special mission. And as my students, I hope, know that Shakespeare is not a philosopher but a playwright, a dramatist, so Baldwin would have us know that a writer is not a psychologist or a sociologist. We are further told that an important part of the writer's responsibility is to examine attitudes, to penetrate the surface in order to discover the motivating causes and reasons behind mankind's actions. In large manner, this is what Baldwin the essayist does. He is concerned with what makes life what life is. And he finds that attitudes, both those of the individual and those of society, are the source from which actions spring. To understand that this is so, the writer does not merely record what happens. He probes. And one writes best—no, Baldwin would say that one writes *only*—out of his own experience: what the writer can really say is dependent upon what he has experienced. For the world and himself are his subject, and only to the extent that he can see the world and himself as they are does he achieve what must be achieved by one who is a writer. This thought, of course, does not originate with Baldwin. It is akin to Faust's quest for experience. It is also Whitmanesque and Emersonian. In a much more constricted and pragmatic sense, it is the thought of Stephen Crane. What Baldwin believes of the writer is what Emerson meant when he said that the scholar must show facts amid appearances. For the writer must constantly see the reality of himself and of the world and interpret this for mankind. Baldwin actually says that the writer "must excavate and recreate history"; for it is he only who has "learned anything from" history.[1] I certainly cannot agree with the exclusiveness of Baldwin's appraisal of the writer—teachers, for example, do a lot of creating too, both from their knowledge of history and, most importantly, from their knowledge of literature: *what* man has chosen to write about and *how* he has written about it. At the same time, one certainly appreciates the high estimate Mr. Baldwin makes of the literary artist and the significance of his role. When the writer does anything short of probing to find and reveal the "buried consciousness of this country,"[2] he has not kept the faith and succeeds in becoming nothing. He is no writer.

Writing of himself, Baldwin states that he is determined "to be an honest man and a good writer."[3] It is to be hoped that he has satisfied his standards of honesty. Unquestionably, he is a great essayist. He is so because of the experiences he has lived, his understanding of them in the social context, and his commitment and remarkable ability to relate these experiences so that his readers relive and comprehend them.

The world he unfolds is broad enough. He writes profusely of life in America; and he writes of France, Sweden, Switzerland, and Germany. He makes critical appraisals of such prominent personages as Richard Wright, Faulkner, Mailer, Ingmar Bergman, Malcolm X, and Elijah Muhammad. Other world figures appear in his essays also, notably Dr. Martin Luther King. Baldwin has a lot to say about his family, especially his father. And though no specific essays are devoted to them, jazz and the blues, Americanism, sex, the police—by all means the police—Christianity, and religion are significantly treated in his text. Always informative and instructive, at times Baldwin reveals philosophic insights that cause his readers to grow in wisdom and stature. And by no means can Baldwin's style be overlooked. He commands the language. His use of italics gives his prose the richness of oral speech—conversation, really. And he is a master of punctuation. He *has* to be; for he likes at times to write long, rambling, all-inclusive sentences, in which academic grammar, by the by, is occasionally sidestepped, as the sentences flow or wind to their interesting conclusions. He is at his best when the world he reveals is *his* world, when he writes of the experiences *he* has had and reveals his personal reactions. And at his best, he is hard to top.

Baldwin makes it pretty clear that he hated his father. Now who am I, who have never *seen* James Baldwin and have only heard of his father through the son's writings—who am I, a student of literature, not of psychology, to doubt this man's appraisal of his relationship with his father? But I do. I find it difficult to believe that he *hated* his father, or perhaps I should say that he *hates* his father. Obviously there was great distance between them. Some of it was physical. James was the oldest child of a second marriage. But James's mother was contemporary with the youngest daughter by the father's first marriage, and James himself was nine years younger than the last son by the earlier marriage. So an immediate, ingrained difficulty was the age barrier. But there was much more to it than that. The family was large—there were ten children, with pregnancies coming regularly. And the children, writes Baldwin, "were all, absolutely and mercilessly, united against" their father.[4] In fact, they were "terrified of the man we called my father.... "[5] Elsewhere, Baldwin further explains that when the elder Baldwin "took one of his children on his knee to play, the child always began to cry.... I do not remember, in all those years, that one of his children was ever glad to see him come home."[6] The full reason for this alienation and hatred is never really stated in the essays. Perhaps it could not be. But it appears that the father's personality, his inability to let his children know what he might have felt toward them, the harsh conditions within which they (and *he*) had to survive, his own apprehension and fear of whites—it appears that these (along with the age difference) were insurmountable contributors to the hostility between father and son.

Baldwin manifests his antipathy in many essays. The feeling was indeed deep and terrifying. We are told in *The Fire Next Time*[7] that he had resolved to kill his father rather than the other way around. The feeling of animosity continued even toward the end of his father's life, actually until the last time Baldwin saw him on his feet. But from my own vantage point as an interested and sympathetic onlooker, and notwithstanding Baldwin's description of the corpse and his account of himself before and at the funeral, another aspect of Baldwin's evaluation stands out significantly. He tells us that upon reflection he realizes that he did not understand "this man . . . until he was past understanding." What the son came to understand is that the dignity that his father so stubbornly and stoically possessed had nothing external to nourish it, and little internal. Life was hard, bitter. He was a *black* black man before the present re-evaluation of color and its pursuant sloganed pride in blackness. He was the son of a slave. He had grown up in the South —the recalcitrant South. He both hated and feared whites. He had next to no friends. He died insane. He did so, as his distinguished son so eloquently puts it, because of

> his merciless children, ... the pregnancies, the births, the rats, the murders on Lennox Avenue, the whores who lived downstairs, his job on Long Island—to which he went every morning wearing a Derby or a Homburg, ... looking like the preacher that he was, and with his black lunch-box in his hand.[8]

All these took their toll, submerging him irretrievably. On top of all this was an experience that might have been even more debilitating. The situation was crucial in that he was robbed of the modicum of peace that every living person must somehow be able to find in the privacy of his own soul. The love of Baldwin the father, according to Baldwin the son, was an "unreciprocated love for the Great God Almighty."[9] But even God's rejection was not all. The final crushing blow that destroyed the father (and this time Baldwin calls him "Daddy") was the ultimate realization that as a result of a quarrel that separated them, he would never again see his favorite son (by his first marriage), "his darling, the apple of his eye, . . . and this broke his heart and destroyed his will and helped him to the madhouse and the grave. . . . "[10] The family "had not known that he was being eaten up by paranoia, and the discovery that his cruelty" to them "had been one of the symptoms of his illness was not, then, enough to enable" them, "then, to forgive him."[11] But as James Baldwin himself grew in wisdom and understanding, he wished that his father "had been beside me so that I could have searched his face for the answers which only the future would give me now." The hatred, it seems, did not last.

Religion receives prominent attention in the essays. It would have to, in that it was a major function in the upbringing of James Baldwin. His father had been a preacher, an unsuccessful one; and the youthful James tried his hand at bringing the souls to Jesus. James gave up the habit but his father held on, becoming even more bitter in the process. The elder Baldwin "never, at bottom, forgave the white world (which he described as heathen) for having saddled him with a Christ in whom, to judge at least from his treatment of him, they themselves no longer believed."[12] Religion, the church, Christianity are a large part of the concerns of Baldwin. In actuality, they are also a large part of the concerns of Negro life, as the essays before us reveal.

Every thinking American Negro who dares to buck his own tradition and be really honest with himself, at least in the privacy of his own mind, must inevitably be struck by the chicanery, the hypocrisy, the lies that are a daily way of life in white-Christian America. Not only are Negroes made to feel the hurt that is inwoven into their lives, but they see, and remark about, sometimes jovially, the antagonisms and brutality that whites show toward each other. And one need not look at national scandals to comprehend my meaning. One can look at close range, on the job, in the community to see the point. In a much milder time than ours, Boccaccio and, in another, Voltaire—to cite only two—exposed basic immoralities that were woven into the fabric of the religious garment. Baldwin does also. It was the awareness of white America at close range that helped to embitter and madden the economically and racially victimized father of James Baldwin. On the other hand, of course, the awareness has made black Christians—I wish to be neither irreverent nor offensive, but sometimes there is incongruity in the sound

—far more Christian than Christians. In some indeed remarkable instances, it has caused them to develop the leadership and cohesive followership that surely the love of God would demand. Baldwin speaks well indeed of Martin Luther King (calling him always Martin), but it is almost inevitable that to talk honestly of American Christianity is to talk of malfeasance. And *this* is what Baldwin largely writes of when he considers religion. To find equanimity, brotherhood among Christians when the black Christian is involved is difficult. What a friend we have in Jesus may not be readily demonstrable either.

James Baldwin is as caustic as he pleases. Writing about how this continent became Americanized, he says of the Negro that

> his shameful history was carried, quite literally, on his brow. Shameful; for he was heathen as well as black and would never have discovered the healing blood of Christ had not we braved the jungles to bring him these glad tidings.

(I am obliged to interrupt the thought for a moment to call attention to Baldwin's use of *we*. Here is a technique that Baldwin uses. It is a way of stepping outside his own blackness while yet remaining in it to tell the black man's story. Baldwin the writer thus identifies with his reader, becomes him, in order to help, if not force, the white reader to see an onerous problem sympathetically, through Baldwin's eyes.) He continues the above:

> As he accepted the alabaster Christ and the bloody cross...he must, henceforth, accept that image we then gave him of himself.... [13]

Elsewhere, Baldwin explains the phenomenon that made a Negro slave into a Christian. Underlying the transformation is the fact that "the rejected desire is an elevation of status, acceptance within the present community"—a fact that many black people today vocalize against but with which the present writer heartily concurs. Baldwin continues:

> Thus the African, exile, pagan, hurried off the auction block and into the fields, fell on his knees before that God in Whom he must now believe; Who had made him, but not in His image. This tableau, this impossibility, is the heritage of the Negro in America: *Wash me,* cried the slave to his Maker, *and I shall be whiter, whiter than snow!* [14]

The problem Baldwin raises is complex and gnarled. It recognizes and emphasizes the awful significance of color. (In my youth, my childhood in Tulsa, after the concert, as the black people left *their* section of Convention

Hall and the white people theirs, *to join in one line* of admirers who went up to shake Roland Hayes by the hand, I heard a bejeweled white matron exclaim, "Wouldn't it be marvelous if we could only bleach him!") The literalist, who certainly far outnumbers those of us who know, with John Milton, what God's image really is, the essence, the soul—the literalist has seen and yet sees that white God's image is not black, despite the pleas of people like Thomas Fuller, the Anglican Divine, who three hundred years ago postulated that African slaves were God's image in ebony even as the slaver was God's image in white. The knotty problem also raises the question of possibility. How on earth can a black man be equal to a white? *In*equality, in fact, stems from theology. Baldwin has much to say about the role that religion has crushed Negro people into. Remarkably typical is his brilliant analysis in the controversial essay "Everybody's Protest Novel." There he says of Richard Wright's celebrated hero:

> Bigger's tragedy is ... that he has accepted a theology that denies him life, that he admits the possibility of his being sub-human and feels constrained, therefore, to battle for his humanity according to those brutal criteria bequeathed him at his birth.[45]

There he also writes of the "zeal of those alabaster missionaries to Africa to cover the nakedness of the natives, to hurry them into the pallid arms of Jesus and thence into slavery."[16] The whiteness of God, that is, the conception that God is white, is inexorable. Even to James Baldwin himself the fact and its implications were clear. During the period of his early conversion, he wondered why, if white God loved *all* His children, the black children were rejected?

The problem further raises the question about why black people are religious, that is, Christian. To Baldwin, it is axiomatic that they are, in spite of the relatedness of Christianity to their enslavement. They yet stand in awe of God, whom they inherited from their God-embracing slave forebears. And— a matter that had never occurred to me—Baldwin suggests that there are "probably more churches in Harlem than in any other ghetto in this city and they are going full blast every night and some of them are filled with praying people every day."[17] It certainly appears that the rejected believe because they are forced to: they do not enjoy what is to be enjoyed, but religiously wish to. They have a dream. (Ultimately, as everybody knows, they resort to demands.)

That Baldwin is not extolling the Christian faith and church there can be little doubt. He sees matters as they are, including the cruelty and criminality of religious practice. (Lillian Smith did, too.) For its worth, I should state that Baldwin does not eliminate the Negro church from criticism. It too subtly but assuredly preaches hatred—of whites. Both white and black churches substitute for the Pauline virtues "Blindness, Loneliness, and Terror."[18] But his major attack, of course, remains against white Christians, who so flagrantly, conveniently, and unashamedly cast off moral virtues to stress power and politics. Christianity has been arrogant and cruel in its expansion of empires into the lands of others. Baldwin makes it quite clear that the white Christian (that too has an incongruous ring) has robbed the African of his history and his gods. The cruelty of those who manifest to be Christians makes Baldwin believe that "whoever wishes to become a truly moral human being . . . must first divorce himself from all the prohibitions, crimes, and hypocrisies of the Christian church." He concludes by emphasizing that if God cannot make us better, more loving toward all, "then it is time we got rid of Him."[19]

At times in one's life one discovers—here is a great work! It lives. Read this, one thinks, get others to do so, and man and society become better. The Bible, obviously, falls in this category. One ought to read the Sermon on the Mount at least once every year. The advice was given by a graduate professor of mine years ago to his seminar in American writers. The individual adds a cubit to himself when he reads certain works. *The Symposium,* Milton's works, *Faust,* Emerson's essays, those of Du Bois—these are among the monumental treatises that one cannot profitably forgo. What of James Baldwin? Can his name be mentioned here? I suppose that the only safe answer is that time will decide. But already we know that he has something tremendous to say and he says it tremendously. Not unlike my excited student of a decade ago, I would say: read Baldwin! Digest the essays, and society *ought* to be better. The problem, the difficulty is that the word and the deed do not always coalesce. And how many have I taught who did not know who Du Bois was, had next to no conception of Emerson, had not encountered *Paradise Lost* or the *Areopagitica* or *Samson Agonistes,* had never read *any* Plato, and were actually not sold on the Bible! These writings should be known. James Baldwin ought to be also.

Presumably, any reader who has even dabbled in the great literary outpourings that focus attention on the problems of our time will know that Du Bois said at the beginning of this century that the big problem would be, is, the problem of color. Like it or not, Du Bois was right. With all the progress that has been made, including that in the area of human relations, color, that is pigmentation—the superficies that identify and categorize the human being—remains a great divisive threat to social unification, if not to human survival. Baldwin, like Du Bois before him, recognizes and has much to say about this matter. In the process, he holds a mirror up to America. The reflection is ugly.

It is not easy to be a Negro, reasons Baldwin. "Black is a terrible color with which to be born into the world."[20] One is victimized from the start—by virtue of birth, I add. Society not only gives black people an inferior status but *convinces* them "of the reality of this decree; it has the force and the weapons to translate its dictum into fact, so that the allegedly inferior are actually made so."[21] The first and binding stigma was stamped on the blackness of the African when the white missionary joined with the slave trader and slave owner to rob the black man of every identity he had, save the superficial. From that beginning, white America has conveniently absolved itself of responsibility, by ignorantly accepting and by selfishly and fearfully and cruelly clinging to the dictum: What is not white is inferior. And what is inferior is treated so. "This is the crime of which I accuse my country and my countrymen, and for which neither I nor time nor history will ever forgive them, that they have destroyed and are destroying hundreds of thousands of lives and do not want to know it."[22]

Baldwin himself had quite dramatically come to understand what it is to be a Negro. He really experienced this in New Jersey. There, having left the familiarity of Harlem and New York, he learned "that to be a Negro meant, precisely, that one was never looked at but was simply at the mercy of the reflexes the color of one's skin caused in other people."[23] It was then that Baldwin realized his own invisibility. He was to realize it many times over. Nobody knew his name. He came to see, as did Mr. Ellison, the importance, the absolutely necessary importance to the human person, of visibility and recognition. For himself, he vowed not to be spat upon, not to permit the quicksands of the ghetto to suck him in. For both himself and beyond, he insists that what black people want more than anything else is to be treated like men. They neither seek nor wish for protection, because protection emasculates. But "neither the Southerner nor the Northerner is able to look on the Negro simply as a man,"[24] so ingrained is tradition. Hence, the struggle must continue, and "one day, to everyone's astonishment, someone drops a match in the powder keg and everything blows up."[25]

"Negroes want to be treated like men: A perfectly straightforward statement, containing only seven words. People who have mastered Kant, Hegel, Shakespeare, Marx, Freud, and the Bible find this statement utterly impenetrable."[26]

No, it is not easy to be a Negro. One cannot live without a past, but the Negro's past was taken from him. To exist without it is a part of the incongruity that is the American Negro's life. For without that past and with the ever-pressure of the dictum, the black man *is* a victim. Hatred and fear of whites are concomitants to life as the American Negro has had to live it. But *self*-hatred is also, thinks Baldwin, and this attitude is corrupting. He states that he himself at one time despised black people. And in writing of himself in Paris, he honestly says that he was "as isolated from Negroes as I was from whites, which is what happens when a Negro begins, at bottom, to believe what white people say about him."[27] Readers of James Baldwin are well aware that whether he is in any way isolated from blacks or whites, he certainly is not negatively motivated. On the contrary, he has proved himself in word and deed, and he writes of the power of love. What I find sterling to remember are his proclamation about black people and his reaffirmation about life in the United States. I search for no finer statement of the former than the following evaluation of the Conference of Negro-African Writers and Artists, held in Paris during September, 1956:

> It became clear as the debate wore on, that there *was* something which all black men held in common, something which cut across opposing points of view, and placed in the same context their widely dissimilar experience. What they held in common was their precarious, their unutterably painful relation to the white world. What they held in common was the necessity to remake the world in their own image, to impose this image on the world, and no longer be controlled by the vision of the world, and of themselves, held by other people. What, in sum, black men held in common was their ache to come into the world as men.[28]

The reaffirmation about America requires further examination of Baldwin's views about this country.

Attention has already been called several times in the present essay to the cruelty that Baldwin sees in white-Christian America. America destroys Negroes. It teaches black people "to despise themselves from the moment their eyes open on the world."[29] It inculcates fear: that distinctive kind of fear that James heard in his father's voice when the elder Baldwin feared "that the child, in challenging the white world's assumptions, was putting himself in the path of destruction."[30] It walls up blacks "in a ghetto in which, in fact, it intended that ... [they] should perish."[31] It yells "nigger" at blacks and paints them despicable. It once in its constitution defined a Negro "as 'three-fifths' of a man. ... "[32] It makes "violence and heroism ... synonymous except when it comes to blacks."[33] For "white Americans have never in all their long history been able to look on ... [the Negro] as a man like themselves."[34] *He* must accept substandard living nonviolently so that the national and individual white conscience will not be disturbed. Baldwin attempts to *make* his reader understand:

> You must put yourself in the skin of a man who is wearing the uniform of his country, is a candidate for death in its defense, and who is called a "nigger" by his comrades-in-arms and his officers; who is almost always given the hardest, ugliest, most menial work to do; who knows that the white G.I. has informed the Europeans that he is subhuman (so much for the American male's sexual security); who does not dance at the U.S.O. the night white soldiers dance there, and does not drink in the same bars white soldiers drink in; and who watches German prisoners of war being treated by Americans with more human dignity than he has ever received at their hands. And who, at the same time, as a human being, is far freer in a strange land than he has ever been at home. *Home!*[35]

(I had the experience a lifetime ago. I was not in uniform, nor was I abroad. I was *here,* in the United States, traveling with my young wife by train from New York to Oklahoma. The German P.W.'s sat wherever they wished. The diner for us was behind a green curtain! Years later, when I moved to New York to find that Jewish landlords in Flatbush, adjacent to the college in which I would teach their sons and daughters, would not rent an apartment to me, I thought of the superiority of German P.W.'s to American citizens!)

Baldwin knows the intimacies of America. He believes that "white Americans are probably the sickest and certainly the most dangerous people, of any color, to be found in the world today."[36] He writes of this country honestly and eloquently, probing to discover America for us all. And, when he wishes, he writes dispassionately, even about matters that are chock full of that which is emotionally explosive. Consider, for example, the following excerpt, a passage that few, if any, black people could fail to understand but that many white would not wish to comprehend:

> In a society that is entirely hostile, and, by its nature, seems determined to cut you down—that has cut down so many in the past and cuts down so many every day—it begins to be almost impossible to distinguish a real from a fancied injury. One can very quickly cease to attempt this distinction, and, what is worse, one usually ceases to attempt it without realizing that one has done so. All doormen, for example, and all policemen have by now, for me, become exactly the same, and my style with them is designed simply to intimidate them before they can intimidate me. No doubt I am guilty of some injustice here, but it is irreducible, since I cannot risk assuming that the humanity of these people is more real to them than their uniforms.

Most Negroes cannot risk assuming that the humanity of white people is more real to them than their color. And this leads, imperceptibly but inevitably, to a state of mind in which, having long ago learned to expect the worst, one finds it very easy to believe the worst. The brutality with which Negroes are treated in this country simply cannot be overstated, however unwilling white men may be to hear it. In the beginning—and neither can this be overstated—a Negro just cannot *believe* that white people are treating him as they do; he does not know what he has done to merit it. And when he realizes that the treatment accorded him has nothing to do with anything he has done, that the attempt of white people to destroy him— for that is what it is—is utterly gratuitous, it is not hard for him to think of white people as devils. For the horrors of the American Negro's life there has been almost no language. The privacy of his experience, which is only beginning to be recognized in language, and which is denied or ignored in official and popular speech— hence the Negro idiom—lends credibility to any system that pretends to clarify it. And, in fact, the truth about the black man, as a historical entity and as a human being, *has* been hidden from him, deliberately and cruelly. . . .[37]

The above passage appears in that portion of the essay in which Baldwin tells of his meeting with Elijah Muhammad. In my judgment, in at least one instance, that in which whites are identified as devils, it reflects the teachings of Black Muslims more pointedly than it does Baldwin's thinking. However, in his essay, "To Be Baptized," Baldwin both shows and comments upon the awfulness of American whites and actually associates them with devils. About the kindest statement he makes about whites in this regard is that American whites cannot believe that the grievances black people talk about are real. To believe would reveal how terrible whites are and how dishonorable the United States is. Baldwin forces the issue; and we are grateful. He shows a disillusioned reality about mankind, the kind that Dostoyevsky had talked about. Historically, men take advantage of and debase others simply because they are men. It is man's nature to do so. Within this context and beyond it, when we leave the theory to see the practice, Baldwin discards Dr. King's dream. Even prior to what happened after the historic March on Washington, Baldwin had thought that "we could petition and petition and march and march and raise money and give money," but "none of this endeavor would or could reach the core of the matter, it would change nobody's fate." This truth is so awful because certainly at the time he wrote it, James Baldwin believed, "Nothing would ever reach the conscience of the people of this nation. . . ."[38] One would like to believe Baldwin wrong, to *prove* that he is wrong. But Baldwin reminds us that while the rhythmic verse, "Free at last, free at last, praise God Almighty, I'm free at last," the verse to which Dr. King gave his own inimitable personal and spiritual stamp—even while the sounds of jubilation were ringing in our ears and giving so many of us so much exaltation, even *then,* "something like two weeks later," a CORE worker, hysterical, telephoned to tell Baldwin that "a Sunday School in Birmingham had been bombed, and that four young black girls had been blown into eternity. That," concludes Mr. Baldwin, "was the first answer we received to our petition."[39]

Now *despite* all its ills and its cruelty, America, to Baldwin, is home. He loves it, he tells us, "more than any other country in the world."[40] There is something very refreshing about this, because whatever one may wish to say about this perceptive and distinguished essayist, Baldwin is *not* an optimist. He is not a dreamer. Nor is he a liar. Again and again he shows anybody who reads him how ugly our country really is. And just as he denounced that church which blessed the Italians on the eve of their invasion of Ethiopia, he explains the honest feelings of a human being who is black. "I very strongly doubt," says Baldwin,

> that any Negro youth, now approaching maturity, and with the whole, vast world before him, is willing, say, to settle for Jim Crow in Miami, when he can—or, before the travel ban, *could*—feast at the welcome table in Havana. And he need not, to prefer Havana, have any pro-Communist, or, for that matter, pro-Cuban, or pro-Castro sympathies: he need merely prefer not to be treated as a second-class citizen.[41]

Baldwin personally has experienced much of America's inhumanness—what perceptive black American has not! But "America *is* my home,"[42] as he reiterates. And it is precisely because of his love for his country that he "insist[s] on the right to criticize her personally,"[43] an insistence, I might add, which, as he has told us, is both the province and function of the writer.

Much more remains to be said about this brilliant essayist than I have written in these pages. The scope of the present volume necessitates limitations and I am writing from a region of my mind. Nevertheless, there remain a serious consideration or two which must be mentioned, a peccadillo, and other matters that can be alluded to in passing.

To the squeamish, there are always possibilities for faultfinding. I do not refer to the bluntness of Baldwin's language at times; for his vocabulary is to the point. The word is suited to the thought. But Baldwin is sometimes immodest. He doesn't *say* he is the greatest, but he does inform us that "I had made it— . . . television . . . Sardi's . . . could . . . sign a check anywhere in the world, could . . . intimidate headwaiters by the use of a name which had not been mine when I was born . . . "[44] He refers to his "famous face"; he brags a lot in the essay "The Black Boy Looks at the White Boy," in which he squares off with Mailer. He apparently still likes his readers to know of his own familiarity with other famous personages. In point of fact, of course, what he is saying is the truth. (John Milton, Frank Lloyd Wright, and Muhammad Ali speak forthrightly about themselves also.)

I have already mentioned the technique of self-projection which identifies the author with the reader and vice versa. The technique is often expanded to indicate that the reader, mankind, projects himself too. Baldwin shows that one time we do so, to put our best self forward—"the moral of the story (and the hope of the world) lies in what one demands, not of others, but of oneself."[45] And again, "The world in which we live is . . . a reflection of the desires and activities of men. We are responsible for the world in which we find ourselves, if only because we are the only sentient force which can change it."[46] At other times Baldwin explains that people influence and limit their ability to understand by projecting prejudices and fears: "The reason that it is . . . of the utmost importance—for white people . . . to see the Negroes as people like themselves is that the white people will not, otherwise, be able to see themselves as they are."[47] "They have had to believe for many years, and for innumerable reasons, that black men are inferior to white men."[48]

His insights into hatred, what it is and why it is, are penetrating. And it certainly is clear to me that he knows the intricacies and influences of the ghetto far better than many who write of the subject. (He takes the anti-sociological stand. Don't try to improve the ghetto. Do away with it!) And of all the condemnation he makes of policemen, that found in "Fifth Avenue, Uptown," in *Nobody Knows My Name,* is most arresting.

In some instances, Mr. Baldwin is contradictory. And in at least one instance, I find his interpretation to be flatly wrong. He says of Negro teachers in the South, for example, that "it is altogether understandable that they, very shortly, cannot bear the sight of their students." He states further that "the most gifted teacher cannot but feel himself slowly drowning in the sea of general helplessness."[49] These assessments are simply not true. I myself am a product of the "separate" schools. And my generation as well as those who went before and after were taught by some extremely gifted teachers who by no means could not bear the sight of us, but loved and inspired us, contributing significantly to what has resulted in regional, national, and international success of an appreciable number of outstanding persons—an outstanding number for *any* school system. In my turn, I, too, have taught many who themselves now teach, and I have known intimately other public-school teachers whom I revere because of their development of their students. I emphasize the fact. On this score, Mr. Baldwin is wrong.

He is also contradictory. Still writing in the same essay about Negro teachers in the South, he says that many of them "work very hard to bolster the morale of their students and prepare them for their new responsibilities. . . . " And again he states that these teachers "spend their waking day attempting to destroy in their students—and it is not too much to say, in themselves—those habits of inferiority which form one of the principal cornerstones of segregation as it is practiced in the South." These latter two statements are to the point. I know famous scholars and lawyers and medics who were taught by people like these.

Baldwin's discovery of the South was, of course, revealing to him in many ways. Among other things, he first discovered terror there. He found there the great strength that black men have. And he learned something about the lack of class distinction which typified public, commercial entertainment for Negro people in the South. (I see no evidence that he learned how selfish and aristocratic Southern Negroes can be.) I find also that the discoveries are a bit heady to our author. Certainly he is ecstatic when he writes:

> What passions cannot be unleashed on a dark road in a Southern night! Everything seems so sensual, so languid, and so private. Desire can be acted out here; over this fence, behind that tree, in the darkness, there; and no one will see, no one will ever know. Only the night is watching and the night was made for desire. Protestantism is the wrong religion for people in such climates; America is perhaps the last nation in which such a climate belongs. In the Southern night everything seems possible, the most private unspeakable longings; but then arrives the Southern day, as hard and brazen as the night was soft and dark.[50]

In another instance I find that Baldwin is contradictory. I have already cited above his opinion that those who are rejected really wish to be accepted by the larger community. He enlarges on this thought. He himself has striven, perhaps strives, to find peace in the United States, his home. But acceptance remains elusive, and life in America takes him into battle rather than affording peace. Of course, the whole civil-rights movement, about which Baldwin has much to tell, aimed toward acceptance of Negro people as people, like everybody else. The Arkansas persons—the boy, the parent, the white principal, and the white student whom Baldwin writes about in "A Fly in Buttermilk"—were all directed not toward loving the little black child but toward *equality* for Negroes. And in one of my favorites of these powerful essays, "Stranger in the Village," the author informs us—not without sarcasm—how he reacted to the Swiss in an isolated Alpine village in which no Negroes prior to him had ever set foot. Though there were many incidents that would make large numbers of Negro people angry and hurt, Baldwin says that he tried "to be pleasant—it being a great part of the American Negro's education (long before he goes to school) that he must make people 'like' him." (He refers to this as the "smile-and-the-world-smiles-with-you routine." In the case before us, it didn't work.)[51]

There are innumerable instances to support the Negro's wanting acceptance. Baldwin even speaks directly against the black separatists, reminding the readers that to build *one* nation in America has been next to impossible. To build *two* would be catastrophic. All of this is appropriate, knowledgeable, and correct.

But Baldwin has another word on the subject. Here is the contradiction: "There appears to be a vast amount of confusion on this point, but I do not know many Negroes who are eager to be 'accepted' by white people, still less to be loved by them."[52] Two things are apparent here. Baldwin is not saying that *he* is against acceptance. However, he continues in the passage to explain that "blacks simply don't wish to be beaten over the head by the whites every instant of our brief passage on this planet." The fact that he uses "our" appears to identify him with the entire thought.

Baldwin also makes quite clear that Negroes (who, he says, like others before him, know whites better than they know themselves) could not possibly respect the standards by which white people live. He is not referring to technological matters but to that which is basic to mankind, morality, both private and public. Negro people cannot respect these standards, nor really the people who embrace them, because the knowledge that Negroes have of the white Christian world—and of Jews as well—prohibits belief in "the good faith of white Americans."[53] Lack of moral standards and good faith cause the Negro, says Baldwin, to ask: "Do I really *want* to be integrated into a burning house?"[54]

One of the most remarkable and baffling of the essays is "Stranger in the Village," which appears in *Notes of a Native Son*. Baldwin is the stranger, but the village is unnamed. Essentially what we know of it is that it is Swiss. It is isolated. It has no television set, and the only typewriter in the town is Baldwin's, the one he brought with him. There is not a movie house, bank, library, or a theater. The village is small. There are a few radios, a jeep, and one station wagon. The less than a half-dozen hotels are closed in winter, and life in the village seems to end around nine or ten at night. The one schoolhouse in the village is for young children. As I have said above, Baldwin was the only Negro the village had ever seen. He was there on three different occasions during three different years, occupying the chalet of the mother of a friend of his, writing in "this white wilderness" with its "absolutely forbidding landscape." [55] And though everybody there knew him, he remained a stranger. Curious about his physical characteristics: his color—it did not wipe off when he was touched—his hair—it did not emit an electrical shock, even when he had been some time in the sun—the natives were not intentionally unkind (we are told); nor was there a suggestion that he was human: were he to grow his hair really long it would make him quite a coat. He "was simply a living wonder." [56]

Baldwin is, I suppose, kinder than I. When I meet at the American Library Association, as I just have, a visitor (not a member), as I also am, and when she, who comes from Providence, learns that I am from Brooklyn and asks with alacrity, "Bedford Stuyvesant?" I wither her with urbanity and innuendo. When, at the bar, a really charming New York book exhibitor (who was born and bred in New York) begs to ask me a personal question—How is it that I, who grew up in Oklahoma, came by the splendid education I "obviously have"?—I, not needing inspiration from my manhattan, let her know that what her Jewish mother did for her and her brother my Negro mother and father did for me and my sisters and brother. Of course, I was not in their village. When James Baldwin, a stranger in the village, was told that the villagers had just " 'bought' last year six or eight African natives . . . for the purpose of converting them to Christianity," *he* "was careful to express astonishment and pleasure at the solicitude shown by the village for the souls of black folk."[57]("Buying" natives was a kind of overseas adoption. The Swiss were really contributing what some Protestant denominations would call "foreign missions" money, I believe.) Baldwin assesses the purpose of this practice in the manner that his readers would expect him to.

This essay is excellent. It is also distinctive and provocative, in that it reveals an aspect of Baldwin's thought which is quite apart from most of his analyses of the human condition. Here Baldwin states that Negroes are different. In my judgment, he says that Negroes are inferior. He reasons in this manner: He enters the village and the white villagers are astonished to see him, a Negro. But they are by no means awed by him. They do not revere him and elevate him because he is different from any human being they have ever seen. In fact, they mock him, not unkindly, he says. But I take it that feeling his hair and testing the fastness of his color were not acts that were designed to praise him.

Baldwin then pictures how his forebears must have acted in their African village when the first white stranger appeared. They too were astonished. Baldwin says that the white stranger accepted the natives' reaction as a tribute. He had come "to conquer and to convert the natives, whose inferiority in relation to himself is not to be questioned. . . . "[58] What this must mean is that the white stranger knew that the natives were inferior, and that Baldwin does also. "There is a great difference," he says, "between the first white man to be seen by Africans and being the first black man to be seen by whites."[59] Obviously, the situations are not parallel. The Swiss villagers had not *seen* a Negro, but they certainly knew about the heathen Africans and from their radios they would know about the American Negro. Obviously also, the thought of surrendering anything to him never entered their minds, or his. Everybody knows what the role and fate of the Africans were. They became slaves and Christians. History reveals as much. Having so implied, Baldwin next reasons what certainly appears to mean that his Swiss villagers are superior—to him. They regard him as a latecomer to their civilization, "bearing no credentials," and apparently he does also. He writes:

> The most illiterate among them is related, in a way that I am not, to Dante, Shakespeare, Michelangelo, Aeschylus, Da Vinci, Rembrandt, and Racine; the cathedral at Chartres says something to them which it cannot say to me, as indeed would New York's Empire State Building, should anyone here ever see it. Out of their hymns and dances come Beethoven and Bach. Go back a few centuries and they are in their full glory—but I am in Africa, watching the conquerors arrive.[60]

This is a bitter pill. It is defeatism. It describes cultural isolationism and ought chauvinistically, if not logically, to lead blacks to total rejection of Western culture and to separatism. One recalls the complaint that Joyce puts into the mouth of young Stephen Dedalus when Stephen realizes that the language he uses belongs to the British priest. Both Joyce and James Baldwin himself are brilliant illustrations of the antithesis to Baldwin's asseveration.

I must state in contradistinction to Mr. Baldwin that civilization is inherited by the civilized. *Hamlet* is no less mine than are *Sophisticated Lady* or *The Hairy Ape*. A student of mine, a Jew, once announced toward the end of a two-semester, sixteen-hour seminar in the humanities that you've got to be a Jew to understand Kafka. I wanted to flunk him. Indeed! What is clear to me, and I think not so to Baldwin, is, for example, that no uninformed, no uneducated, no *insensitive* or *unappreciative* Greek experiences and enjoys the rapport with Euripides that many Americans do, I among them. In fact, one of my great joys in life is to direct my students—Jews, Italians, blacks, Irishmen (the list could go on)—to the understanding of the great literature of the West. The point is that here, in his assertion that there is something innate in race, I think Baldwin sells himself (and me) quite short.

The remainder of "Stranger in the Village" is powerful and intricate. It goes somewhat beneath the surface to show why it is that white people have found it so difficult, if not impossible, to regard black people as human beings. How poignant is the passage:

> There is a dreadful abyss between the streets of this village and the streets of the city in which I was born, between the children who shout *Neger!* today and those who shouted *Nigger!* yesterday—the abyss is experience, the American experience. The syllable hurled behind me today expresses, above all, wonder: I am a stranger here. But I am not a stranger in America and the same syllable riding on the American air expresses the war my presence has occasioned in the American soul.[61]

"Stranger in the Village" also talks about the vast difference between the African slave and all other slaves. The American Negro slave "is unique among the black men of the world in that his past was taken away from him, almost literally, at one blow."[62] Baldwin illustrates this thought by suggesting that there may well be Haitians who can "trace their ancestry back to African kings,"[63] but the American Negro who tried to discover his ancestry would be stopped by the signature on the bill of sale. We now know, of course, that there is at least *one* remarkable exception to this. But so thoroughly was the American Negro robbed of his past that Baldwin "wonders what on earth the first slave found to say to the first dark child he [*sic*] bore." I would like to answer the query. But I don't know how. Why wouldn't the slave mother say to her child what she remembered? How could the crossing in the slavehold eradicate memories of previous life? The slave songs reveal that the new, devout Christians stole away—away to Jesus. But why would they not have stolen away to talk of yesteryear? My great-grandmother, a mulatto, was freed before her teens. She died when I was a college freshman. I knew Ma intimately. But I have long known that the most remarkable memories I have of her are her tales of the "mountain boomers" (which she never would really identify) and the frequency with which she sang (and hummed!) "When the Saints Go Marching In." It was as though she obliterated her childhood. As Baldwin states, the slaves were so completely robbed of their past that a mother did not relate to her child that which one would have assumed she remembered. Baldwin's summation is superb:

> Despite the terrorization which the Negro in America endured and endures sporadically until today, despite the cruel and totally inescapable ambivalence of his status in his country, the battle for his identity has long ago been won. He is not a visitor to the West, but a citizen there, an American; as American as the Americans who despise him, the Americans who fear him, the Americans who love him—the Americans who became less than themselves, or rose to be greater than themselves by virtue of the fact that the challenge he represented was inescapable.[64]

A few years ago, John Dewey made a list of the twenty books that were most meaningful to him. Were I to list my favorites they would begin with works by the Greeks and the Hebrews. My list would prominently display Shakespeare and Milton, Goethe and Emerson, Du Bois. If I included favorites among current writers, James Baldwin's volumes of essays would have to appear. But there are difficulties within Baldwin. Even just a few years after publication, some of his essays are already dated. They are topical. Some matters that gave him—and me—great cause for grave concern have changed. I am grateful for that! Not disregarding the obvious fact that only the surface has been scratched and that Negroes and American Indians, as Baldwin tells us, remain the most despised Americans by Americans, at the same time, the conscience of portions of white America and some of the aspects of American legality have changed. I attend meetings, for example, in Atlanta and Miami, and eat and socialize there, quite freely, in downtown hotels. The surface has been scratched. Buses are no longer segregated. Black mayors and other elected officials dot the land. The atmosphere is much more relaxed than it was when Baldwin wrote several of his essays. There is even hope, if I may say so—reverently—for the church. Much has changed. Certainly, James Baldwin, the prominent essayist, has contributed significantly to that change—even as Voltaire prodded civilization toward progress in his day.

But there is a great difference between the universal and the timely. Time has dimmed neither Shakespeare nor the best of Montaigne, though on occasion in history time did. Emerson and Du Bois indicate timelessness, although the philosophy of Emerson is too idealistic for our busy, pragmatic society. James Baldwin, too, may possess timelessness. We are too close to tell. We know, however, that he exposes and interprets manfully for us what *our* minds and spirits need to know. He does so in language and style that have already acclaimed his greatness.

In reflecting upon his writings, I recognize that "Many Thousands Gone" may be his most profound expression. "Fifth Avenue, Uptown" and its short companion piece, "East River, Downtown," are remarkable in perception and interpretation. "A Fly in Buttermilk," "Notes for a Hypothetical Novel," almost all of the essays in *No Name in the Street*—all these are favorites, along with "Stranger in the Village," and will probably remain major interpretations of our era. Of the essays on criticism, I yet believe that "Alas, Poor Richard" is Baldwin's best. And *The Fire Next Time* should be read by many more than those hordes who have already read it.

James Baldwin as Poet-Prophet

A. Russell Brooks

*H*owever quietly he goes about it, James Baldwin has a burning mission in life. He ingenuously announces at the end of his introductory remarks to *Notes of a Native Son,* his first and very likely his best book of essays, that he wants "to be an honest man and a good writer."[1] Unlike some successful authors, he must involuntarily equate *good* with *honest* as it applies to *writer.* What we can very well believe he really means is that he wants to be an honest writer; that is, uncompromisingly radical, not in the widely used sense of *extreme* but in the sense of *fundamental,* in disinterestedly probing for sources, causes, and roots. This is an extraordinarily active principle for him as an artist, for it determines and shapes the substance of what he has to say to black and white Americans, principally the latter. Most of what he has written in the approximately twenty years that have elapsed since he wrote the above statement might be considered elaborations on the theme of honesty in the diagnosis of America's race problem.

Baldwin also says in this prefatory note that he dislikes "earnest" people. Earnest in the sense of thoughtful, intense, and unswervingly honest in quest of underlying truth he himself clearly is; earnest in the sense of inordinately zealous, of generating much heat but little light, he is not. The lodestar of his course as a writer is the light of reason that moderates the heat and seeks to efface the darkness—his primary purpose, to look beneath surfaces for sources and causes. This radical approach to truth may be compared with the Socratic view of knowledge as not only having the truth but seeing the reason why it is true. Thus Baldwin's exceptional interest in one's past and the past of one's country or race as bases for understanding the present and foreseeing possible developments. Especially crucial to a writer, he holds, are his own origins. Wherever he was born, he carries these marks with him always and everywhere; and his merit as an artist depends on his acceptance of this fact. Certain other allied concepts, expressed principally in Baldwin's essays and autobiographical comment but often illuminated in his fiction and plays, add up to an image of him which for want of a more accurate designation might be described as poet-prophet.

In *A Rap on Race*,[2] a recent book produced from several conversations between Baldwin and the anthropologist Margaret Mead, Baldwin becomes rather explicit about the task he has pursued all along. He conceives of himself as a poet—not, he hastens to point out, in the sense of one skilled in the externals of poetic technique but in the sense of one who because of his knowledge of "what human beings have been and can become" is a "witness to a possibility" that will not be realized in his lifetime. Thus, in this prophetic potential, poets may be considered subversive and, therefore, disturbers of the peace ("angels troubling the waters"). For this reason, declares Baldwin, they were banned by Plato from his Republic. Here Baldwin seriously and quietly conceives of his art as a high calling, for his responsibility is to the future, his commitment "to the human race." He sees all about him "tremendous national, global, moral waste," and he raises the cry of what to do "to save our children." It was the same urgency—"What of the children?"—that prompted Meridian in *Blues for Mister Charlie*[3] to risk his life and remain in town so that he might reveal the truth and make the white people know the evil they countenanced when they allowed Lyle to go free after he had murdered Meridian's son.

Baldwin distinguishes between what he calls "the fact of prose" and "the fact of the hope of poetry."[4] Applying the first to the twentieth century and "on every single level from television to the White House," he is thinking primarily, it seems, of the current surface facts of American existence. By "the fact of the hope of poetry" he no doubt means the apprehension of historical reality, an imaginative grasp of the more complex aspects of the human condition, and a creative perspective on future possibilities. He says in this conversation with Mrs. Mead that he is using *poetry* "in its most serious sense." In this context Baldwin is not thinking of *poet* as one who writes poetry or *poetry* as that which is written by a poet. Among other considerations, *poet* is used here to embrace one of the concerns of the critic which Matthew Arnold, in *The Function of Criticism at the Present Time,* also assigns to the poet, who as he looks at history and other branches of knowledge should endeavor to "see the object as in itself it really is." He should, in short, look steadily at the increasingly complex world. To do this demands a disinterestedness that is especially difficult for Baldwin, who will never recover from his childhood terror of white cops in Harlem's streets. Rage does sometimes take over, and hate gets the upper hand; but there is yet a greater compulsion: to *see* America beneath the complexities of history—past and present—as in itself it actually is. This compulsion grows out of the conviction that Americans, on pain of their eventual undoing, must take an honest look at themselves and this country, especially in its dealings with the black man. To exert oneself with compassion and with creative insight for bringing this about and to perceive its ultimate results for the children yet unborn is poetry in its profoundest sense—and it is poetry encompassing an element of prophecy.

Isaiah told the people of Israel that they were forsaking knowledge by taking darkness for light and evil for good. He warned them to turn from their foolish ways lest they meet their own destruction. We catch something of the same substance and tone in Baldwin's many warnings to white Americans to avert their doom by looking straight at themselves and straight at blacks so that they can know who and what they are and where they are headed. Meridian, father of the murdered Richard in *Blues for Mister Charlie,* for instance, cries, "What a light, my Lord, is needed to conquer so mighty a darkness? . . . Who, or what, shall touch the hearts of this headlong and unthinking people and turn them back from destruction?"[5] The darkness that Meridian remained in town to fight was the darkness of the white preacher Phelps, who looked on blacks as simple, good-natured people who have deserted their God and hearkened to the counsel of Communists. It was the willful blindness of Jo, wife of Richard's murderer, who was unable to remember any white person who had ever mistreated a Negro. In stubbornly resisting the light that Parnell offered in his liberal newspaper, the whole town turned their eyes away from the injustices against which the black student Jerome and others were demonstrating: denial of licenses to black electricians and plumbers, refusal of the use of parks and swimming pools to blacks, denial of their right to register and vote, and denial to them of police protection.

Isaiah also enjoined his people to look at "former things" in order to know what things were yet to come. Baldwin often urges blacks, as well as whites, to do just that. When he attempted to look into his own past, how far back did he try to see? He believes that for all practical purposes the American black man's past began when the first slave stepped off the ship onto American shores. One day in London's British Museum when a Jamaican asked him where he was from, he answered New York. "Yes, but where are you from?" the Jamaican further inquired. And then, he finally asked, "Where are you from in Africa?" Baldwin—not so fortunate in this regard as Alex Haley says he was—was frustrated in having no way of finding out where he came from in Africa.[6] He had heard that Haitians could trace their ancestry back to African kings, "but any American Negro wishing to go back so far will find his journey through time abruptly arrested by the signature on the bill of sale which served as the entrance paper for his ancestor."[7] The Afro-American was thus robbed of his past in one fell swoop. Baldwin, then, considers his relationship to Africa a discontinuous one, and accordingly devotes his attention to that past which he can examine and which can therefore have meaning for him. Contrasting the African's past with his own and those of other American Negroes, he wrote that the African has suffered privation, injustice, and cruelty, but not, like the American Negro, "the utter alienation of himself from his people and his past. His mother did not sing 'Sometimes I Feel Like a Motherless Child,' and he has not, all his life long, ached for acceptance in a culture which pronounced straight hair and white skin the only acceptable beauty."[8]

The Harlem that Baldwin depicts is the Harlem that cancels his need to go back a thousand years in order to know his roots. When he was ten years old, two cops beat him "half to death,"[9] because, he states, history was written in the color of his skin. He believes this is the central fact in the history of America, and until we face that fact we will continue to be murdered in many ways. Some will even be dead while they live. This past the black man will never overcome: it is "blood dripping down through leaves, gouged-out eyeballs, the sex torn from its socket and severed with a knife." To say that blacks have forgotten it would be meaningless and sentimental. Even though Oedipus did forget the thongs that bound his feet when he was cast away as a child, Baldwin goes on to say, the imprints of them were still on his feet, and their marks spelled the doom that eventually overtook him.[10] A man may have forgotten the hand that struck him when he was a child, but the terror remains and will forever be a part of him.

It is especially valuable to a writer to know his past. The novelist Richard Silenski in Baldwin's *Another Country* failed as a writer because he denied his origins. The fifth son of a Polish carpenter immigrant, he was ashamed to speak Polish when he was growing up—"and look at him now," lamented his wife, Cass; "he doesn't *know* who he is."[11] Never able, as a result of this denial, to get beneath the surface to things "dark, strange, dangerous, difficult, deep," he wrote a disappointing, superficial book. Baldwin was careful to avoid his character's fate. When he was in Europe, he was afraid he had buried too deep some of the things of his past that he had seen and felt. In order to remember them, to reach back and recall how he must have talked when he "was a pickaninny," he would often listen to Bessie Smith records. She helped to reconcile him to being a "nigger."[12] His first trip South, taken after he became an adult and started his writing career, taught him much about himself and his people that he had not fully realized before. A Northern Negro coming South for the first time, he observed, "is in a position similar to that of the son of the Italian emigrant" on his first trip to Italy. As he nears his father's village, he perhaps experiences the odd sensation of seeing himself "as he was before he was born"[13] or the kind of person he would have been if indeed he had been born in this village. Baldwin thus believes, as was said centuries ago, that the unexamined life is not worth living and that no writer, for whatever reason, can afford to delude himself about his origins.

How can Baldwin, then, reconcile lengthy sojourns in Europe with emphasis upon holding on to his true heritage? He left America for Europe at age twenty-four, remaining there nearly ten years and publishing before returning to America his first two novels, *Go Tell It on the Mountain* and *Giovanni's Room,* and his first book of essays, *Notes of a Native Son.* We read in his second book of essays, *Nobody Knows My Name,* that he left this country because he doubted he could "survive the fury of the color problem here." Paris helped him find his identity, for there he discovered that he was "as American as any Texas G.I."[14] Later, to get his "balance," he went to the mountains of Switzerland and played blues records, which helped to recreate for him the life from which he had been a fugitive for a number of years.

While on the continent, Baldwin was able to come to terms with himself and to reassess his own country, for which during the past twenty years he has several times asserted his love. His European experiences have had other salutary results for him. It was good to enjoy freedom from the stigma on intellectual effort in a place where writers are a part of "an old and honorable tradition."[15] There he could listen to and talk with all kinds of people in all levels of society. But best of all—and here we catch glimpses of the poet-prophet—Baldwin, in Europe, experienced a sense "of the mysterious and inexorable limits of life, a sense, in a word, of tragedy." In wedding the vision of the Old World with that of the New, he continued, "it is the writer, not the statesman, who is our strongest arm. Though we do not wholly believe it yet, the interior life is the real life, and the tangible dreams of people have a tangible effect on the world."[16]

Knowing his roots are in America, knowing this is his home, yet not at home here and weary of finding a true anchor, Baldwin returns occasionally and heeds the advice that he has Luke in *The Amen Corner* give his son, David: "Son, don't try to get away from the things that hurt you. The things that hurt you—sometimes that's all you got. You got to learn to live with those things—and—use them."[17] He came home and took part in the civil-rights demonstrations, but he espouses no particular economic or political school of race uplift and does not consider himself a spokesman for the Negro. He is, as far as a man of so emotional a nature can manage, a disinterested observer, an interpreter of America in its disposition of the black situation. He points out the white man's blind spots and warns him of dire events should he fail to heed the increasingly clear and urgent danger signals. His words are sometimes whiplashes; more often, impassioned but restrained warnings of the fire next time.

Baldwin claims the right to criticize America, for although she feeds him, as she did Claude McKay, "bread of bitterness" and sinks her "tiger's tooth" into his throat, he loves her. Despite all his years in Europe, he has never sounded like an expatriate. The moment he got off the ship in France he did not rejoice but was shocked when he realized that he was nothing but an American and that, willy-nilly, American blacks and whites belonged to each other. If the black man wants to change his situation, he must see it for what it actually is: he has been "formed by this nation, for better or for worse, and does not belong to any other—not to Africa, and certainly not to Islam."[18] A peculiar fact about American history, a feature "that distinguishes Americans from other people is that no other people has ever been so deeply involved in the lives of black men, and vice versa."[19] Accepting this anomalous fact for what it is could eventually result, Baldwin would like to hope, in such a reconciliation as would erase the importance of being either black or white.

Baldwin believes Americans are prone to talk and write about America's ills but opposed to discussing their symptoms. A close examination is long overdue, he holds, and can come only "if we are willing to free ourselves of the myth of America and try to find out what is really happening here."[20] Constantly evading this responsibility has brought about a kind of incoherence that further blots out the reality that all but stares us in the face. It is a doggedly deliberate, obdurate incoherence—the kind a person would have if a friend had just murdered his mother and put her in the closet and both of them knew the corpse was there and that they might stumble on it any minute but they did not discuss it.

The white man's confusion arises partly from his almost unconsciously assuming that a person can be considered apart from the various forces that have gone into his making, and from his failure to understand that the experiences of white men since they settled America have made of them a unique and "unprecedented" people with a unique past, a past that now has little to do with Europe. By perceiving this uniqueness, Americans can end alienation from themselves and clarify their true relationship to Europe. They need also to reconstitute their thinking on what constitutes a true majority in this country. In his essay, "In Search of a Majority,"[21] Baldwin points out that the original Anglo-Saxon stock (or mixture of Teuton and Celt) has been diluted by hordes of people from other parts of the world; yet the Anglo-Saxon image of "hard work and good clean fun and chastity and piety and success" —honored mainly in the breach—has a false but powerful influence and discounts what ought to be America's true majority. Beneath this conqueror-image, writes Baldwin, are hidden "a great many unadmitted despairs and confusions, and anguish and unadmitted crimes and failures."

Before there can be any clear thinking about minorities, then, Americans must find out what the American image hides. In fact, they cannot very well discuss the state of their minorities until they themselves have a sense of what and who they are. Nor can they achieve this awareness so long as they continue to make the black man invisible. Sociological reports, study commissions, and investigating committees, of which Americans are so fond, hide more than they reveal—namely, the Negro's complexity, his basic humanity. In dehumanizing the black man, Americans dim their eyes and blunt their sensibilities, thus dehumanizing themselves.

Baldwin makes no claims to extraordinary moral and spiritual insight, nor is there any intention here to establish such claims for him. His high seriousness as a writer, his sense of the infinite worth of the human personality, his unwavering faith in the ultimate benefits from clear thinking and unobstructed vision, and his acute assessments of the American experience occasionally lead him, nevertheless, to speculations of immense reach. Here he resembles the kind of poet he says Plato shunned. When his speculations embrace future developments, as they often do, his utterances are warnings and prophecies issuing more from the workings of a sound mind and an adequate heart than from spiritual revelation.

A theme in Baldwin's essays concurrent with that of the white man's treatment of the Negro and of the white man's consequent degradation is the sense of the black man's redeeming power for America and America's great need of what the black man has to offer. One summer night in Birmingham as Baldwin talked with the Reverend Mr. Shuttlesworth—a night when both were in mortal danger of being tracked down and shot because of their involvement in the civil-rights demonstrations—Baldwin noticed a look of deep sorrow on Shuttlesworth's face when he expressed concern for Shuttlesworth's safety, a look that seemed to indicate that he was "wrestling with the mighty fact that the danger in which he stood was as nothing compared to the spiritual horror which drove those who were trying to destroy him."[22] It was the anguish that the French movie director in Baldwin's short story "This Morning, This Evening, So Soon" spoke of when he said that the

American Negro, like the European, knows about suffering, and since the West is in the hands of the Americans, it is to be regretted that most Americans know little of what suffering is.[23] Realizing the great potential that blacks hold for America, Baldwin, addressing his nephew in *The Fire Next Time,* wrote that if integration has any meaning in America, it is that blacks, with compassion, will force their white brothers to see themselves as they are, stop running from reality, and make America what it has to be.[24]

Baldwin applies an Old Testament prophecy to contemporary history, less as a pronouncement of irrevocable doom than as a warning: destruction once came by water, but it will be by fire next time. If the few awakened blacks and whites do not arouse the conscience and awaken the consciousness of the rest of their fellow Americans, thereby ending "the racial nightmare," achieving America, and changing the history of the world, this prophecy will be fulfilled in our time.[25] He asserts his preference for kindness and generosity instead of violence, but the persistence of poverty and rage has ominous possibilities. His two-year-old great-nephew will not go through what he has experienced, even if it calls for blowing up the Empire State Building.[26] He believes American blacks have no business in Vietnam "aiding the slave master to enslave yet more millions of dark people and also identifying themselves with the white American crimes."[27] Blacks, after all, may some day need their allies, for soon the American white man may have none. In fact, the time is approaching when even the bent South African farmer will stand up straight.

Still doggedly determined to hold on to his long-suffering optimism, Baldwin expresses a desperate hope not just for America but for all the West: white people must—there is no option—go through the same fire that produced the rage in Aretha Franklin's music. It is in this journey, this ordeal that the hope of the West lies, for it must "change the Western assumptions, and make it a larger civilization than it has ever been before."[28] In the Epilogue, on next to the last page of his last book of essays, *No Name in the Street,* this hope is still alive, as Baldwin heralds the birth of the new world, which is "ready to be born." It will not be easy to bring it about, he writes, but that is our responsibility to the newborn.

The poet-prophet speaks in Baldwin when he likens the vision of the artist to that of the revolutionary. Both are possessed by it and both find themselves not so much following it as being driven by it.[29] This vision prompts the artist to an endless search, an endless questioning through which he comes to a knowledge of himself. And the questions he asks himself assist him in his understanding of the experience of others and his understanding of the world. It is possible for a person to face only in others what he can face in himself. "On this confrontation," Baldwin declares, "depends the measure of our wisdom and compassion. This energy is all that one finds in the rubble of vanished civilizations and the only hope for ours." [30]

Thematic Patterns in Baldwin's Essays

Eugenia W. Collier

A writer, like everybody else in the world, operates from a set of basic assumptions about the nature of life and of people. His self-image and indeed his image of the universe arise from these assumptions, which are fashioned by his experiences and observations as he makes his way—*gropes* his way, as it were—through the years. If one examines a writer's works perceptively (compassionately), one can detect a pattern that reveals, though through a glass darkly, that writer's basic assumptions, which have colored his works.

I have tried to read everything written or recorded by James Baldwin, because I think he is one of the most brilliant minds of our times; he is also a virtuoso literary stylist. I do not always agree with his conclusions; moreover, I have ambivalent feelings about his long sojourn in Europe. Nevertheless, I feel that Baldwin has a great deal to say to our times and that in our present desperate state, we had better listen. In examining his works from beginning to end, I seem to have detected a basic assumption that unifies them all: that on all levels, personal and political (which ultimately boils down to personal), life is a wild chaos of paradox, hidden meanings, and dilemmas. This chaos arises from man's inability—or reluctance—to face the truth about his own nature. As a result of this self-imposed blindness, men erect an elaborate facade of myth, tradition, and ritual behind which crouch, invisible, their true selves. It is this blindness on the part of Euro-Americans which has created and perpetuated the vicious racism that threatens to destroy this nation.

In his brilliant essays Baldwin unravels the complexities of our times—and since time is three-demensional, these complexities involve our history and our projected future as well as our turbulent present. From the essays collected in his first volume of essays, *Notes of a Native Son,* to those in his latter edition, *The Fire Next Time,* Baldwin probes the multiple dualities in which we are caught. Considered together, Baldwin's essays are a study in chaos.

The style of the essays reinforces this duality. The early essays in particular are highly ironic—savagely so at times—and irony involves double meanings, unspoken nuances of meaning, ambiguity. Most impressive in this respect are those essays (e.g., "Many Thousands Gone") in which Baldwin juxtaposes "American" and "Negro," speaking with the voice and viewpoint of a white man, referring to Americans as "we," to Negroes as "they." The style of each essay is highly polished, extremely controlled. With the expertise of a native guide on a safari, Baldwin leads the reader through long and intricate sentences, the phrases and clauses strung together like crystal beads in a necklace. The smooth, controlled style is an effective contrast to what it is explaining—the mad chaos of American life.

To explain chaos is, in itself, a significant task, for the better we know our situation, the more able we are to deal with it. But Baldwin does more. He offers solutions. They are not solutions that we in our present state are likely —or even, perhaps, *able*—to attain. But they make a great deal of sense, and for the sake of our future we had better take heed.

The paradoxes in American culture, according to Baldwin, arise largely from this nation's refusal to face the truth about itself—its history, its nature, the direction in which it moves toward its future. Obscuring the picture is a bright and totally false system of idealistic myths called "the American dream," which is itself a part of the problem. One is reminded of an attractive girl with an offensive body odor, who prefers to spray on perfume rather than to wash. At the core of this nation's self-deception is white racism.

As a result, American life is riddled with paradoxes. In "Down at the Cross"[1] Baldwin explains that the American dream itself is so shaky that we dare not look at it too closely: in spite of our stated convictions, people do not want to be equal but superior, and freedom is always "hard to bear." Consequently, we are confused. "We are controlled here by our confusion, far more than we know, and the American dream has become something much more closely resembling a nightmare. . . . Privately, we cannot stand our lives and dare not examine them; domestically, we take no responsibility for (and no pride in) what goes on in our country; and, internationally, for millions of people, we are an unmitigated disaster."[2]

Because we are afraid to face our national self, we retreat into a superficial passion for order: "Our passion for categorization, life neatly fitted into pegs, has led to an unforeseen, paradoxical distress; confusion, a breakdown of meaning. Those categories which were meant to define and control the world for us have boomeranged us into chaos; in which limbo we whirl, clutching the straws of our definitions."[3]

It is inevitable, then, that our cherished ideals are in truth the exact opposite in practice. The myth that success is possible for anyone who really tries: "The American equation of success with the big time reveals an awful disrespect for human life and human achievement. The equation has placed our cities among the most dangerous in the world and has placed our youth among the most empty and bewildered."[4] The myth of social mobility: "Where everyone has status, it is perfectly possible, after all, that no one has."[5] The myth of individuality: "The American ideal, after all, is that everyone should be as much alike as possible."[6] The myth of the Protestant ethic: "In spite of the Puritan-Yankee equation of virtue with well-being, Negroes had excellent reason for doubting that money was made or kept by any very striking adherence to the Christian virtues; it certainly did not work that way for black Christians."[7]

Black Americans are, in fact, inextricably involved in the confusing paradoxes of this nation. Repeatedly Baldwin points out that white people cannot face the savagery of their attitudes and actions toward blacks and so constantly and simultaneously perpetuate and violate their own myths. As a result, both blacks and whites are demoralized. He says "this is a warfare waged daily in the heart, a warfare so vast, so relentless and so powerful that the interracial handshake or the interracial marriage can be as crucifying as the public hanging or the secret rape. This panic motivates our [whites'] cruelty, this fear of the dark makes it impossible that our lives shall be other than superficial; this, interlocked with and feeding our glittering, mechanical, inescapable civilization which has put to death our freedom."[8]

Certainly there is no freedom for the black man. Virtually all the American institutions have failed him, from the most private to the most public— " . . . the unrehabilitated houses, bowed down, it would seem, under the great weight of frustration and bitterness they contain; the dark, the ominous schoolhouses from which the child may emerge maimed, blinded, hooked, or enraged for life; and the churches . . . niched in the walls like cannon in the walls of a fortress."[9] On all levels the black man is caught.

Paradoxically, however, the white man, too, is trapped. Over and over, Baldwin points out that when one denies another's humanity, one is also abridging one's own, that one cannot be free while one robs another of freedom. "The ways in which the Negro has affected the American psychology are betrayed in our popular culture and in our morality; in our estrangement from him is the depth of our estrangement from ourselves. We cannot ask, What do we *really* feel about him?—such a question merely opens the gates on chaos. . . . Our dehumanization of the Negro then is indivisible from our dehumanization of ourselves; the loss of our own identity is the price we pay for the annulment of his."[10] It is the white American, in fact, who is enslaved by his own false beliefs, for the black man has never believed the myths about this nation, and has tended "to dismiss white people as the slightly mad victims of their own brainwashing."[11]

In such a culture, the truth is often obscured by appearances. Baldwin looks behind the obvious and brings basic truths into view. Religion, for example, often masks irreligious values. The church, Baldwin points out in "Down at the Cross," is often devoid of love, is a citadel of hatred and despair. The first principles of the church, rather than Faith, Hope, and Charity, are Blindness, Loneliness, and Terror. The plethora of black churches is not a sign of faith and goodwill, but actually a backdrop for "a complete and exquisite fantasy revenge. White people own the earth and commit all manner of abomination and injustice on it; the bad will be punished and the good rewarded, for God is not sleeping, the judgment is not far off."[12]

Baldwin's literary criticism draws aside the curtain on many concealed truths about ourselves and our attitudes. For example, "Sentimentality, the ostentatious parading of excessive and spurious emotion, is the mask of dishonesty, the inability to feel; the wet eyes of the sentimentalist betray his aversion to experience, his fear of life, his arid heart; and it is always, therefore, the signal of secret and violent inhumanity, the mask of cruelty."[13] Baldwin's views on the hidden truth of the protest novel are well known—that far from being a tool for liberation, the protest novel merely reinforces the false image of blackness, an image that the Euro-American cherishes.

Concerning this image Baldwin has much to say. In several essays, but in "Many Thousands Gone" in particular, he explains the psychological necessity for the white man to construct an image of black inferiority and to hold this image frantically between himself and the truth—the truth, that is, about the humanity of blacks and the inhumanity of whites. Paradoxically, the image reflects not black reality but white guilt.

In the midst of numerous paradoxes and masked truths, the black American faces, on all levels, a fantastic number of irresolvable dilemmas—about his self-concept, his parents and his children, his art, and certainly his relationships to white people as well as to black people from other lands and to his native land. Baldwin explains the basic dilemma on a personal level. In his "Autobiographical Notes" he explains, "I was a kind of bastard of the West . . . I was an interloper; this was not my heritage. At the same time I had no other heritage which I could possibly hope to use—I had certainly been unfitted for the jungle or the tribe."[14] He regards Africans with "an awful tension between envy and despair, attraction and revulsion."[15] Yet he points out the impossibility of acceptance in white America, for those who do find acceptance " . . . do so at the grave expense of a double alienation; from their own people, whose fabled attributes they must either deny, or, worse, cheapen and bring to market; from us, for we require of them, when we accept them, that they at once cease to be Negroes and yet not fail to remember what being a Negro means—to remember, that is, what it means to us."[16]

The other dilemmas rise from these. And they are numberless and pervasive. The dilemmas of the parent: " . . . how to prepare the child for the day when the child would be despised and how to create in the child—by what means?—a stronger antidote to this poison than one had found for oneself."[17] Those of the artist: " . . . I was, in effect, prohibited from examining my own experience too closely by the tremendous demands and the very real dangers of my social situation."[18] Those of the Negro leader: " . . . the nicely refined torture a man can experience from having created and having been defeated by the same circumstances."[19] Those of the serviceman pledged to die for his country, who is "far freer in a strange land than he has ever been at home."[20] And so on through every aspect of life.

The chaotic complexities that Baldwin describes would seem beyond any possibility of solution. Yet Baldwin does envision solutions. They are solutions that demand more of us, I think, than we are likely to be able to give at this time. But then, "A man's reach . . . " and so forth. The answers are surprisingly simple.

First one needs a base of personal philosophy, rooted in two ideas: (1) " . . . the acceptance, totally without rancor, of life as it is, and men as they are: in the light of this idea, it goes without saying that injustice is commonplace"; and (2) "that one must never, in one's own life, accept these injustices as commonplace but must fight them with all one's strength."[21]

Then one must come to grips with one's worth. "Know whence you came. If you know whence you came, there is really no limit to where you can go."[22] Self-knowledge (of both weaknesses and strengths) is necessary because "one can only face in others what one can face in oneself."[23] This means an establishment of one's own black identity, which in turn means providing a standard for white people rather than, as in the past, trying to follow their standards. "The only thing white people have that black people need, or should want, is power—and no one holds power forever."[24]

Knowing one's worth, one can—indeed, one *must*—accept white people with love. For " . . . these men are your brothers—your lost, younger brothers. And if the word *integration* means anything, this is what it means: that we, with love, shall force our brothers to see themselves as they are, to cease fleeing from reality and begin to change it."[25]

From a personal assertion of identity, it is necessary to establish an American identity. Baldwin insists that blacks and whites in America are inalienably meshed in each other's fates. "Whether I like it or not, or whether you like it or not, we are bound together forever. We are part of each other. . . . These walls—these artificial walls—which have been up so long to protect us from something we fear, must come down."[26] In several essays Baldwin points out that in order to destroy these walls and live harmoniously, America must reexamine its attitudes, rid itself of the fantasies that have inhibited realistic and compassionate appraisal, and stop thinking of itself as a white nation bound for the certain death of white nations. "The price of this transformation is the unconditional freedom of the Negro; it is not too much to say that he, who has been so long rejected, must now be embraced, and at no matter what psychic and social risk. He is *the* key figure in this country, and the American future is precisely as bright or as dark as his."[27]

The solution to chaos, then, lies in the individual's acceptance of himself, which involves rejection of the "safe" life and requires the courage to face his life *absolutely*. On a nationwide scale it means acceptance of our history, destruction of damaging myths and false images, and an unswerving gaze at reality. Here I myself become confused. My personal belief is that white America cannot do these things any more than a mental patient can behave rationally simply by deciding that that is the best thing to do. Still I cannot gainsay that this is the only solution that I know of, short of armed revolution.

Baldwin's vision is not of a monolithic society but of tranquility within our duality, an acceptance of our twoness. We must accept, with love, ourselves and each other. It can be done, Baldwin says. It *must* be done. "If we—and now I mean the relatively conscious whites and the relatively conscious blacks, who must, like lovers, insist on, or create, the consciousness of the others—do not falter in our duty now, we may be able, handful that we are, to end the racial nightmare, and achieve our country, and change the history of the world. If we do not now dare everything, the fulfillment of that prophecy, re-created from the Bible in song by a slave, is upon us: *God gave Noah the rainbow sign, No more water, the fire next time!"* [28]

The choice is clear.

Baldwin as Short-Story Writer

Style, Form, and Content in the Short Fiction of James Baldwin

_____ Harry L. Jones

The short fiction of James Baldwin appears largely in the collection enti-tled *Going to Meet the Man.* This volume contains eight pieces, written over a period from 1948 to 1965. Five of the works, "The Outing," "Previous Condition," "Sonny's Blues," "This Morning, This Evening, So Soon," and "Come Out the Wilderness," had been published previously, while "The Rockpile," "The Man Child," and the title story, "Going to Meet the Man," appear for the first time in this collection. Two of the pieces, "The Rockpile" and "The Outing," are obviously culls or unused remnants from *Go Tell It on the Mountain* and ought best to be considered in connection with that work. They will not, therefore, be discussed here. An examination of Bald-win's short fiction should provide a basis for some studies on his development as a writer, for the short works seem to contain in microcosm the universe that later manifests itself in Baldwin's major works.

Baldwin's short works are not notable for their presentation of action. In some, the real plot is so slender as to be almost nonexistent; in others, Bald-win begins by creating a situation, goes on to introduce a conflict or com-plication, adds an episode here and there, and concludes without a denoue-ment or resolution of the conflict or complication.

"Sonny's Blues" is the most perfectly realized story in the collection, that is, if one is operating in a scheme that insists on a cyclical structure and a fitness of formal elements to formal whole. There is nothing wasted in the story; even the flashback is structural. Albeit leisurely paced, the story does move from situation, complication, climax, to denouement. While there is some problem with the realization of the character of the narrator, even he is more fully presented than many of the other characters in the short works, and since he serves as a foil to Sonny, the narrator functions well largely because Sonny is so fully developed. Sonny is the artist-in-exile, the soul out of step with mainstream society, marching to the beat of a different drummer. He is the same person as Baldwin's narrator in "Previous Condition" and "This Morning, This Evening, So Soon," and he will eventually develop into Rufus Scott of *Another Country*.

As a depiction of the artist-in-exile, Sonny is superb. The statement on the artist's dilemma in connection with the philistines of straight society is as good as Kafka's realization of the same problem in "A Hunger Artist." Sonny tries to explain the artist's internal drive to creation by saying,

> "It's terrible sometimes, inside, . . . that's what's the trouble. You walk these streets, black and funky and cold, and there's not really a living ass to talk to, and there's nothing shaking, and there's no way of getting it out—that storm inside. You can't talk it and you can't make love with it, and when you finally try to get with it and play it, you realize *nobody's* listening. So *you've* got to listen. You got to find a way to listen. . . . Sometimes you'll do *anything* to play, even cut your mother's throat. . . . Or your brother's. . . . Or your own."[1]

This statement does not simply serve as an expression of Sonny as an artist-in-exile, but its structural worth is made clear when the narrator-brother is in the club in the Village listening to Sonny play. Suddenly the narrator understands as he has not throughout the earlier portions of the story that

> . . . the man who creates the music is hearing something else, is dealing with the roar rising from the void and imposing order on it as it hits the air. What is evoked in him, then, is of another order, more terrible because it has no words, and triumphant, too, for that same reason. (P. 137)

Later, when the combo hits a groove that transports him, the narrator goes on to remark:

> They were not about anything very new. He and his boys up there were keeping it new, at the risk of ruin, destruction, madness, and death, in order to find new ways to make us listen. For, while the tale of how we suffer, and how we are delighted, and how we may triumph is never new, it always must be heard. There isn't any other tale to tell, it's the only light we've got in all this darkness. (P. 139)

This is heady stuff, for Baldwin here, and in the whole story, has come very close to symbolizing the impulses of Dionysus and Apollo, with a nod to Dionysus. The only jarring note in the total structure is that all of this effort goes to Sonny's rendition of "Am I Blue," a pop blues tune that carries about as much weight in the repertory of soulful blues as a poem by Edgar A. Guest would carry among the metaphysical poets.

With respect to plots, the remaining stories go downhill from "Sonny's Blues." The title story, "Going to Meet the Man," is a full story, concluding in a resolution of its conflict. Jesse, the central character wants to make love to his wife but is unable to do so. He lies in bed and recalls a lynching that took place during his boyhood, and he is aroused. Awakening his wife, Jesse says, "Come on, sugar, I'm going to do you like a nigger, just like a nigger, come on, sugar, and love me just like you'd love a nigger." (P. 249) As story, this is not much. Baldwin expends his best efforts not with his current situation but with the flashback to the castration and burning of a black man. In the flashback the writing is so graphic that one almost hears the howls of the victim and smells the burning flesh. The significance of the story, however, lies in its relationship to Baldwin's ideology.

In his famous essay on Wright entitled "Alas, Poor Richard," Baldwin wrote:

> In most of the novels written by Negroes until today . . . there is a great space where sex ought to be; and what usually fills this space is violence. . . . The violence is gratuitous and compulsive because the root of the violence is never examined. The root is rage. It is the rage, almost literally the howl, of a man who is being castrated. I do not think that I am the first person to notice this, but there is probably no greater . . . body of sexual myths in the world today than those which have proliferated around the figure of the American Negro. This means that he is penalized for the guilty imagination of the white people who invest him with their hates and longings, and is the principal target of their sexual paranoia.[2]

From these statements it is clear that "Going to Meet the Man" is Baldwin's artistic attempt to render this ideology on the relationship between violence and sexuality, between white guilt and black suffering. Even the language of the essay and the story are the same in key respects. The danger in a story of this type is that the ideological content tends to smother the narrative as narrative.

The three stories "Previous Condition," "This Morning, This Evening, So Soon," and "Come Out the Wilderness" have several things in common. In the first place, all three central characters are black and are involved in some aspect of interracial sex. Ruth in "Come Out the Wilderness" is at the end of her affair with Paul, a white man she has been living with. The narrator in "This Morning, This Evening, So Soon" is a successful black singer, married to Harriet, a Swede, and living in Paris. The voice of "Previous Condition" is a black actor who is supported in bad times by Ida, a married Irish woman. All three characters are estranged, alienated, and cut off from their suggested roots in the black community.

All three stories are episodic rather than cyclical in structure; they introduce a problem at the beginning but end without a resolution or denouement. Ruth knows at the outset that Paul plans to leave her soon, and she is very much upset and knows that she must set a new course for her life. At the end of the story, Paul still has not left; Ruth is still very much upset, and, as for the course of her life, the story ends with " . . . she did not know where she was going." (P. 225) The actor is unemployed, homeless, and in a condition where he, too, must do something. He confronts a landlady and gets thrown out of a room lent to him by a white friend; he meets his girlfriend and has lunch and some drinks with her; he finally ends up in a Harlem bar, where, when asked by a woman for whom he has bought a beer, "Baby . . . what's your story?" he replies, in the final line, "I got no story, Ma." (P. 100) The singer has reluctantly accepted a contract to return to the United States. There is a considerable uneasiness about the trip. He goes out one night, meets a group of black-American students, barhops with them, and the story ends with his return to his Paris apartment.

Finally, in each of the stories, Baldwin has created an episode where the central character has a renewed contact with the black community. Ruth has an interview with Mr. Davis, a black man in her office, who wants her reassigned as his secretary. The singer barhops with the black-American students. The actor winds up in a Harlem bar. But nothing happens in the episodes; they serve neither to heighten nor to resolve the dilemma in which the character finds himself at the outset. As structural components, the episodes are completely nonfunctional.

None of these seeming difficulties obtain if one looks at these stories not so much as stories but as serial structures that present a series of episodes from various lives. It would then be the lives themselves, rather than the narrative action surrounding the lives, that would illustrate whatever Baldwin wished to illustrate. Indeed, Baldwin himself set forth such a writing plan in his "Notes for a Hypothetical Novel":

> Let's pretend that I want to write a novel concerning the people or some of the people with whom I grew up, and since we are only playing, let us pretend it's a very long novel. I want to follow a group of

lives almost from the time they open their eyes on the world until some point of resolution, say, marriage, or childbirth, or death. And I want to impose myself on these people as little as possible. That means that I do not want to tell them or the reader what principle their lives illustrate, or what principle is activating their lives, but by examining their lives I hope to be able to make them convey to me and to the reader what their lives mean.[3]

Here, the principle of a kind of whole-life conceptualization of character might explain one of the recurring features of Baldwin's style in the short fiction: the use of flashbacks. All of the stories discussed in this essay use the flashback as a case of recall on the part of the central characters. These characters are only partially drawn in their first presentation, and their attitudes, postures, to say nothing of the organizing principles of their lives, unfold only gradually. Most of the revelation of character comes as the characters recall from the past the specific incidents that account for the nature of their being in the present.

Baldwin's great strength in his short fiction lies in his creation of patterns of static reference, presenting descriptions or affective states in his characters. None of the pieces in this collection, even those episodic pieces that lack final resolution, are lacking in these superbly written passages. One such passage occurs in "The Man Child" in a description of Jamie and his dog:

> Jamie had a brown and yellow dog. . . . They had always been there, they had always been together: in exactly the same way, for Eric, that his mother and father had always been together, in exactly the same way that the earth and the trees and the sky were together. Jamie and his dog walked the country roads together. . . . He walked as though he were going to walk to the other end of the world and knew it was a long way but knew that he would be there by morning. . . . His head was carried in a cloud of blue smoke from his pipe. Through this cloud, like a ship on a foggy day, loomed his dry and steady face. Set far back, at an unapproachable angle, were those eyes of his, smoky and thoughtful, eyes which seemed always to be considering the horizon. (P. 62)

This is excellent writing. The embellished style, however, does not have much to do with the story that Baldwin is telling. It can be justified structurally as a means of contrasting this Jamie state with the act of murder which he commits at the end of the narrative or as an example of the murder victim's benign view of his unexpected murderer, but both of these approaches seem to strain the text a bit, and the passage might be best seen as an instance of Baldwin's use of the unstructured aesthetic, a beautiful passage set down in the midst of narrative as an end in itself and for the conative impact it has on the reader.

Not all of the passages in which Baldwin makes use of patterns of static reference are as nonfunctional as the above. Sometimes the passages are used partly as characterizing devices or merely as externals to indicate affective states of characters. An example of the former occurs in "Previous Condition," where the actor, listening to the music of Beethoven in a room he expects to be thrown out of, in a flashback recalls a happier time when he and his friends were at an outdoor concert. He recalls,

> I sat with my knee up, watching the lighted half-moon below, the black-coated, straining conductor, the faceless men beneath him moving together in a rhythm like the sea. There were pauses in the music for the rushing, calling, halting piano. Everything would stop except the climbing soloist; he would reach a height and everything would join him, the violin first and then the horns; and then the deep blue bass and the flute and the bitter trampling drums; beating, beating, and mounting together and stopping with a crash like daybreak. When I first heard the *Messiah* I was alone; my blood bubbled like fire and wine; I cried; like an infant crying for its mother's milk; or a sinner running to meet Jesus. (P. 90)

Apart from its betrayal of Baldwin's folk-preacherly background in the concluding simile and the overall affective impact that such a passage must have on the reader, in terms of the structure of the narrative the passage is one illustration of the sensitivity of this artist-in-exile type, and it prepares for the intensity of his emotional response on later being evicted from his white friend's room by the white landlady.

The actor knows he is not welcome in the room his white friend has let him use, and he expects any moment to hear the landlady's knock on the door. The knock comes, and Baldwin's narrator says,

> When I opened the door the landlady stood there, red-and-white-faced and hysterical. . . .
>
> Her glasses blinked, opaque in the light on the landing. She was frightened to death. She was afraid of me but she was more afraid of losing her tenants. Her face was mottled with rage and fear, her breath came rushed and little bits of spittle gathered at the edges of her mouth; her breath smelled bad, like rotting hamburger on a July day. (P. 91)

The intent of the passage is clear: to indicate the internal or affective state of the narrator. But the description proves much more affective as an external suggesting the narrator's state of mind than the earlier statements, "I began to be angry. I wanted to kill her." (P. 91)

As well constructed as "Sonny's Blues" is as narrative, part of its effectiveness is due to the same structural patterns of static reference. While the denouement of the story is the narrator's realization of the possibility of music or creative art as an instrument of redemption, this resolution has been prepared for much earlier in the story, when the narrator at home observes a group of religious street-singers outside his window:

> The woman with the tambourine, whose voice dominated the air, whose face was bright with joy, was divided by very little from the woman who stood watching her, a cigarette between her heavy, chapped lips, her hair a cuckoo's nest, her face scarred and swollen from many beatings and her black eyes glittering like coal. Perhaps they both knew this, which was why, when, as rarely, they addressed each other, they addressed each other as Sister. As the singing filled the air the watching, listening faces underwent a change, the eyes focusing on something within; the music seemed to soothe a poison out of them; and time seemed, nearly, to fall away from the sullen, belligerent, battered faces, as though they were fleeing back to their first condition while dreaming of their last. (P. 129)

The connection with the conclusion of the story comes when the narrator remarks, "Then I saw Sonny, standing on the edge of the crowd." (P. 129)

One could go on to reproduce these passages one by one, since none of the short fiction seems to be lacking in them, but a final example will here suffice. The singer in "This Morning, This Evening, So Soon" has not only become alienated from his American home, but he has found life, love, family, and a land in Paris. None of this is explicitly stated; it comes seeping through, implicitly, in the singer's description of his relationship to the River Seine, as he says,

> I know the river as one finally knows a friend, know it when it is black, guarding all the lights of Paris in its depths, and seeming, in its vast silence, to be communing with the dead who lie beneath it; when it is yellow, evil, and roaring, giving a rough time to tugboats and barges, and causing people to remember that it has been known to rise, it has been known to kill; when it is peaceful, a slick, dark, dirty green, playing host to rowboats and *les bateaux mouches* and throwing up from time to time an extremely unhealthy fish. (P. 155)

The story itself is another example of Baldwin's loosely jointed, episodic structures, but a passage like this does much to show us a character's life and the principle that life illustrates.

A final assessment of Baldwin's short fiction shows that the author leaves something to be desired in the creation of the kind of cyclical structures that make for good narrative art. He often uses the short story as a means of artistically imposing his ideological positions on the nature and purposes of fiction. He is limited to the use of flashbacks as a means both of character development and of plot resolution. But Baldwin stands out as a writer of patterns of static reference which are used as instances of the unstructured aesthetic, or as a means of showing affective states of characters or producing a telling conative impact on his readers. In any case, the short fiction presents the promise of all that is to come in Baldwin's later development as a writer of novels.

James Baldwin's
"Previous Condition"
A Problem of Identification

_____ Sam Bluefarb

*I*n James Baldwin's story "Previous Condition" (1948) a young black actor (read artist, intellectual, or both, for actor) attempts to find some form of identification in the white world; but ironically he also fails to find even a place for himself in the black world. He is a not-so-daring young man on a flying trapeze between two unattainable poles.

The opening of the story sets its tone. The first paragraph adumbrates, through its imagery, the plight of the Negro not only in the story but in the United States. Peter, the young actor, wakes up in a cold sweat, alone in a room, shaking with fear. He may have had a nightmare, which, transferred to the waking-up, has him observe: "The [bed] sheet was gray and twisted like a rope."[1] The allusion of this simile should be fairly obvious.

In the second paragraph, Peter tells us: "I couldn't move for the longest while. I just lay on my back, spread-eagled. . . ." (P. 83)—suggesting an earlier form of torture-punishment.

This story of the alienated and invisible man in miniature—it antedated Ralph Ellison's novel *Invisible Man* by some four years—portrays the hero's sensitivity and intellectuality, which form the ingredients of his invisibility; it thus reveals the plight of the black artist-intellectual in the white world, but it goes even further to reveal that individual's plight in the black world. In this respect, "Previous Condition" is as powerful a piece of writing as any of Baldwin's essays, for it poses a twofold problem of identification for a certain category of Negro—the Negro intellectual.

That Baldwin makes Peter an actor is interesting, since Baldwin himself has been interested in the theater and has even done a stint of playwriting himself. However, Baldwin, being the professional that he is, makes Peter an actor as a kind of metaphor for the artist-intellectual, which of course permits him to place Peter in "double jeopardy"—his alienation as a Negro and his alienation as an artist in America, both thoroughly "American" ingredients.

Perhaps Baldwin chose acting for Peter's profession as a kind of provocation to white sensibilities, since for the Negro, being black and being an actor in the mid-forties (when the story was written) would be an almost impossible combination. As Peter tells us, speaking of a play in which he has recently appeared but which has had a short run:

> I played a kind of intellectual Uncle Tom, a young college student working for his race. The playwright had wanted to prove he was a liberal, I guess. But, as I say, the show had folded and here I was, back in New York and hating it. I knew that I should be getting another job, making the rounds, pounding the pavement. But I didn't. I couldn't face it. It was summer. I seemed to be fagged out. And every day I hated myself more. Acting's a rough life, even if you're white. I'm not tall and I'm not good looking and I can't sing or dance and I'm not white; so even in the best of times I wasn't in much demand. (PP. 83–84)

But Peter's problem is as much his alienation as an intellectual as his alienation as a Negro. He is patronized by the white liberals—in the persons of the "Jewboy" Jules Weissman (Whiteman?) and the white Protestant Ida —and he is not understood by his fellow Negroes; indeed, as we see before the story ends, he is regarded with greater suspicion by them than by his white friends.

There is, of course, the lack of communication inevitable in such a situation. Jules and Ida both "know" Peter intellectually, understand his problems intellectually, sympathize with him intellectually—but they cannot *feel* with him. Between Jules and Ida, then, there is little true understanding of Peter's problem—how can there be?—"liberal" as they are.

There are a number of attempts at communication on the part of the white "liberal" world (Jules and Ida)—all unsuccessful. At one point in the story, after Peter has been evicted from his room by his white landlady, Ida attempts to lecture Peter. The lecture, in the face of Peter's virtually insurmountable problems, is a simple-minded "appeal to reason":

> "It's no better anywhere else".... "In all of Europe there's famine and disease, in France and England they hate the Jews—no-

thing's going to change, baby, people are too empty-headed, too empty-hearted—it's always been like that, people always try to destroy what they don't understand—and they hate almost everything because they understand so little—" (P. 96)

Jules, too, attempts to console Peter over the eviction: "Cheer up, baby. The world's wide and life—life, she is very long." (P. 92) (Curiously, both Ida and Jules address Peter as *baby,* a gratuitous familiarity, and Jules's "The world's wide," may have been an ill-concealed "The world's *white!*") Both forms of consolation fail, however, and Peter is left, as he has been all along, alone. His answer to Jules at this point is, quite appropriately, "Shut up. I don't want to hear any of your bad philosophy." (P. 92)

The white bigot of a landlady tells him that he must leave her rooming house, because "I can't have no colored people here. . . . All my tenants are complainin'. Women afraid to come home nights." (P. 91) But if these words enrage Peter all the more, he can at least understand them. The landlady who spits them out is at least the tangible enemy, the ofay. He knows where *she* stands. It is the intangible and perhaps more insidious enemy that proves a tougher problem for Peter. This enemy is embodied perhaps in such well-meaning but innocent white liberals as Jules and Ida, who in their bumbling ways are ineffective precisely because they try so hard to be effective. Perhaps this is true of many white liberals *vis-à-vis* "the problem"—they try too hard, and thus turn into what I have called white Uncle Toms.

Jules and Ida each lecture Peter—Ida as the "voice of reason"; Jules as Job's comforter. Yet neither Jules nor Ida can really know (with their entire beings) Peter the Negro, just as his own people cannot know Peter the artist-intellectual.

Jules's lectures are gratuitous (though he isn't as vocal as Ida), but they are still the verbal equivalent of Ida's rapping Peter across the knuckles with a piece of silverware in a restaurant for talking himself down. Except that where Jules is the "philosopher," Ida is the "activist," who engages (and enrages) Peter by her brash familiarities (the incident of the knuckle-rapping).

Jules, the sympathetic "Jewboy," as Peter calls him, knows persecution too—though only at a second, or perhaps third, remove. Yet Jules in America cannot know, or could not have known, the intense experience of the European Jews under Hitler. As I have said, Jules, after all, is a Jew living in *America*—a point that cannot be stressed too much in this context—but Peter is a *Negro* living in America. There lies the vast difference. Thus Jules, no matter his "Jewish understanding" as fellow victim, may sympathize with Peter, but he cannot really empathize with him.

Ida, Peter's girl, though a "liberal," is still the white-bitch goddess (that symbol of success and "making it" in the white world) toward whom Peter has ambivalent attitudes. For both guilt and shame are present in Peter, since he could easily be accused of being a sexual Uncle Tom—the "black buck" to satisfy the voracious white nymphomaniac.

While the whites differ from each other—from personal sympathy (Jules Weissman), to "understanding" (Ida), to outright fear and hatred (the bigoted landlady)—in the end it is all one blank white wall that Peter faces. His eventual return to Harlem, to his "previous condition" (really not his *previous* condition) only serves to underline his lack of contact with the white world.

Back in Harlem, Peter sees the sights and the sounds he knows so well, but these give him little comfort either:

> I got off [the subway train] in Harlem and went to a rundown bar on Seventh Avenue. My people, my people. Sharpies stood on the corner, waiting. Women in summer dresses pranced by on wavering heels. . . . There were white mounted policemen in the streets. On every block there was another policeman on foot. I saw a black cop.
> God save the American republic. (P. 99)

Peter's journey is no mere journey, then, to Harlem, or back into his "previous condition"; it is a journey to the end of his own personal night. And although he attempts to return to his "previous condition," to "my people," he finds that this too is impossible. It actually is worse than "knowing one's place and keeping it." The title of the story thus reveals its theme, though with intense irony—especially when Peter, after his harsh experiences in the white world ("liberal" or racist) returns to Harlem to find a place for himself there. For even in Harlem he finds himself alone, misunderstood, the object of suspicion. He is thus a stranger in his "own land" (Harlem, that is); but of course he is an even greater stranger in that greater land of which Harlem is only a part, though still a most significant—and barometric—part.

Peter's inability to identify with either group—black or white—represents of course the true source of his alienation, as a Negro in the white society and as an artist-intellectual in the black. He can identify neither with Jules nor with Ida, for a world of time and color separates them from him; yet he cannot identify with his own people, as represented—perhaps unfairly on Baldwin's part—by the old Negro woman he meets in the Harlem bar. For all she can tell him—and she pulls no punches—is "Nigger . . . you must think you's somebody" (P. 99)—which goes unanswered since Peter cannot communicate with her either. "I didn't seem to have a place," (P. 100) Peter tells us after this experience. And, curiously, in these words lies the core of the story. They have become a refrain, which is adumbrated when Jules asks Peter, on the occasion of the latter's eviction from the rooming house, how he, Peter, has fared. Peter's answer, as may be recalled, is an ironic "No room at the inn," (P. 92) an answer that has biblical undertones an intellectual—especially a black intellectual—would make in the bitterness of his lot, an answer that has its echoes two thousand years after the incident that inspired it.

With whom, then, can Peter identify? Obviously, at this stage, with no one —unless it be with other black intellectuals, which in itself would become a form of separatism and therefore alienation. Thus, he is too bright and sensitive for the black Harlem milieu of bars and honky-tonks and too black for the white world, whether "liberal" or racist. Peter stands between the two, though unable to bridge the gap between them. Thus, like Ellison's invisible man, he can truthfully say:

> . . . there was nothing except my color. A white outsider coming in would have seen a young Negro drinking in a Negro bar, perfectly in his elements, in his place, as the saying goes. But the people here [in the bar] knew differently, as I did. *I didn't seem to have a place.* (P. 100) [Italics mine]

In attempting to bridge the gap between the white world and the black, perhaps before those worlds are ready for it, Peter fits in, in neither.

Thus the story ends as it begins, a young black intellectual suspended between two worlds—is it too much to identify Peter with Baldwin himself?— neither of which he feels "at home" in, neither of which really wants him, and perhaps, even more important, neither of which *he* wants.

The story further ends on a note of indecision, as indeed it does today when, most poignantly for both blacks and whites of goodwill, neither can seem to "join hands" as completely as they would like to. Encapsulated, then, in this story, lies the true dilemma of black and white in the second half of the twentieth century.

James Baldwin: The Black and the Red-White-and-Blue

_____ John V. Hagopian

James Baldwin is one of the most accomplished and sophisticated American writers of today, and from a strictly literary point of view it is unfortunate that he expends so much of his energy on non-fiction. To be sure, his essays are sensitive accounts of the complex spiritual and moral predicament of the Negro intellectual, but, as Baldwin himself once said (in *Notes of a Native Son),* he does not want to be a Negro—he wants to be a writer. Yet we find him still expending his creative energies on the genre of the protest essay, which he no doubt finds more satisfactory than the protest novel but which is nevertheless a way of being a Negro rather than a writer. That he has gained enormously in skill since *Giovanni's Room* is clear from his story, "This Morning, This Evening, So Soon" *(Atlantic Monthly,* September, 1960). It is a work that deserves to take its place as one of the most important short stories written since the war, not only because the theme of the Negro girding himself to take his rightful place in American society is significant in our postwar cultural history, but because *as literature* it is a very fine piece of work.

"This Morning, This Evening, So Soon" appears to be a relatively simple story, but it is full of subtle and surprising complexities. A young American Negro, who has for twelve years been living in Paris, where he has established a family (a Swedish wife and a seven-year-old son) and has found fame as a singer and actor, has decided to return to America. He is full of anxiety, especially for his son, who may suffer the spiritually crippling effects of American anti-Negro prejudice. But the experiences and reminiscences of his last twenty-four hours in Paris make him feel "very cheerful, I do not know why," and he finds himself smiling at the prospect of taking his son "all the way to the new world."

The story is divided into three sections, which might have been subtitled: I. Family, II. Friend, III. Strangers; hence, it moves from the intimate center of the unnamed narrator's experiences outward into public life and society. Simultaneously, the narrator—and the reader—gains more and more insight into the complexities and changes in the current of his emotions, although much happens that he does not fully understand. The "I" narrator tells us (in the present tense) about the events as they happen and (in the past tense) about his reminiscences, together with his own interpretations, which are often too explicit:

> Everyone's life begins on a level where races, armies, and churches stop. And yet everyone's life is always shaped by races, churches, and armies; races, churches, and armies menace, and have taken, many lives.

Such comments give the reader the false notion that he is getting the meaning as well as the action from the narrator. Intelligent as the narrator is, and trained as he is to be wary, observant, and critical, such observations are appropriate to his character and are often apt and to the point. But he has had prejudices of his own ("I had always thought of Sweden as being populated entirely by blondes"), is super-sensitive to every act and gesture by a white man that might conceivably be interpreted as anti-Negro ("was it my imagination or was it true that they seemed to avoid my eyes?"), and often speaks ("she is only an American like me") and feels ("I feel very cheerful, I do not know why") in ways that he does not fully understand. Hence the narrator does not, however much he may seem to, do all the reader's interpretive work for him. In fact, the fundamental meaning of the story remains implicit.

In the opening lines of the story, the narrator cites the members of the family circle: his wife Harriet; his sister Louisa, who has come to Paris for a brief holiday before accompanying him and his family back to America; his son Paul, to whom America is "only a glamorous word"; and "the director of the film," who remains unnamed at this point because he is not important until we reach the second section of the story. The strangers of the third section are, of course, not mentioned because the narrator is speculating on events as they occur and does not know what is going to happen. Many of the undercurrents of the opening section will not have much impact on the first reading, because Baldwin holds back the vital information that the narrator and his sister are Negroes until after he has established his characters as a family unit. Only on second reading can we realize the tactfulness of Harriet when she explains to their son that his father's crankiness at breakfast "is because he is afraid they will not like his songs in New York. Your father is an *artiste, mon chou,* and they are very mysterious people, *les artistes.*" The Negro question is avoided because "Harriet does not so much believe in protecting children as she does in helping them to build a foundation on which they can build again, each time life's high-flying steel ball knocks down everything they have built." And only on second reading can we understand the reason why Louisa must seem to Paul "peculiarly uncertain of herself, peculiarly hostile and embattled," or the sinister significances of her insistence to Harriet, "We have *got* some expressions, believe me. Don't let anybody ever tell you America hasn't got a culture. Our culture is as thick as clabber milk." It is in this atmosphere of family love that the narrator's fears emerge: "Paul has never been called any names before"; in America he and Harriet would never have been able to love each other; he fears "all the threats it holds for me and mine." And he shrewdly observes that "Harriet is really trying to learn from Louisa how best to protect her husband and her son." The sum total of this first section is an image of a family group full of love and goodwill facing a threatening experience in which each is eager to help and protect the other.

After Harriet and Louisa leave to spend an evening in Paris and after Paul has been delivered to the safe-keeping of the concierge, the narrator returns to his apartment to await the visit of Vidal, the director of the film that has made him famous. On the balcony he smokes, looks at Paris, where he has "always felt at home," meditates and reminisces: "I love Paris, I will always love it, it is the city which has saved my life . . . by allowing me to find out who I am." It was in Paris eight years before that he fell in love with Harriet just before returning to America for the funeral of his mother—"I felt . . . for the first time that the woman was not, in her own eyes or in the eyes of the world, degraded by my presence." He was afraid of America and eager to return to her. New York seemed like "some enormous, cunning and murderous beast, ready to devour, impossible to escape," and he was especially vulnerable because he "had forgotten all the tricks [of appearing subservient to the whites] on which my life had once depended." There are few subtleties in this transitional part of the story. The narrator is ambivalent about America, fears it but is attracted to it: "I was home." There is a fine little sketch of the noise and power of New York, capped with the observation that "the human voices distinguish themselves from the roar by their note of strain and hostility." When his sister Louisa, who met him at the ship, directed the cabdriver to the New Yorker Hotel, the narrator was surprised, for Negroes had always been discriminated against there. Obviously the country was changing, but Louisa's optimism was cautious: "this place really hasn't changed very much. You still can't hear yourself talk."

The second section of the story begins with the arrival of Jean Luc Vidal, a "tough, cynical, crafty old Frenchman," a former Gaullist, whose wife and son were lost in the war and who had spent time in a Nazi prison. This man is very fond of the young Negro whom he has made into an international star in a film significantly entitled *Les Fauves Nous Attendent*. But Vidal has done more for him than that; he has taught him to express and thus to relive his deep-felt hatreds through his art and has exposed the self-pitying anti-white prejudice that prevents him from responding to any white man as an individual just as effectively as anti-Negro prejudice blinds white people to the individuality of Negroes: "I am a French Director and I have never been in your country and I have never done you any harm—but . . . you are not talking to Jean Luc Vidal, but to some other white man, whom you remember, who has nothing to do with me." To Vidal, the narrator can speak openly of his fears at returning to a country where "I always feel that I don't exist, except in someone else's—usually dirty—mind . . . I don't want to put Harriet through that and I don't want to raise Paul there." Vidal reassures him that his return needn't be permanent, that his new status and the prospects of great wealth are worth the risk. At the end of this dialogue, the two leave for their evening out.

Section three begins with their arrival at a discotheque where they encounter a group of American Negro students, two girls and two young men. The most attractive of the girls approaches them, astonished at her luck "because it's in the papers that you're coming home." These Negroes, like the narrator, obviously regard America as "home" despite the conditions of their life there. Their dialogue reveals their fear and hatred of the whites, but also their belligerent determination to fight back. One says, "I fear you are in for some surprises, my friend. There have been some changes made." Then "Are you afraid?"

"A little."
"We all are," says Ada, "that's why I was so glad to get away for a little while."

As the group goes bar-hopping, they are joined by an Arab named Boona, an erstwhile prizefighter from Tunis and an acquaintance of the narrator. Though he is a disreputable fellow and obviously does not fit with the group, the narrator cannot send him away for fear of appearing to display prejudice against Arabs. One of the Negro girls asks Boona, "Wouldn't you like to go back [to Tunis]?" and he replies, "That is not so easy." (The significance of this will be dealt with in a moment.) During the course of the night, Boona steals money from the purse of one of the girls; he is confronted, denies it—"Why she blame me? Because I come from Africa?" In this section of the story the narrator makes no commentaries on the action, and when the girl decides not to press the point ("I'm sure I lost it. . . . It isn't worth hurting your feelings"), we can only assume that she has observed the Arab's desperation and is therefore willing to endure the loss of the money. The party breaks up at dawn, and the narrator goes home, stopping at the concierge's apartment to pick up his son: "I feel very cheerful, I do not know why." The concierge, referring to their trip to America, says, "What a journey! *Jusqu-au nouveau monde!"*

> I open the cage [of the elevator] and we step inside. "Yes," I say, "all the way to the new world." I press the button and the cage, holding my son and me, goes up.

The symbolism of the ending is clear. Although this Negro and his son are in the cage of their Negro skins, they are rising in the world. But what, exactly, has happened to explain or justify this optimism? The answer is that as the story moves in wider and wider orbits around the central character, we see that his original feeling that everything was divided into his oppressed self and the hostile world was false, that he is part of a history and a humanity that is far more complex than that. The narrator cannot identify himself simply as an oppressed person, for much of the world does *not* oppress him. He finds love not only from his Negro sister but from a Swedish woman who marries him and gives him a son and from a French film director who teaches him some hard truths about life. In the film he had been obliged to portray a mulatto boy who hated "all dark women and all white men" and he had not been throwing himself fully and honestly into the role. Vidal had goaded him:

> "Have you never, yourself, been in a similar position?"
> I hated him for asking the question because I knew he had the answer to it. "I would have had to be a very lucky black man not to have been in such a position."
> "You would have had to be a very lucky *man*."
> "Oh, God," I said, "please don't give me any of this equality—in—anguish business."
> "It is perfectly possible," he said sharply, "that there is not another kind."

Vidal then gave him a stern lecture on history, pointing out that the white men—especially the French—are paying for their history of abuse of the colored peoples and that if revenge is what the Negro wants he will certainly have it. He then strikes home with a telling blow "How will you raise your son? Will you teach him never to tell the truth to anyone?" The narrator then recalled how he had held his own father in pity and contempt for not being able to prevent or even to prepare him for the humiliation and the anguish of Negro life in Alabama. "But for Paul . . . I swore I would make it impossible for the world to treat Paul as it had treated my father and me." But since the story does not end at that point, this must be taken as a temporary and transient stage in the narrator's development. And Vidal's wisdom, too, is by no means the last word.

The last word apparently has to do with Boona, i.e., with the contrast between the Arab from Tunis and the Negro from America, neither of whom wishes to go home. But their situations are not quite the same, as the narrator comes to realize; there is a profound difference in their racial histories. The Arabs do not identify themselves as Frenchmen, but the Negroes are Americans. In his balcony meditation, the narrator had mused on the plight of the Arabs in Paris and how their treatment had caused such a degeneration among them. "I once thought of the North Africans as my brothers" and responded to "their rage, the only note in all their music which I could not fail to recognize." Yet because "they were perfectly prepared to drive all Frenchmen into the sea and to level the city of Paris" he could not identify with them—partly because he owed his spiritual life to France and partly because his own rage against America is the anger one feels against the wrongs of a country he loves ("waiting for the first glimpse of America, my apprehension began to give way to a secret joy, a checked anticipation"). Furthermore, he had discovered aboard ship during his first voyage home that the white Americans "who had never treated me with any respect, had no respect for each other." True, they quickly came to call each other by their first names, but their friendliness "did not suggest and was not intended to suggest any possibility of friendship." And earlier in the story he had observed that the whites "could not afford to hear a truth which would shatter, irrevocably, their image of themselves." But he shares with his sister Louisa the conviction that if the whites could be brought to confront the Negro honestly and to accept him for what he was—not only a fellow human being but a permanent and unshakable part of his American culture—the entire culture could be made whole and healthy. Louisa had said that even the Negro must be brought to realize this truth:

That's what I keep trying to tell those dicty bastards down South. They get their own experience into the language, we'll have a great language. But, no, they all want to talk like white folks. . . . I tell them, honey, white folks ain't saying *nothing*. Not a thing are they saying—and *some* of them know it—they *need* what you got, the whole world needs it.

It is this kind of racial pride that the Arabs in France do not share with the Negroes in America, that has been buttressed by the narrator's observation of understanding and kindness displayed by the Negro tourists toward Boona. That is what makes him cheerful at the end. It is an achievement that he has come to feel a whole man in France; it is a greater achievement that he can face with pride the prospect of being a Negro in America.

"Sonny's Blues" James Baldwin's Image of Black Community

_____ John M. Reilly

A critical commonplace holds that James Baldwin writes better essays than he does fiction or drama; nevertheless, his leading theme—the discovery of identity—is nowhere presented more successfully than in the short story "Sonny's Blues." Originally published in _Partisan Review,_ in 1957, and reprinted in the collection of stories _Going to Meet the Man,_ in 1965, "Sonny's Blues" not only states dramatically the motive for Baldwin's famous polemics in the cause of black freedom but also provides an aesthetic linking for his work, in all literary genres, with the cultures of the black ghetto.[1]

The fundamental movement of "Sonny's Blues" represents the slow accommodation of a first-person narrator's consciousness to the meaning of his younger brother's way of life. The process leads Baldwin's readers to a sympathetic engagement with the young man by providing a knowledge of the human motives of the youths, whose lives normally are reported to others only by their inclusion in statistics of school dropout rates, drug usage, and unemployment.

The basis of the story, however, and its relationship to the purpose of Baldwin's writing generally, lies in his use of the blues as a key metaphor. The unique quality of the blues is its combination of personal and social significance in a lyric encounter with history. "The Blues-singer describes first-person experiences, but only such as are typical of the community and such as each individual in the community might have. The singer never sets himself against the community or raises himself above it."[2] Thus, in the story of

Sonny and his brother an intuition of the meaning of the blues repairs the relationship between the two men who have chosen different ways to cope with the menacing ghetto environment, and their reconciliation through the medium of this Afro-American musical form extends the meaning of the individual's blues until it becomes a metaphor for black community.

Sonny's life explodes into his older brother's awareness when the story of his arrest for peddling and using heroin is reported in the newspaper. Significantly, the mass medium of the newspaper with the impersonal story in it of a police bust is the only way the brothers have of communicating at the opening of the story. While the narrator says that because of the newspaper report Sonny "became real to me again," their relationship is only vestigially personal, for he "couldn't find any room" for the news "anywhere inside. . . ." (P. 103)

While he had had his suspicions about how Sonny was spending his life, the narrator had put them aside with rationalizations about how Sonny was, after all, a good kid. Nothing to worry about. In short, the storyteller reveals that along with his respectable job as an algebra teacher he had assumed a conventional way of thinking as a defense against recognizing that his own brother ran the risk of "coming to nothing." Provoked by the facts of Sonny's arrest to observe his students, since they are the same age as Sonny must have been when he first had heroin, he notices for the first time that their laughter is disenchanted rather than good-humored. In it he hears his brother, and perhaps himself. At this point in the story his opinion is evidently that Sonny and many of the young students are beaten and that he, fortunately, is not.

The conventionality of the narrator's attitude becomes clearer when he encounters a nameless friend of Sonny's, a boy from the block who fears he may have touted Sonny onto heroin by telling him, truthfully, how great it made him feel to be high. This man who "still spent hours on the street corner . . . high and raggy" explains what will happen to Sonny because of his arrest. After they send him someplace and try to cure him, they'll let Sonny loose, that's all. Trying to grasp the implication, the narrator asks: "You mean he'll never kick the habit. Is that what you mean?" He feels there should be some kind of renewal, some hope. A man should be able to bring himself up by his will, convention says. Convention also says that behavior like Sonny's is deliberately self-destructive. "Tell me," he asks the friend, "why does he want to die?" Wrong again. "Don't nobody want to die," says the friend, "ever." (P. 108)

Agitated though he is about Sonny's fate, the narrator doesn't want to feel himself involved. His own position on the middle-class ladder of success is not secure, and the supporting patterns of thought in his mind are actually rather weak. Listening to the nameless friend explain about Sonny while they stand together in front of a bar blasting "black and bouncy" music from its door, he senses something that frightens him. "All this was carrying me some place I didn't want to go. I certainly didn't want to know how it felt. It filled everything, the people, the houses, the music, the dark, quicksilver barmaid, with menace; and this menace was their reality." (P. 107)

Eventually a great personal pain—the loss of a young daughter—breaks through the narrator's defenses and makes him seek out his brother, more for his own comfort than for Sonny's. "My trouble made his real," he says. In that remark is a prefiguring of the meaning the blues will develop.

It is only a prefiguring, however, for by the time Sonny is released from the state institution where he has been confined, the narrator's immediate need for comfort has passed. When he meets Sonny, he is in control of himself, but very shortly he is flooded with complex feelings that make him feel again the menace of the 110th Street bar where he stood with Sonny's friend. There is no escaping a feeling of icy dread, so he must try to understand.

As the narrator casts his mind back over his and Sonny's past, he gradually identifies sources of his feelings. First he recalls their parents, especially concentrating on an image of his family on a typical Sunday. The scene is one of security amidst portentousness. The adults sit without talking, but every face looks darkening, like the sky outside. The children sit about, maybe one half-asleep and another being stroked on the head by an adult. The darkness frightens a child and he hopes "that the hand which strokes his forehead will never stop." The child knows, however, that it will end, and, now grown up, he recalls one of the meanings of the darkness in the story his mother told him of the death of his uncle, run over on a dark country road by a car full of drunken white men. Never had his companion, the boy's father, "seen anything as dark as that road after the lights of the car had gone away." The narrator's mother had attempted to apply her tale of his father's grief at the death of his own brother to the needs of their sons. They can't protect each other, she knows, "but," she says to the narrator about Sonny, "you got to let him know you's *there*." (P. 119)

Thus, guilt for not fulfilling their mother's request and a sense of shared loneliness partially explain the older brother's feeling toward Sonny. Once again, however, Baldwin stresses the place of the conventional set of the narrator's mind in the complex of feelings as he has him recall scenes from the time when Sonny started to become a jazz musician. The possibility of Sonny's being a jazz rather than a classical musician "seemed—beneath him, somehow." Trying to understand the ambition, the narrator asked if Sonny meant to play like Louis Armstrong, only to be told that Charlie Parker was the model. Hard as it is to believe, he had never heard of Bird until Sonny mentioned him. This ignorance reveals more than a gap between fraternal generations. It represents a cultural chasm. The narrator's inability to understand Sonny's choice of a musical leader shows his alienation from the mood of the postwar bebop subculture. In its hip style of dress, its repudiation of middlebrow norms, and its celebration of esoteric manner, the bebop subculture makes overtly evident its underlying significance as an assertion of black identity. Building upon a restatement of Afro-American music, bebop became an expression of a new self-awareness in the ghettos by a strategy of elaborate nonconformity. In committing himself to the bebop subculture Sonny attempted to make a virtue of the necessity of the isolation imposed upon him by his color. In contrast, the narrator's failure to understand what Sonny was doing indicates that his response to the conditions imposed upon him by racial status was to try to assimilate himself as well as he could into the mainstream American culture. For the one, heroin addiction sealed his membership in the exclusive group; for the other, adoption of individualistic attitudes marked his allegiance to the historically familiar ideal of transcending caste distinctions by entering into the middle class.

Following his way, Sonny became wrapped in the vision that rose from his piano, stopped attending school, and hung around with a group of musicians in Greenwich Village. His musical friends became Sonny's family, replacing the brother who had felt that Sonny's choice of his style of life was the same thing as dying, and for all practical purposes the brothers were dead to each other in the extended separation before Sonny's arrest on narcotics charges.

The thoughts revealing the brothers' family history and locating the sources of the narrator's complex feelings about Sonny all occur in the period after Sonny is released from the state institution. Though he has ceased to evade thoughts of their relationship, as he did in the years when they were separated and partially continued to do after Sonny's arrest, the narrator has a way to go before he can become reconciled to Sonny. His recollections of the past only provide his consciousness with raw feeling.

The next development—perception—begins with a scene of a revival meeting conducted on the sidewalk of Seventh Avenue, beneath the narrator's window. Everyone on the street has been watching such meetings all his life, but the narrator from his window, passersby on the street, and Sonny from the edge of the crowd all watch again. It isn't because they expect something different this time. Rather it is a familiar moment of communion for them. In basic humanity one of the sanctified sisters resembles the down-and-outer watching her, "a cigarette between her heavy, chapped lips, her hair a cuckoo's nest, her face scarred and swollen from many beatings. . . . Perhaps," the narrator thinks, "they both knew this, which was why, when, as rarely, they addressed each other, they addressed each other as Sister." (P. 129) The point impresses both the narrator and Sonny, men who should call one another "Brother," for the music of the revivalists seems to "soothe a poison" out of them.

The perception of this moment extends nearly to conception in the conversation between the narrator and Sonny that follows it. It isn't a comfortable discussion. The narrator still is inclined to voice moral judgments of the experiences and people Sonny tries to talk about, but he is making an honest effort to relate to his brother now and reminds himself to be quiet and listen. What he hears is that Sonny equates the feeling of hearing the revivalist sister sing with the sensation of heroin in the veins. "It makes you feel—in control. Sometimes you got to have that feeling." (P. 131) It isn't primarily drugs that Sonny is talking about, though, and when the narrator curbs his tongue to let him go on, Sonny explains the real subject of his thoughts.

Again, the facts of Sonny's experience contradict the opinion of "respectable" people. He did not use drugs to escape from suffering, he says. He knows as well as anyone that there's no way to avoid suffering, but what you can do is "try all kinds of ways to keep from drowning in it, to keep on top of it, and to make it seem . . . like *you*." That is, Sonny explains, you can earn your suffering, make it seem "like you did something . . . and now you're suffering for it." (P. 132)

The idea of meriting your suffering is a staggering one. In the face of it the narrator's inclination to talk about "will power and how life could be—well, beautiful" is blunted, because he senses that by directly confronting degradation Sonny has asserted what degree of will was possible to him, and perhaps that kept him alive.

At this point in the story it is clear that there are two themes emerging. The first is the theme of the individualistic narrator's gradual discovery of the significance of his brother's life. This theme moves to a climax in the final scene of the story when Sonny's music impresses the narrator with a sense of the profound feeling it contains. From the perspective of that final scene, however, the significance of the blues itself becomes a powerful theme.

The insight into the suffering that Sonny displays establishes his priority in knowledge. Thus, he reverses the original relationship between the brothers, assumes the role of the elder, and proceeds to lead his brother, by means of the blues, to a discovery of self in community.

As the brothers enter the jazz club where Sonny is to play, he becomes special. Everyone has been waiting for him, and each greets him familiarly. Equally special is the setting—dark except for a spotlight, which the musicians approach as if it were a circle of flame. This is a sanctified spot, where Sonny is to testify to the power of souls to commune in the blues.

Baldwin explicates the formula of the blues by tracing the narrator's thoughts while Sonny plays. Many people, he thinks, don't really hear music being played except insofar as they invest it with "personal, private, vanishing evocations." He might be thinking of himself, referring to his having come to think of Sonny through the suffering of his own personal loss. The man who makes the music engages in a spiritual creation, and, when he succeeds, the creation belongs to all present; "his triumph, when he triumphs, is ours." (P. 137)

In the first set, Sonny doesn't triumph, but in the second, appropriately begun by "Am I Blue," he takes the lead and begins to form a musical creation. He becomes, in the narrator's words, "part of the family again." (P. 139) What family? First of all, that of his fellow musicians. Then, of course, the narrator means to say that their fraternal relationship is at last fulfilled as their mother hoped it would be. But there is yet a broader meaning, too. Like the sisters at the Seventh Avenue revival meeting, Sonny and the band are not saying anything new. Still they are keeping the blues alive by expanding it beyond the personal lyric into a statement of the glorious capacity of human beings to take the worst and give it a form of their own choosing.

At this point the narrator synthesizes feelings and perception into a conception of the blues. He realizes Sonny's blues can help everyone who listens be free, in his own case free of the conventions that had alienated him from Sonny and that dimension of black culture represented in Sonny's style of living. Yet at the same time he knows the world outside of the blues moment remains hostile.

The implicit statement of the aesthetics of the blues in this story throws light upon much of Baldwin's writing. The first proposition of the aesthetics that we can infer from "Sonny's Blues" is that suffering is the prior necessity. Integrity of expression comes from "paying your dues." This is a point Baldwin previously made in *Giovanni's Room* (1956) and which he elaborated in the novel *Another Country* (1962).

The second implicit proposition of the blues aesthetics is that while the form is what it's all about, the form is transitory. The blues is an art in process and in that respect alien from any conception of fixed and ideal forms. This will not justify weaknesses in an artist's work, but insofar as Baldwin identifies his writing with the art of the singers of blues, it suggests why he is devoted to representation, in whatever genre, of successive moments of expressive feeling, and comparatively less concerned with achieving a consistent overall structure.

The final proposition of the aesthetics in the story "Sonny's Blues" is that the blues functions as an art of communion. It is popular rather than elite, worldly rather than otherwise. The blues is expression in which one uses the skill one has achieved by practice and experience in order to reach toward others. It is this proposition that gives the blues its metaphoric significance. The fraternal reconciliation brought about through Sonny's music is emblematic of a group's coming together, because the narrator learns to love his brother freely while he discovers the value of a characteristically Afro-American assertion of life-force. Taking Sonny on his own terms, he must also abandon the ways of thought identified with middle-class position, which historically has signified for black people the adoption of "white" ways.

An outstanding quality of the black literary tradition in America is its attention to the interdependence of personal and social experience. Obviously, necessity has fostered this virtue. Black authors cannot luxuriate in the assumption that there is such a thing as a purely private life. James Baldwin significantly adds to this aspect of the tradition in "Sonny's Blues" by showing that artful expression of personal yet typical experience is one way to freedom.

Fire as the Symbol of a Leadening Existence in "Going to Meet the Man"

Arthenia Bates Millican

James Baldwin's collection of short stories, *Going to Meet the Man,* was published in 1965, a year after *Blues for Mister Charlie,* his first published play. The title story in the collection and the play sing the blues for "Mister Charlie," the white racist, who is intent on keeping the black man in his place—more specifically in the Southern region of the United States. Baldwin has drawn attacks on these works from several critics[1] who consider the "blues" effect "trivial" because he labors to bring new light to the same-old-story-worth-telling-once-more of whites against blacks. Furthermore, he has employed the everlasting, inescapable symbol as the locus for both works. In fact, Joseph Featherstone expresses the opinion that the whole "racial fuss" in *Blues for Mister Charlie* and "Going to Meet the Man" stems from the author's concern for the white man's inability to display his sexual virility at will.[2]

The chronology of works in an author's canon may have everything or nothing to do with the ordering of his perception. But to build a premise, we will assume that *Blues for Mister Charlie* was written a year before "Going to Meet the Man." That way we can assume that Baldwin portrayed a white racist in the play who is freed of his crime (murder) by the law. In the meantime he informs us that something happens to that man, the human being, who is freed by the law of the land. Escape from crime in this manner places the absolution from that crime on the back of the criminal. He will either repent in humility or remain adamant in the decision of the law and lose his humanity. We are left with the white racist, unshaken and unredeemed in *Blues for Mister Charlie.* If there is any vestige of justice in the South, which is based on Christian ethics or secular morals, Lyle Britten is lost. He is, like the protagonist in William Melvin Kelley's *Dem,* left smarting in a tub of hot water gazing at the ceiling—not the sky. Jesse, the lawman, is one step above them.

Perhaps no one who witnesses the spectacle of a man "in fire," "on fire," or "under fire" can resist voicing the simple query—"Why?" "Going to Meet the Man" gives the case history of Lyle Britten, in broader dimensions, to answer that query. Fire is used in "Going to Meet the Man" as a symbol of frustration, which Jesse, the protagonist, experiences as a boy of eight, as a young adult (no doubt in his twenties), and as a deputy sheriff forty-two years old. Through Jesse's reverie, we can rebuild the framework for his destruction, which, of course, exempts the decadence of the racist society that helped to form him. Baldwin does this by grafting upon Jesse's consciousness the necessity for him to keep the black man in *his* place.

Fire, in a literal and symbolic sense, is frequently used by Baldwin in his non-fiction as well as in his fiction. The ready example in non-fiction is *The Fire Next Time,* which emerges as a searing, torturous personal account of the writer as a youth growing up in Harlem. Besides, there is a candid, mind-jolting portrayal of what America has done to the black man. The ready example in fiction is *Go Tell It on the Mountain,* where the saints, one by one, give vent to the lightning power of the Holy Ghost that purifies the sinner's heart with tongs of fire. So often implications in Baldwin's works take us to the fire and brimstone of hell, to the overwhelming heat of passion and lust, to the well-fed bonfire set to scorch the black criminal hanging from a tree. Notwithstanding the power of Baldwin's literal engagement with fire, we want to touch upon realities that transcend the limitations of the obvious. By way of symbolism, Baldwin uses fire in "Going to Meet the Man" as a device to achieve coherence as he dissects the inner mind of Jesse, the deputy sheriff who must cope with black civil-rights demonstrators because he is the *law.*

The story begins and ends in Jesse's nuptial bed. The "nighttime reverie" is at first a recapitulation of his "brutal day" among the blacks who staged a demonstration while voter-registration took place at the county court house. What had annoyed him most of all was the singing—the continuous singing of the blacks, which pierced his consciousness so severely that he longed to escape from "the castle of his own skin." But he could not escape, though he had the desire to escape. The memories of the day opened a vista to past encounters—the not-so-distant past, and the distant past, where the white-black encounter began for him. The reverie, borne upon the device of a remembered song, has a "simple river-run structuring that is flawless," according to David Littlejohn.[3]

To measure the descent of Jesse, who is "nameless" though not fatherless, let us select two referents that will allow us to sense the leadening weight that attends him as he rises or grows from boyhood into manhood. If he moves in space, it is a "descent into the maelstrom"—Poe's phrase. The platform of white supremacy on which Jesse *must* stand is a maelstrom—simply defined as "a powerful, often violent whirlpool sucking in objects within a given radius." To reconstruct Dante's cosmography in order to establish a hierarchy of ethical, moral or religious (spiritual) values, let us consider the cone, the artist's rendering of the Inferno, as a plane representing the complex of heaven, purgatory and hell. The top, or the wider area, may represent heaven; the middle area, purgatory; the bottom area, hell. In the area of hell, at the lowest point, according to Dante, Satan is frozen in a pool of ice. The chill, Jesse's temporary impotence the night of the reverie, intimates that he is frozen in hell. If heaven symbolizes warmth, happiness, enlightenment, joy, or peace, hell symbolizes the absence of these "virtues." Therefore, the "river-run structure" of Jesse's reverie is flawless in the artistic sense; but what Baldwin depicts in terms of Jesse's sense, ultimately the human sense, is overwhelmingly flawed. Jesse has been under fire—frustrated because of his engagement with the white-black, love-hate thing all of his life. Becoming a deputy sheriff at the age of forty-two, Jesse makes his ascendant step to a rage-sorrow thing that renders him the semblance of a man. And that is what the blacks will confront when they step out to vie for liberty, equality, and fraternity.

Jesse's experience of a lynching at the age of eight comes from a father's will to train a white boy the way he should go so that in later times he will be anchored to the moorings of white superiority. The initiation rites left Jesse, the boy, with too much burdensome knowledge. The coalescence of the good and bad, pleasant and unpleasant—picnic and fire, love and hate—opposites forged into what might be called a single wedge of experience, makes way for a continuum of unresolved conflict in his mind.

The love-hate entanglement that rests upon Jesse's mind is set forth in "Going to Meet the Man" through Baldwin's depiction of outright occurrences under review in Jesse's reverie.

The first important incident in Jesse's life is the lynching of the black man in Harkness who "knocked down old Miss Standish." The excitement in the air, the preparation of food, and the care his mother took in "dressing up" gave Jesse (then an eight-year-old boy) the impression that they were going on a Fourth of July picnic. When he asked his father if they were going on a picnic, his father replied: "That's right, we're going on a picnic. You won't ever forget this picnic."[4] At the lynching, Jesse sat on his father's shoulder so that he could see the black man hanging above the bonfire. The boy saw a man "bigger than his father and black as an African jungle cat, and naked." (P. 246) The boy sensed the value of his chance to observe the "stylized" lynching by the look on his father's face. "His father's face was full of sweat, his eyes were peaceful. At that moment Jesse loved his father more than he had ever loved him. He felt that his father had carried through a mighty test, had revealed to him a great secret which would be the key to his life forever." (P. 248) Later, his father said that he anticipated a night of conjugal bliss after enjoying the lynching and the picnic. The strange kind of horrified fulfillment experienced by Jesse as a boy with his father's prompting may suggest that "there is in this barbaric anti-human rite a genuine primeval satisfaction."[5]

This idea of love in a general and specific way, in connection with the lynching, stands in contrast to the idea of hate in the same way. The idea of love, which enabled the boy to understand his place in the scheme of a Southern bureaucracy, balances with the idea of hate, which he must perpetuate to maintain his place in that bureaucracy. When Jesse was coming home from the lynching, he realized that he had not seen Otis, a black playmate his age, for three days. He asked his father about Otis, and his father said that Otis' people were afraid to let him out. When Jesse said: "Otis didn't do nothing," his father replied: "Otis *can't* do nothing, he's too little. . . . We just want to make sure Otis *don't* do nothing. . . . And you tell him what your Daddy said, you hear?" And the boy answered, "Yes sir." (P. 240) Thus, Jesse is commissioned as a guardian of the white Southerner's trust at the age of eight.

Behind the scene, a moment of personal involvement with the black criminal intensified Jesse's sense of guilt and fear as potently as his father's personal involvement excited sexual passion. During the gelding scene, the crowd screamed because of the horrifying excitement. The sound of the boy's voice is enveloped with that of the crowd, but he is screaming for a different reason. Baldwin writes: "The dying man looked straight into Jesse's eyes—it could not have been as long as a second, but it seemed longer than a year. Then Jesse screamed and the crowd screamed as the knife flashed, first up and then down." (P. 248) The thought of Otis made Jesse sick after the Harkness experience. The pattern was set for Jesse's frustration in the coalescence of the love and hate entanglement. He had loved Otis (the black race), yet he must now hate him in order to perpetuate the ideals of *his* race.

If we follow a chronological sequence, the second phase of Jesse's reverie takes us to the not-too-distant past, when he worked as collector for a mail-order house. His dealings with "nigger" mail-order customers mark the state in his life when he is all-knowing and debonair about race relations. His lessons on race, taught well during the period of orientation, present him now as an authority on the "niggers"; he is sure of their love (respect) for him, and he is sure that they deserve disrespect (hate) because they deliberately choose to be brutes. The issues are seemingly clear: white is white and black is black. Yet the love-hate entanglement persists.

On one hand Jesse saw his black customers as a group of people who enjoyed laughing and talking and playing music when they were not "pumping out kids every five minutes." Seemingly they did not have a care in the world as they stood in the door in the sunlight just looking foolish—seemingly not thinking of anything but getting back to what they were doing. They seemed to appreciate him, greeting him with "Yes suh, Mr. Jesse. I surely will, Mr. Jesse. Fine weather, Mr. Jesse. Why, I thank you, Mr. Jesse." (P. 231) He could easily demonstrate his role then as a Southern patriarch whom they loved. Jesse was sure of that "love." Baldwin writes:

> Hell, they all liked him, the kids used to smile when he came to the door. He gave them candy, sometimes, or chewing gum, and rubbed their rough bullet heads. . . . (P. 231)

And of course, his nights in Black Town with black paramours came with the territory.

But on the other hand, he hated "niggers." They were not progressive: "They had been living in a civilized country for years but their houses were dark, with oil cloth or cardboard in the windows, the smell was enough to make you puke your guts out." (P. 231) He was, therefore, justified (according to his orientation) in demonstrating his authority as a preserver and destroyer of his mail-order customers.

The unexpected assault of a fatherless and nameless black boy on Jesse's whiteness is not only preemptive of the rise of the black man in the generic sense, but also of his rise as an individual who demands dignity for himself (the black male) and for his women as a whole and for each of them, also, as individuals. The scene is brief but important in that it serves as a throttle to reverse the pattern of the love-hate entanglement. The nameless boy says, I love myself but I hate you Mister Charlie. The black boy's love, though, bears a closer relationship to love in its truest sense. It springs from a sense of personal loyalty and devotion instilled in him by "Old Julia" which is of course, untutored. He is able to see through the shambles of Jesse's "love" for blacks and denounces it outright. He considers the white man's "love" as the *raison d'être* for black hate.

"Old Julia," one of Jesse's mail-order customers, was to him "a nice old woman." He had not seen her for years so he stopped to ask a boy, about ten years old, if she still lived in the house.

> JESSE: Old Julia home? . . .
> BOY: Don't no Old Julia live here.
> JESSE: This is her house. I know her. She's lived here for years.
> BOY: . . . You might know a Old Julia some place else white man. But
> don't nobody by that name live here . . . .
> JESSE: Hey! Old Julia! . . . She's gone out? . . . Well, . . . tell her I passed by and
> I'll pass by next week . . . . You want some chewing gum?
> BOY: I don't want nothing you got, white man. (PP. 234–35)

The recollection of his encounter with the boy brought to memory his first assessment of the boy's action—disgust over the antics of a crazy black kid. But then an unspoken vigil between the two of them brought a different impression. Jesse broke the silent combat—their eyeing each other—by calling out, "Hey Old Julia!" He realized that in that moment

> . . . only silence answered him. The expression on the boy's face did not change. The sun beat down on them both, still and silent; he had the feeling that he had been caught up in a nightmare dreamed by a child. . . . It had that feeling—everything familiar, without undergoing any other change, had been subtly and hideously displaced: the tree, the sun, the patches of grass in the yard, the leaning porch and the weary porch steps and the card-board in the windows and the black hole of the door which looked like the entrance to a cave, and the eyes of the pickaninny, all, all, were charged with malevolence. *White Man.* (P. 234)

The young, debonair salesman was made aware of the presence of a "New Negro" who would foster the same old love-hate scheme (thus the "familiar feeling"), but the love (respect) formerly reserved for him (the white race) had suddenly turned to hate (disrespect).

The civil-rights demonstration led by blacks in Jesse's hometown was a typical phenomenon of the 1960s. Blacks who had been in the army knew the tactics of combat and employed them during the rebellion. The sentiment was that dynamite had fallen into the wrong hands, for the once peaceful town was rocked by explosions every night. The night of the reverie, Jesse heard cars as they hit the gravel road not far from his house going to the black college. He knew that the cars were coming from everywhere, bringing people out of the state who would face the lawmen at the court house the next morning.

Baldwin exercises care in portraying Jesse, the deputy sheriff of forty-two who is now a lawman, "the lyncher" in special uniform. Despite the sherriff's faults,

> he tried to be a good person and treat everybody right: it wasn't his fault if the niggers had taken it into their heads to fight against God and go against the rules laid down in the Bible for everyone to read! Any preacher would tell you that. He was only doing his duty: protecting white people from the niggers and the niggers from them selves. (PP. 235–36)

He had never thought of blacks in relation to God or heaven before the confrontation, but the singing blacks helped him to decide that "God was the same for everyone, he supposed, and heaven was where good people went— he supposed." (P. 235) The Jesse who is "the law" must do his duty as a lawman; however, he is no longer the debonair Jesse. He is a refined version of the deputy sheriff in Rulesville, Mississippi, who became "the law" after he had assisted his brother in the Emmett Till murder of 1955.

Jesse, the deputy sheriff, has the job of stopping the black singers. He decides that they can be stopped by manhandling the leader, who might silence his followers to avoid physical harm to himself. His guess is wrong. He puts the prod to the ringleader, who jerks and screams. Big Jim C., Jesse's superior, and his boys had already whipped him severely. Jesse bullies the leader, commanding: "You make them stop that singing . . . you hear me? . . . and you are going to stop coming down to the court house and disrupting traffic and molesting the people and keeping us from our duties and keeping doctors from getting to sick white women and getting all them Northerners in this town to give our town a bad name—!" As he talked, "he kept prodding the boy. . . . The boy rolled around in his own dirt and water and blood and tried to scream again as the prod hit his testicles." (PP. 232–33) He stopped because he had not been ordered to kill the black ringleader.

No doubt the continuous singing of the blacks, the haunting melodies that had dominated his consciousness during the Harkness experience, caused him to rage in order to mitigate his guilt and self-denigration. Even though the leader was still, maybe dead, Jesse continued to rave: "You hear me? . . . You had enough? . . . You had enough? You going to make them stop that singing now?" (P. 233) The singing went on. Impulsively,

> His foot leapt out, he had not known it was going to, and caught the boy flush on the jaw. *Jesus,* he thought, *this ain't no nigger, this is a goddam bull.* (P. 233)

Jesse tried to recall something deep within his memory as the youth passed out. As soon as the leader gained consciousness he spoke to Jesse:

> "My grandmother's name was Mrs. Julia Blossom. *Mrs.* Julia Blossom. You going to call our women by their right names yet. —And those kids ain't going to stop singing. We going to keep on singing until every one of you miserable white mothers go stark raving out of your minds." (P. 233)

The youth passed out again and Jesse remembered that he was the black boy who had insulted him years before. He "wanted to go over to him and pick him up and pistol whip him until the boy's head burst open like a melon. He began to tremble with what he believed was rage, sweat, both cold and hot, raced down his body. . . ." (P. 235)

For all his brutality, Baldwin considers Jesse, the deputy sheriff, a rightful American product. He says in "Notes for Blues,"

> . . . we, the American people, have created him, he is our servant; it is we who put the cattle-prodder in his hands and we are responsible for the crimes that he commits.[6]

He expresses the belief, also, that

> it is we who have locked him in the prison of his color. . . . It is we who have forbidden him, on pain of exclusion from the tribe, to accept his beginnings, when he and black people loved each other, and rejoice in them, and use them . . . .[7]

Finally, he says,

> It is we who have persuaded him that Negroes are worthless human beings, and that it is his sacred duty, as a white man, to protect the honor and purity of his tribe.[8]

If Baldwin can muster the strength to issue these views to account for the making of Lyle Britten, it is certain then that the depiction of Jesse is meant to be sympathetic. His lack of a surname indicates that he is a scapegoat for the white-racist ideal.

The "sorrows" attending Jesse's outrage seem plausible. No one seemed capable of finding the right method to cope with the effects of the black demonstration on the white populace. The men who were his models and had been friends to his father "had taught him what it meant to be a man. He looked to them for courage now." (P. 236) But the ease of former years had vanished. "They were soldiers fighting a war, but their relationship to each other was that of accomplices in a crime." (PP. 238–39) "Each man in the thrilling silence which sped outward from their exchanges, their laughter, and their anecdotes, seemed wrestling, in various degrees of darkness, with a secret which he could not articulate to himself, and which, however directly it related to the war, related yet more surely to his privacy and his past." (P. 238)

Jesse remembered the man in the fire, the boy on the swing, the boy in the cell and realized as he looked forward to another day that the singing of the blacks did not have the obscure comfort of former years. He knew that the young people had changed the words to the song. He knew now that "they hated him, and that this hatred was blacker than their hearts, blacker than their skins, redder than their blood, and harder, by far, than his club." (P. 238) He came to the conclusion that when the young blacks sang they were singing white folks into hell rather than blacks into heaven. Even when he had gained the obscure comfort from the songs from other years, the blacks had perhaps intended to consign him and other white men to hell.

"Going to Meet the Man" dramatizes Baldwin's idea about the confrontation of forces outside and within ourselves to initiate a first step in redeeming our humanity. One virtue of Jesse, the deputy, is that, through the reverie, he faces his experiences and expresses the desire to be born again to more pleasant experiences if not to the reality of universal brotherhood. A somewhat lengthy statement from Baldwin's recent work, *No Name in the Street,* states the value of confrontation:

> The black and white confrontation, whether it be hostile, as in the cities and the labor unions, or with the intention of forming a common front and creating the foundations of a new society, as with the students and the radicals, is obviously crucial, containing the shape of the American future and the only potential of a truly valid American identity. No one knows precisely how identities are forged, but it is safe to say that identities are not invented: an identity would seem to be arrived at by the way in which the person faces and uses his experience. It is a long drawn-out and somewhat bewildering and awkward process.[9]

Blacks, according to Baldwin's idea in *The Fire Next Time,* feel that if outright confrontation with whites fails to assure their rise to power, "at least they are well placed to precipitate chaos and to ring down the curtain on the American dream."[10]

For Jesse, chances seem slim for forging a new viable personality from his own experiences. He decides to use his experiences with black paramours to incite his wife to the abandonment that she might use with a black lover. His desire to be born again is suggested by his desire to drown his disturbing memories in the sensuality that he attributes to lovemaking with blacks. The very suggestion of his ordering his wife to imagine that he is a black lover to insure conjugal bliss from the virginal font, the source of Southern purity, substantiates Baldwin's claim that whites are victims of an uncertainty that leads them to distrust their own reactions. He writes:

> It is this individual uncertainty on the part of white American men and women, this inability to renew themselves at the fountain of their own lives, that makes the discussion, let alone the elucidation, of any conundrum—that is, any reality—so supremely difficult. The person who distrusts himself has no touchstone for reality—for the touchstone can be only oneself.[11]

Thus, the white man is himself in need of new standards to release him from the confusion that bars him from fruitful communion with the depth of his own being.[12]

The final comment on Jesse's desire to "die" in order to become once more a refreshed, if not a renewed, being, is based on his misreading of "sensuality" as a white interpreter of the black experience. Baldwin says that "ironic tenacity" in blacks is, to whites, synonymous with sensuality. "White Americans do not understand the depths out of which such an ironic tenacity comes, but they suspect that the force is sensual, and they are terrified of sensuality and do not any longer understand it. The word 'sensual' is not intended to bring to mind quivering dusky maidens or priapic black studs."[13] In its truest manifestations, "to be sensual," says Baldwin, "is to respect and rejoice in the force of life, of life itself, and to be *present* in all that one does, from the effort of loving to the breaking of bread."[14]

Fire is the symbol of the frustrations in the life of Jesse the boy, the young salesman, and the deputy. His frustrations have prevented him from priming the depths of his own personality because he must do what his forefathers ordained for him. Even though he desires to be freed from the unpleasant experiences caused by the white-black conflict in his native Southern town, he is unable to escape the burden of his heritage. His situation is almost hopeless. According to Baldwin, "the crimes we have committed are so great and so unspeakable that the acceptance of this knowledge would lead literally, to madness. The human being, then, in order to protect himself, closes his eyes, compulsively repeats his crimes, and enters a spiritual darkness which no one can describe."[15] This "spiritual darkness" is beginning to enshroud Jesse.

"Going to Meet the Man," in its bare outline, may be "an angry sermon and a pain-wracked lament . . . which sings the blues for the white man's moral crisis as much as for the black man's frustration and agony"[16] just like

Blues for Mister Charlie. But when Jesse turns to "the frail sanctuary of his wife" for ultimate comfort (regeneration), he becomes Nicodemus the Pharisee, who asked the Master: "How can a man be born when he is old?" Baldwin's answer is in accord with the Christian ethic—he must be reborn or purified in the fire of devastating experiences to forge a better self. This self is "the man" each one is going to meet the next morning and the next night, until he counts his days with "yesterday's seven thousand years."

_____ Baldwin as Playwright

James Baldwin as a Playwright

Carlton W. Molette

At first glance, the whole subject of Baldwin as a playwright seems destined to be rather uncomplicated. After all, he has had only two plays professionally produced, and subsequently published. But the depth of Baldwin's characters simply does not permit uncomplicated answers to questions of some substance. Baldwin's characters—those in his plays—have the same kind of depth and complexity with which the characters in his novels are endowed. After all, he is a novelist; and novelists—the good ones—are supposed to be able to do that: create characters of great depth and complexity. But novels provide ways of delving into character that plays do not have at their disposal. And the concern here is with plays.

I will leave it to the literary critics to examine Baldwin's literature—to examine Baldwin as a writer. I am a theater worker, and I will confine my concern to Baldwin as a playwright, and to the plays that he has wrought. I would further like to emphasize that plays are *wrought,* not written. This is an important concept to reckon with. Writers work wherever and whenever they will. Playwrights must work with and for the other theater workers, or theater-wrights. Plays are events that occur, not words that are written. So, to examine James Baldwin as a playwright is to examine something that only seldom, and quite inadvertently, has to do with things literary. My concerns with any script have largely to do with such questions as: Does it come alive on the stage? Does the action of the play flow smoothly and continuously? Will it hold the attention of the audience? Will it have meaning and worth for the audience? There have been many great writers throughout history who have not been able to *wright* a play that is successful, according to the above criteria.

Remarkably enough, James Baldwin's very first play, *The Amen Corner,* is one of the most successful Afro-American plays that I have seen. The play was first presented at Howard University, and directed by Owen Dodson. At its best, the collaboration of playwright and director causes the work of both to be better than it would have been otherwise. Baldwin's influence upon Dodson and Dodson's influence upon Baldwin have, undoubtedly, made a better theatrical event than either would have been able to produce without the collaborative interchange that took place while the premiere production of *The Amen Corner* was in rehearsal. *The Amen Corner* is built upon the rhythms of the Afro-American church. The action of the play flows smoothly and effortlessly to the rhythms of the language and of the music of the play. This flow of the action includes the transitions back and forth between the three locales of the play. The dominant force in the play is the rhythm. The congregation is swept up in this rhythm. The congregation is compelled to participate. I say "the congregation" because this play is more of a black church ritual than it is a play in the sense that modern Western culture defines a play. So one of the major goals in this particular collaborative effort between playwright and director must be to affect the congregation in a way very similar to that of the black church ritual. This effect might be called a purgation of the emotions. Two of the most important means of creating this purgation of the emotions have already been suggested. First, there is the rhythmic response from the congregation to the events on stage. Secondly, the very response of those who are gathered together reinforces the rhythm and the sense of belonging, of community, of togetherness within the congregation. Both of these are important elements in the traditional black church ritual.

The Amen Corner is also more a black church ritual because of its content. *The Amen Corner* is about love—about the enduring strength that love gives —about the love between (not among) four people who comprise a particular black family. In addition to family love, there is an extended-family love that surrounds the congregation on the stage (the actors) and the congregation in the auditorium (the audience). There is a love that transcends all the petty bickering, the jealousies, the family fights. And this love is made to come alive in the theater via the same ritual techniques that the black church uses. As a black ritual event, *The Amen Corner* works. The first professional production was moving as theater ought to be but seldom is. But was it moving because of something contained in James Baldwin's script? The professional premiere was produced and directed by Frank Silvera, designed by Vantile Whitfield, and performed by a phenomenally impressive cast, headed by Bea Richards. The cast also included Maidie Norman, Juanita Moore, Robert DeCoy, Isabell Sanford, Whitman Mayo, and Gloria Foster. It is highly doubtful that such a cast could have been put together—even by Frank Silvera—if there had been some other meaningful work available to black actors in Los Angeles at the time. But, the point I want to make is this: With a cast like that one, one might be moved by a play that is only mediocre to fairly good. It has happened before. But there have been other productions of this play. The range in production quality has been rather wide. I have seen audiences moved by this play even when it was not particularly well produced. Now, that is something special.

On the other hand, the play is not perfect. And people do expect critics to find fault with things. Ironically enough, *The Amen Corner* is at its worst as a play precisely when it is at its best as literature. There are several two-character scenes between the members of the Alexander family that are true literary gems. They are also the scenes of greatest character revelation. They actually tell us too much about the characters. Now, all that is told needs to be told; but some of it ought to be told through means other than words. That is what actors are supposed to use their "instruments" to do. The emotional tonality of these scenes makes it mandatory that the tempo be slowed; thus, the rhythm becomes less pronounced. On these few occasions, in act two of a three-act play, the action slows down, and the word becomes far more important than the deed. In the theater, that usually means trouble. This is especially a problem with the scenes that involve the father (Luke), because he is confined to his sickbed, making visual interest through movement very difficult to achieve, as well.

Of course, the Frank Silvera production was able to mask this flaw in play construction quite effectively. As the mother (Margaret), Bea Richards was capable of maintaining interest with her voice alone. And the language in these scenes is beautiful and powerful in and of itself. On the other hand, we are frequently told essentially the same thing for several speeches in a row. The use of repetition can work very well when the goal is to create a rhythmic response from the congregation. But in these quiet, introspective, two-character scenes, repetition primarily serves to increase the playing time of the scene. Having pointed out what I consider to be the major flaw of the play, I must add that, when I directed a production of *The Amen Corner,* I was not willing to cut a single one of those words.

I have never directed Baldwin's other play, but I think I would have virtually the same reaction to the words in *Blues for Mister Charlie* if I were placed in a position of deciding on some specific words that could just as well be omitted. I seriously doubt that there are any. One of the most illuminating moments that I have spent in a theater was spent in watching a particular scene in *Blues for Mister Charlie.* This particular scene is a soliloquy. I am sure that, if I had read the scene prior to seeing it performed, I would have said, "It will not work on the stage. It is too long. And besides, soliloquies are no longer acceptable as a principal means of character revelation." Fortunately, I was privileged to witness a truly gifted actress, Miss Diana Sands, perform the soliloquy before I had an opportunity to say all of those incorrect things. But again the question arises, Is it the play? Or did Miss Sands make it work in spite of the script rather than because of it? After all Diana Sands could transform even *The Owl and the Pussycat* into an arresting evening of theater. I am afraid that, in the hands of a lesser artist than Miss Sands, that soliloquy could be transformed from the highpoint to the lowpoint of the play. On the other hand, this soliloquy does not stand out as a readily perceived flaw. The play is too complex, really, for anything to stand out as a readily perceived anything. Again Baldwin has wrought a play in which its worst theatrical characteristics are its best literary characteristics. As a piece of literature, the complexity of *Blues for Mister Charlie* is an admirable trait; as a theatrical event, that same complexity is its major flaw.

But, before we get into the details of the above assertion, let us look for a moment at both of these plays, and the times out of which they grew. *The Amen Corner* is a play of the 1950s. It tells a story of love and hope for a better tomorrow. The story is told in an uncomplicated, straightforward manner. It grew out of the years just before college students were marching, arm in arm, to the strains of "We Shall Overcome." On the other hand, *Blues for Mister Charlie* grew out of the years just before Watts, and the others, burned. *Blues for Mister Charlie* is a "protest" play. It is a complicated, angry play. It is a play that is self-consciously black. When blacks do protest plays, to whom do they protest? To whites, of course. So *Blues for Mister Charlie* is largely aimed at a white audience. This is not intended to imply that the play says nothing to blacks. On the other hand, *The Amen Corner* does not protest to whites; it informs, educates, illuminates blacks. The play was first staged on the campus of a black university. It is not self-consciously black. The play assumes that there are some elementary aspects of black culture that do not require explanation within the body of the play. It assumes, in effect, a black audience. It is not an anti-white play, it is an a-white play.

Blues for Mister Charlie tries to be all things to all people. It tries to explain whites to blacks and blacks to whites. That probably requires two different plays. That is certainly one major reason for the complexity of the play. And, since plays must be absorbed in the span of time it takes to perform them, complexity can be a liability. Conversations among average white audience members in the theater lobby during intermission and following *Blues for Mister Charlie* all seemed to revolve around the fact that there was content that the blacks understood that the whites did not. "What are *they* laughing at?"—meaning the blacks in the audience—the whites kept asking each other. But the reverse situation applied as well. The white characters were frequently not understood, or not accepted as valid, by the black audience members. Actually, blacks did not want to face an essential truth in the character of Lyle Britten. That truth is that Lyle is not some kind of a demonic redneck character. Lyle is *not* a bad guy—just ask Lyle, he'll tell you. Baldwin says, "No man is a villain in his own eyes." So most blacks in the audience were presented with a character that they either refused to admit was there, or refused to admit was true. What they wanted was some kind of wild-eyed, nigger-hating, stereotyped redneck villain. Instead they got a real man who was backed into a corner, not by Richard Henry but by the system.

But that is only one of a number of paradoxes. Richard Henry thinks he must destroy "Mr. Charlie" in order to achieve his own salvation. On the other hand, he knows that the system is programmed to destroy him if he attempts to destroy the man. He knows that he cannot realistically expect to beat the whole system singlehandedly. So he knows that his act of destruction perpetrated against "Mr. Charlie" will inevitably result in his own destruction. Yet he wants to live. He is not suicidal. Still a third paradox. And this one clearly marks this as a statement of 1960s point of view. The leader of the white community and the leader of the black community get together to tell each other how much progress they are making within the system. But even they know that it is a lie.

In addition to these, and other, paradoxes, *Blues for Mister Charlie* is made even more complicated by a number of fluctuations. There are fluctuations in at least three major aspects of the production: time, locale, and acting style. Time fluctuates between time present and time past. The locale of the play also fluctuates between two distinctly different atmospheres. There are black locales and white locales. There is a fluctuation between two distinct acting styles. Most of the performance requires an illusionistic, representational style of acting—one in which the action of the play revolves around relationships between the actors. But there is some fluctuation into the realm of soliloquy that requires quite a different approach, or style, for the actors. When the play moves into the realm of soliloquy, a less illusionistic style is necessitated—one that requires the actor to relate more inwardly to his own character; and at the same time, more outwardly to the audience, but not to the other characters.

Blues for Mister Charlie fluctuates among eight different combinations of these six elements: black atmosphere, white atmosphere, time present, time past, representational style, soliloquy style. If the play is to have its optimum effect upon the audience, the audience must be able to keep up with these fluctuations. Further, the audience must manage this without devoting a great deal of concentration to the effort. After all, primary attention must be devoted to receiving the message, not to determining the where, the when, and the how of the transmission of the message. In spite of all these complexities, the play can work as a play. The inherent complexities do create production problems. Actually, the script would work better as a film than it does as a play. But Baldwin has achieved one very important requisite for *wrighting* a play. Further, this acheivement is undoubtedly why the play works, despite its complexity. Baldwin has not attempted to provide complete verbal transitions for all of these fluctuations and paradoxes.

I am sure that such restraint must be difficult for a novelist to achieve. Such restraint must be particularly difficult for a novelist to achieve because it requires that one artist turn his creative efforts over to someone else before it can be completed. So the transitions are achieved through the use of music, lighting, scenery, costume, and, of course, acting. That requires from the playwright a trust of and a reliance upon many other artists. The ability to accomplish that collaborative working relationship may very well be the reason for Baldwin's success as a playwright where so many other novelists have failed.

Certainly, Baldwin would be an even better playwright if he would gain more experience in the theater. But who can blame him for not doing so? After all, his first obligation is the physical and artistic survival of James Baldwin. Given the present system of producing plays professionally in the United States, we are lucky indeed to get one play per decade from the likes of James Baldwin.

James Baldwin in the Dilemma of the Black Dramatist

_____Darwin T. Turner

In his two dramas—*Blues for Mister Charlie* (1964) and *The Amen Corner*, produced professionally in 1965 but written during the 1950s—James Baldwin reflects two divergent positions of contemporary black dramatists. Ironically, in the earlier of the two—*The Amen Corner*—he more closely resembles Afro-American dramatists of the 1970s than in *Blues for Mister Charlie*, even though the latter play not only aroused sensation among theatergoers in general but also evoked admiration from many blacks.

The issue that distinguishes one group of contemporary black playwrights from another is whether the black writer should direct himself to a white audience—to entertain them, or to educate them about black people—or should direct himself to a black audience—to educate them to awareness of their needs. Many people fail to appreciate the dilemma. They argue that a writer should not concern himself with the cultural or racial identity of his audience. Such an attitude, however, is naive and academic in a society in which blacks and whites cling to differing visions of the realities of black life. What white Americans have learned of black life through Joel Chandler Harris, Thomas Dixon, Margaret Mitchell, and William Faulkner is often their only vision of the reality of that life. Black people know, however, that the white literary view frequently ignores or contradicts the facts of black life. One group's reality is the other group's stereotype.

Traditionally, black writers have directed their works to the white population, either to achieve personal rewards or to serve black people by winning support from whites. This habit has governed black playwrights even more because they have known that they must win box-office support from white patrons. Consequently, Langston Hughes (*Mulatto,* 1935) appealed for sympathy for a mulatto who wants to be identified publicly as his white father's son. Lorraine Hansberry (*A Raisin in the Sun,* 1959) taught that, despite their lack of money, urban blacks possess and practice such revered American virtues as pride, decency, and hard work, and define "the good life" in ways identical to those of American whites. LeRoi Jones (*Dutchman,* 1963) denounced whites who, stereotyping blacks as dull-witted and imitative sexual studs, destroy any blacks who refuse to conform to the stereotype. All these sought to educate white audiences.

In contrast, since 1965 a group of black playwrights, following the lead of Imamu Amiri Baraka (LeRoi Jones), has consciously directed its work toward black audiences in what is called Black Arts drama. Such playwrights propose to educate blacks to awareness of their needs for liberation, either by teaching them to know their enemies or by making them aware of the internal problems of black communities.

In his dramas, James Baldwin has followed both paths of contemporary black playwrights—most consciously writing for white spectators when he seems to be denouncing them (*Blues for Mister Charlie*), most effectively creating for black audiences when he seems unaware of any audience (*The Amen Corner*). Yet the varying reactions to the two plays clearly illustrate the problem of the black playwright. Sensational, melodramatic, and written for whites, *Blues for Mister Charlie* provoked controversy that increased the attention accorded to it. The more thoughtful, more realistic, more credible *The Amen Corner* waited a decade for professional production, then appeared almost without comment. The question that arises is, Can a black be respected simultaneously as an artist and as a faithful portrayer of black life if his reputation depends upon an audience that neither knows nor cares about the world depicted by that black, but is concerned only with the effect of that world on the lives of white Americans?

Blues for Mister Charlie tells the story of Richard Henry, a black youth, who temporarily found success in the entertainment world in the North before drug addiction ended his career. When he returns to his home in the South, he discovers love, which gives him a new strength. But, unwilling to relapse to the subordinate position required for blacks in his community, he provokes a confrontation with Lyle Britten, a white store-owner, whose murder of a black man has been overlooked by white keepers of law and order. Because Richard Henry insults the white store-owner by asserting his own economic and sexual superiority, Richard is killed. The white murderer is acquitted, however, because his wife claims that Henry tried to assault her. The traditional lie succeeds because another witness, Parnell, who considers himself a friend of black people, cannot force himself to deny publicly the words of a respected Southern white woman. As the play ends, the Reverend Meridian Henry, Richard's father, has begun to understand that he cannot depend upon white men of good will to effect improvements in interracial relationships. Instead, blacks themselves must effect the change, and must arm themselves for protection against whites.

When Baldwin wrote the play, protest marches were timely and popular subject matter. Still fresh in the minds of black people was the torture-murder of young Emmett Till* in Mississippi by white men subsequently acquitted by a white jury. Furthermore, the play appealed to many young blacks because Richard Henry was the first black stage character in their lifetime to attack white society boldly.

Nevertheless, *Blues for Mister Charlie* is written for a white audience. It is patterned on the protest tradition, modified only slightly—perhaps because Baldwin remembered that, in earlier years, he had denounced that tradition. Lyle Britten, the antagonist, is treated so gently that, whereas blacks despise him, whites can find sympathy. To blacks he is an arrogant and vulgar brute, characterized by the very lust and coarseness with which racists stereotype blacks. An adulterer, he raped a black woman whom he regarded merely as an exploitable sex object. He murdered her husband when the husband objected to the illicit relationship. Recalling the sexual pleasure he found in the woman, he arrogantly presumes that she found equal pleasure in him. He murders Richard because he cannot hold his own in a verbal duel. Yet he sees himself—and undoubtedly many whites see him—as a good-natured white American who loves his child, works hard at his business, and professes to have no ill will toward blacks.

The wife, whose lie results in her husband's acquittal, is handled less gently; nevertheless, Baldwin carefully provides white spectators with an excuse for her behavior. Conscious of aging into a weak position in the marriage race, she considered herself lucky to find Britten. Now, fearful of losing her husband, she will do anything necessary to protect him.

Other characters familiar to white audiences through literature at least are Parnell, an ineffectual liberal supported by the wealth of his dead father and motivated by the memory of his love for a black girl; Meridian Henry, a minister whose dignity recalls the temper that James Weldon Johnson ascribed to the creators of the spirituals; Richard Henry, a rebellious and arrogant black youth who boasts of the white women he has known; and Juanita, who attracts and inspires Parnell and the Henrys.

*Till was accused of whistling at or flirting with a white married woman. The fifteen-year-old youth was not accused of attacking her physically.

Because of his own belief in the necessity of integration, Baldwin suggests the interrelationship of blacks and whites by stage directions for shadowy images of whites appearing in the background during the black scenes and the sounds of black church services as a background for the white scenes. Less obviously, he suggests the similarity of blacks and whites by ascribing to whites the moral weaknesses stereotypically identified with blacks and by ascribing to blacks the virtues traditionally identified with whites. For example, as I noted earlier, Lyle Britten exhibits the carnality that white society has projected as a dominant characteristic of black men. In contrast, the Reverend Meridian Henry displays the courage identified with whites. Baldwin even draws comparison between Henry's proposal to take a gun to church and the manner in which American pioneers armed themselves for protection against "savages."

Despite the interest of blacks in the boldness of Richard Henry, the play seems to speak more directly to whites than to blacks. *Blues for Mister Charlie,* like works by some white Americans of the 1960s, calls upon the Parnells of America to defend their convictions even if such action pits them against their neighbors. Otherwise, black men of peace and goodwill, like Meridian Henry, must use weapons to defend themselves.

In contrast, although it was written in the 1950s, when many black writers were promoting integration, *The Amen Corner* seems more clearly designed as a drama written about black experience for a black audience. In this respect, it resembles Black Arts drama, in which the dramatist presumes that he must write without concern for the white spectator, who exists outside the black experience and without comprehension of it. I do not wish to imply that Baldwin consciously designed the play for the education of a black audience. Instead, I am suggesting that he found strength in writing meaningfully about an experience he knew while assuming that his audience would be equally familiar with that experience.

The Amen Corner is the story of the lesson in godliness learned by Sister Margaret, a minister who demands moral perfection from her congregation. She disapproves of a parishioner's driving a liquor truck; she wishes her son to have no life outside the church. She even suggests that a young wife consider leaving her husband in order to discover purity in God. Although Margaret considers herself so flawless as a leader that she volunteers to guide a Philadelphia congregation to the path to God, her power is challenged by her son and by members of her own congregation, who envy her position and resent her autocratic rule. Her situation is further complicated by the return of her musician-husband who, she has said, deserted her. Dismayed by discovery of this allegation, Luke, the husband, little by little forces Margaret to recall the past and to perceive the truth that her venture into religion was not a response to a call from God but a flight motivated by her own fear of life. When Margaret lost a child because she was too undernourished to give it life-strength, she blamed her husband. Knowing her need for someone to protect her and finding no such strength in Luke, she fled into a fanatic abjuration of the flesh, into the worship of a merciless God. Simultaneously, because Luke needed comfort, which he could not find in Margaret, he turned to drinking. After her desertion, he tried to forget love by involving himself totally in his musical career, but he knew that a career could not be an adequate substitute for the human love he needed. Despite her efforts to abjure her need for love, Margaret finally admits that her greatest wish always has been to be a woman and a wife. Her discovery comes too late. She loses both husband and career. After Luke dies, her new sense of herself as a human being in love incapacitates her to preach the authoritarian, wrathful message that has enslaved her congregation. Ironically, then, at the very moment at which a new understanding of and compassion for human beings makes her most fit to be a minister, she loses her position. However, hope remains for her son, David. Enlightened, educated by the experience of his parents, he leaves the church, not to flee into music as a refuge (as his mother had fled to a merciless God) but to seek in music a means of expressing his people and their needs.

Freeing himself from the need to create characters familiar to white spectators, Baldwin projected individuals who are known within the black culture: a hypocritical churchgoer who professes to support her minister while she simultaneously agitates and leads a rebellion against the minister; a male gossip who resents female authority. Such freedom of portrayal extends to the major characters. Although Luke, like Meridian Henry, may be somewhat idealized as a man who blends emotion with wisdom derived from experience, Margaret appears vividly as an excessively arrogant, compassionless minister who must learn her humanity and her need for human love.

Baldwin's theme in *The Amen Corner* is not restricted to black people. The need for love and understanding is propounded as emphatically in *Another Country*, where Baldwin shows that white, middle-class people must learn to love each other. This theme, in fact, dominates Baldwin's work: human beings must learn to give themselves totally to other human beings if humankind is to survive. Nevertheless, he seems to develop this recurrent thesis more credibly within the traditionally religious context and church setting of *The Amen Corner* than in the topical, political situation of *Blues for Mister Charlie*.

In short, in *The Amen Corner* Baldwin achieved a success in theme and characterization surpassing his effort in *Blues for Mister Charlie*. His success, I feel, did not result solely from his re-creation of a church setting that was familiar to him but from his presumption that his audience required no interpretation, no modification, because it already knew the cultural setting. Thus Baldwin achieved an artistic freedom rarely granted a black dramatist except when he works within the theater of a black community.

The question raised earlier in this essay, however, remains to challenge the black artist and students of black culture. If the black artist, like artists of any group, writes most effectively about his own culture, how severely is his growth restricted by publishing houses which will promote his work only when it appeals widely to audiences of a different culture? *Blues for Mister Charlie* appeared as a separate volume within a year after its production on the professional stage. *The Amen Corner*, artistically superior, was produced first at a black college, then remained unpublished for many years, until it finally appeared in the Dial Press edition of 1968.

Given such conditions, is it any wonder that most supporters of Black Arts literature disdain efforts to secure production through the established and white-controlled publishing companies? Black artists will remain forever in an untenable position if they must modify their knowledge of black life to conform to the visions of reality maintained by those who have remained aloof from that black life. Yet fame and fortune in America require publication by white-controlled companies and production before white audiences. *The Amen Corner* is art; *Blues for Mister Charlie* earned sensation and money for Baldwin.

A *Note on* Blues for Mister Charlie

Waters E. Turpin

W hen I read the reviews of *Blues for Mister Charlie*, I was tempted to squelch the desire to see it. The chief objection of the critics was that it was "badly written." When with misgivings I finally did see the play, I had my skepticism about critics further justified, for the reason the reviewers tagged the play "badly written" is that they did not know (or didn't care to discover) what the playwright's purpose was, nor did they recognize the manner of its projection.

The play has no direct plotline; rather, its scenes weave in and out of one another like the segments of a nightmare from which one awakes screaming, yet which seizes one immediately as one attempts to recapture sleep. Or again, these scenes flow like the turgid, repetitive rhythms of a syncopated blues that has no end. What other way—authentically—could Baldwin have conceived his piece, considering the material he had chosen? For it is not only a dramatic use of the Emmett Till lynching, but it is also a distillation of all the maimed and lynched, all the brutish sadism of three centuries of the Negro's American experience. It *had* to be a nightmare to be authentic, and it *had* to be a blues, a *Blues for Mister Charlie*.

Baldwin's good fortune was twofold in this production. He had a cast sparked by Diana Sands and Al Freeman as Juanita and Richard respectively—Juanita, who in the trial scene assumes the symbolism of all Negro women here in America who have suffered the loss of their men to the lynchers; Juanita, who cries aloud in anguished hate: "I hope I'm pregnant. I *hope* I am! One more illegitimate black baby—that's right, you jive mothers! And I am going to raise my baby to be a man. A *man*, you dig?"—and Richard, the Emmett Till-like rebel who screams his defiance at his murderer even as the gun spits death into him during the lynch scene. Baldwin also had a sensitive, imaginative director, Burgess Meredith, who must have sensed the phantasmagoria that the playwright had striven to induce. And Meredith also must have been able to realize that, for the Negro, life in America has to assume the fantastic. So for me, *Blues for Mister Charlie* is what its author had to contrive—an expressionistic outcry that captures the distilled agony of this racially tormented, mid-twentieth-century America.

_Baldwin's Raps and Dialogues

James Baldwin
Portrait of a Black Exile

———————————Kenneth J. Zahorski

F or centuries, readers have received great pleasure and considerable mental stimulation from the recorded conversations of the knowledgeable, articulate, and witty. Readers of Boswell's monumental biography of Samuel Johnson, for example, do not soon forget the verbal pyrotechnics delightfully displayed whenever Johnson and his celebrated circle gathered for punch and conversation. Although the recorded dialogue between Margaret Mead and James Baldwin in *A Rap on Race*[1] does not display the genteel polish and urbane wit of many of the Johnsonian exchanges, it does possess an abundance of thought-provoking ideas, illuminating insights, and memorable passages. Perhaps most importantly, however, it provides the careful reader with a deeper understanding of the convictions, values, attitudes, hopes, fears, and biases of one of the most important and influential black writers of the twentieth century.

The fact that we probe so deeply into Baldwin's complex and enigmatic character in this unique work can in large part be explained by the particular techniques used in generating and recording the dialogue between Mead and Baldwin. Those who have tired of reading tasteless and hollow interviews consisting of bland responses to inane questions will happily discover that this sterile approach has not been used in *A Rap on Race*. In a concise editorial note the genesis of this work is explained, and its format described:

> Margaret Mead and James Baldwin met for the first time on the evening of August 25, 1970. They spent approximately one hour getting acquainted. On the following evening they sat down to discuss race and society. Their discussion was resumed the next morn-

ing and again that night. The entire conversation lasted approximately seven and one half hours. It was tape-recorded, and this book, *A Rap on Race,* is the transcript made from those tapes.[2]

The title, *A Rap on Race,* is in a way misleading; it implies that the reader is to hear Baldwin's views only on racial issues. In reality, this is a rap session with a much broader base. Indeed, Baldwin shares with us his thoughts about a wide variety of vital and volatile social, moral, and political issues.

On American materialism: "I have always had a quarrel with this country . . . about the standards by which it appears to live. People are drowning in things. They don't even know what they want them for. . . . You can't sleep with a yacht. You can't make love to a Cadillac, though everyone appears to be trying to. . . . I think the great emotional or psychological or effective lack of love and touching is the key to the American or even the Western disease."[3]

On Democracy: "Democracy should not mean the leveling of everyone to the lowest common denominator. It should mean the possibility of everyone being able to raise himself to a certain level of excellence."[4]

On the American judicial system: "I think that one can make the absolutely blanket statement that no black man has ever been tried by a jury of his peers in America. And if that is so, and I know that is so, no black man has ever received a fair trial in this country."[5]

On violence: "There has always been, perhaps not *only* in America, but certainly in this country, . . . a strain of violence. Violence has always been a kind of door to the whole legend of the Western, the cowboys-and-Indians nonsense. I have always considered that whole legend a kind of insult to the human race. You know, the glorification of the slaughter of people becoming a door to American folklore. It says a great deal to me about this country and about the way people are unconsciously trained—schooled—to accept violence."[6]

But, of course, Baldwin's most passionate concern—nay, obsession—is with race. Very early in his conversation with Mead he confesses: ". . . that one problem is a problem which has obsessed my life. And I have the feeling that that one problem, the problem of color in this country, has always contained the key to all the other problems. It is not an isolated, particular, peculiar problem. It is a symptom of all the problems in this country."[7] And as the dialogue progresses, Baldwin's remarks on race become more fervent, and even prophetic: ". . . the salvation of America lies in whether or not it is able to embrace the black face. If it cannot do that, I do not think the country has a future."[8]

It is with this kind of candor, and conviction, that Baldwin comments on nearly every aspect of the black condition in *A Rap on Race*. He explains the genesis, and significance, of the "Black Power" movement: "You simply find your situation intolerable and you set about to change it, and when you do that, you place yourself in a certain kind of danger: the danger of being excessive, the danger of being wrong. That is the only way you ever learn anything, and it is also the only way the situation ever changes."[9] He candidly discusses the sexual problems connected with race, specifically pointing out how much anguish and frustration the myth of the black man's sexual prowess has caused him and his black brothers: "Then there's the great problem of white women. They come to you for the most part as though you're some exotic—well, they really come to you as though you're some *extraordinary* phallic symbol."[10] And, above all, he eloquently describes the long-lasting effects of slavery, the white man's almost total ignorance of black culture, and the black man's long, tortuous, and as yet unfulfilled, quest for identity and dignity. It is difficult to dispute B. A. Bannon's observation that in *A Rap on Race*, ". . . Baldwin cut loose with some of the most deeply felt and anguished statements about the relations between black and white in America he has yet made."[11]

Integrally related to James Baldwin's attitudes toward the racial crisis are his ambivalent feelings about being an American. Both circumstances are unquestionably responsible for much of his frustration, disillusionment, and despair; and the evidence provided by *A Rap on Race* strongly suggests that he still has not fully come to grips with either his racial or his national identity. Mead discovers this early in her dialogue with "Jimmy" when she remarks in her characteristically positive fashion: "I think one of the very important things you have done is to keep on saying that, after all, you are an American."[12] But Baldwin's response is an unenthusiastic, and clearly reluctant, admission that he simply is "not anything else."[13] He then goes on to explain that he did not truly discover that he was an American until he got off the boat in France at the age of twenty-four. "I became an American in a foreign country. . . . That experience . . . really says something of utmost importance about the moral life of the West . . . : the fact that I had to leave my country in order to realize that I was a part of it, or that it was a part of me."[14]

Baldwin does make it clear, however, that he was not always disenchanted with his native land; he sadly remembers that there was once a time when he believed that America "could [have] become what it has always presented as what it wanted to become."[15] Unfortunately, his hope of better things from his homeland gradually gave way to disappointment as he discovered the grim truth about the black man's slim chances for happiness in America. Baldwin confides that his disappointments began early in life. Harlem, his birthplace and childhood home, he refers to as "a dreadful place,"[16] and a "kind of concentration camp"[17] which not many people survive. His father, he painfully recalls, had to engage in the "most awful kind of hard labor"[18] in order to feed his nine children. And, Baldwin assures Mead, it was not only his parents' suffering that turned him against his country. In a later reminiscence of his youth in Harlem he offers poignant testimony that he suffered more than his own share of pain and humiliation: "When I was ten years old—I'm very small now; when I was ten I was much, much smaller— two cops who were not ten *beat* me half to *death*. . . . I was ten and nearly died because of history written in the color of my skin."[19]

It is reasonable to assume that such agonizing and traumatic experiences would have forced Baldwin into completely forsaking his country while still a very young boy. Not so, reveals Baldwin. His faith in America's potential remained with him throughout the painful Harlem years, and even into his expatriate sojourn in Paris. But all hope disintegrated with the assassination of Martin Luther King, a man he deeply loved and admired: ". . . I am sorry, no matter how this may sound: when Martin was murdered for me that hope ended."[20] And with this termination of hope came profound disillusionment and "exile." It is a strong word, with very strong implications, but it must be recognized as the one that Baldwin uses time and time again in describing his current state of affairs. His final statement on his relationship with America is bleak, and seemingly conclusive: "I am an exile. But I was an exile long before I went away. Because the terms—this is the point, for me— the terms on which my life was offered to me in my country were . . . entirely intolerable and unacceptable. . . . My country drove me out. The Americans drove me out of my country."[21]

The immediate, and long-term, effects of Baldwin's self-imposed exile have for some time been the focus of copious critical speculation. Although this kind of conjecture will certainly not come to an end as a result of Baldwin's revelations in *A Rap on Race,* he does make clear, once and for all, how profoundly important his flight to Europe was in helping him gain a clearer perspective on himself, and on the entire racial problem. Shortly after the initial taping session commences, Baldwin emphasizes the therapeutic effect his stay in Paris had upon him. Evidently, a kind of catharsis occurred there which was to prove vital to his immediate mental and emotional stability:

> I got to France, and everything came pouring out. I started breaking
> up bars, knocking down people. I spent a year in Paris tearing up the

town. Of course, I got torn up too, finally ended up in jail. It took a year—to get to jail, I mean. Even when I was doing it I realized what was happening, but I couldn't stop it. I knew it all finally had to come out. And finally, when I was *absolutely* flat on my back and kind of humiliated with myself because I knew I had behaved very badly, it was over. Something was over.[22]

But clearly something that was not over for the youthful expatriate was his soul-wrenching quest for spiritual identity. It is a self-confessed fact that Jimmy Baldwin turned his back on the church at the age of seventeen, but we know that his concerns and doubts and questions about religion continued to plague him. In the powerfully written final section of *Go Tell It on the Mountain,* John Grimes, with the help of his God, and his friend Elisha, finally "comes through" his threshing-floor ordeal; James Baldwin, the transcript of *A Rap on Race* would lead us to believe, still furiously struggles there. Indeed, he admits that he is still "obsessed" by the "whole question"[23] of religion, and that he continues to view the Christian church as "meaningless."[24] His most vehement and bitter observations on religion, though, are aimed directly at *white* Christians, whom he simply cannot "understand"[25]: "I remember the photographs of white women in New Orleans, several years ago, during the school integration crisis, who were standing with their babies in their arms, and in the name of Jesus Christ they were spitting on other women's children, women who happened to be black, women with *their* babies in their arms. I have never been able to understand that at all."[26]

It would be unjust to leave the reader with the impression that all of Baldwin's utterances in *A Rap on Race* are full of despair and totally devoid of hope. There are notes of optimism. For instance, Baldwin sees hope for his present life, and future, as a result of the fact that he has not forsaken his heritage: "I thought to myself years ago, It is a very good thing that I didn't try to escape from my roots because I would now be in terrible trouble."[27] And later on in the taping session he delivers what is undoubtedly his most optimistic pronouncement: "You know my fury about people is based precisely on the fact that I consider them to be responsible, moral creatures who so often do not act that way. But I am not surprised when they do. I am not that wretched a pessimist, and I wouldn't sound the way I sound if I did not expect what I expect from human beings, if I didn't have some ultimate faith and love, faith in them and love for them."[28]

Unfortunately, these hopeful statements are decidedly in the minority. Hanging over this entire work is the aura of frustration, bitterness, despair, and anguish. One cannot be blamed for wondering if Baldwin ever fully came to grips with himself in Paris. In his exchange with Mead he gives the distinct impression that he is still desperately struggling for racial, national, and spiritual identity. Perhaps these unresolved struggles are at least partially responsible for the kind of disillusionment that Baldwin reveals in the last two paragraphs of the transcript, where he passionately, and eloquently, confesses:

> I don't *really* like my life, you know. I don't really want another drink. I've seen enough of the world's cities to make me vomit forever. But I've got something to do. It has nothing in it any longer for me. What I wanted is what everybody wanted. You wanted it, too. Everybody wanted it. It will come. It comes in different shapes and forms. It is not despair, and the price one pays is everybody's price.
>
> But on top of that particular price, which is universal, there is something gratuitous which I will not forgive, you know. It's difficult to be born, difficult to learn to walk, difficult to grow old, difficult to die and difficult to live for everybody, everywhere, forever. But no one has a right to put on top of that another burden, another price which nobody can pay, and a burden which really nobody can bear. I know it's universal, Margaret, but the fact that it is universal doesn't mean that I'll accept it.[29]

A Rap on Race obviously cannot provide the reader with answers to all the questions that Baldwin's complicated life and complex writings have generated. However, it is a uniquely valuable work in that through it the reader gains a profoundly personal perspective on this renowned black writer. It is true that he has given us intimate glimpses of himself in clearly autobiographical novels, such as *Go Tell It on the Mountain,* and in his highly personal essays, but more of his soul is exposed in *A Rap on Race* than in any one of these other works. Indeed, this contention is supported by Baldwin himself, who, after reading the transcript for the first time, candidly admitted: "It makes me nervous. I'm more naked in this book than I've ever been, but I cannot take it back. It would be dishonest."[30]

Power and Morality as Imperatives for Nikki Giovanni and James Baldwin
A View of A Dialogue[1]

A. Russell Brooks

Nikki Giovanni is a bright light among young black poets, college students, and little old ladies. What does it matter if her luster is somewhat dimmed for "revolutionary-minded" youths, who originally comprised the greater portion of her following? She still attracts an enthusiastic crowd of young and old alike on her poetry-reading and speaking circuits. James Baldwin—essayist, fiction writer, and sometime dramatist—is a light of a different sort. Neither a poet (except, perhaps, in a generic sense) nor a young man, his incisive and searching style has gained for him a worldwide reputation, mainly among the more mature and intellectually inclined, as the Number One Scourge of the America he loves too much to abandon and fears too much to inhabit. Ms. Giovanni, though still essentially militant in outlook, changed almost abruptly from supporter of the black revolution to harbinger of black love. Baldwin in all his twenty-odd years as a writer has appreciably altered neither his intellectual nor his emotional stance on blacks and whites and black-white relations. The Baldwin of 1973 is, by and large, the Baldwin of 1953.

A Dialogue[1] presents nothing actually new in attitudes or ideas from either participant in this conversation that took place in 1971, but it does bring into focus an emphasis which is significant in terms of the direction that their respective careers have taken and are likely to take in the future.

This can be seen in their approach to questions of power and morality, the implications of which might be of value as one attempts to assess their achievement.

The conversation nearly takes the form of an interview, for Ms. Giovanni sparks the talk in the direction that she wants it to take as she introduces all but one or two of the topics and, for the most part, listens to Baldwin's rather lengthy responses. They talk mainly about Baldwin's living in Europe, his "Everybody's Protest Novel," the prevalence of white characters in his fiction, recent black literature, the present generation, junkies, the black man-black woman question, and power versus morality, a topic that Ms. Giovanni brought up more than once. Readers who have high regard for Baldwin's views and much admiration for his powers of expression may, nevertheless, find themselves more curious about what the younger writer has to say, since her image at this time is somewhat more fluid than the older and more solidly established Baldwin.

Baldwin had just praised Ms. Giovanni's generation for their improved attitude toward themselves when she observed that, after all, there were two kinds of people in the world, master and slave, and that it was for her principally a matter of power and not morals. To the question, What does it profit a man to lose his soul and gain the world? she would reply, "The world! That's what it profits him." You can have Jesus, but no matter how polluted the world is, give it to her, "Or I'll take it." Shall we attribute this catchy retort to the irresistible appeal that rhetoric has for her, as also for many of the younger black poets? A brief look at her career up to this point may suggest the extent of her retreat from the advocacy of power, particularly power through revolution.

In *Black Feeling, Black Talk/Black Judgement*[2] she writes in an unnamed poem—"Poem (No Name No. 3)"—that the black revolution is passing Negroes by (*Negroes* as distinguished from *blacks*) and that "tomorrow is too late to properly arm yourself." In a prose piece, "Letter to a Bourgeois Friend Whom I Once Loved (and Maybe Still Do If Love Is Valid)," she wrote that there was no place for emotion in what she must do—upset his world, "even if I don't like doing it because likes or dislikes have nothing to do with what has to be done." In "Of Liberation" she declared, "All honkies and some negroes will have to die." The death of the "responsible Negro" (that is, one who teaches tolerance) she believed was the first step toward her liberation, as she stated in "Concerning One Responsible Negro with Too Much Power." In "For Saundra" she thought it time for her to clean her gun and check her kerosene supply. There is a foreshadowing of a different temper, a different accent, in "Nikki-Rosa," in which Ms. Giovanni said she did not want white people to write about her, for they will probably never know she was happy as a child and that "Black love is Black wealth."

Re: Creation[3] appeared only a few months after *Black Feeling* was issued, but an abrupt change is reflected in the poet's mood and in her conception of her role in life and what she considers worthy of her energies and time. She dedicated it to her little boy Tommy, who has "defined" her nature and given her a new name—Mommy—which now happily controls her life. In "Revolutionary Dreams" she wrote of once having had militant dreams of taking over America, but she woke up and discovered that she would indeed have a revolution if she "dreamed natural/dreams of being a natural/woman doing what a woman/does when she's natural." Some of the poems unabashedly express longing for sex and the joys of its consummation. In *Gemini*,[4] her book of autobiographical essays, she said she did not want her son to be a George Jackson and have to die. Martin Luther King was supposed to have waked the people up. If they are not awake yet, maybe their dreams are too good for us to disturb them. Furthermore, she concluded, black people may not want a revolution, after all. Some of the pieces in this book sound the revolutionary alarm, but they were written *earlier* than the poems in *Re: Creation*.

Ms. Giovanni's latest book of poems, *My House*,[5] moves still further from revolution, from the power idea, and still further in the direction of the wealth that is black love. In "When I Die," her concern is in *touching* a life, for she knows that "touching was and still is and will always/be the true/ revolution." Perhaps this new revolution, like the moat that surrounds the castle of her skin (in "Poem") will free her poetic spirit and be "filled/with dolphins sitting on lily pads and sea horses ridden by starfish." This is the herald of a new Nikki Giovanni, one of light fancy and nimble imagination. We will be on the watch so that we can see to what heights her new freedom of spirit will allow her to soar—and, more importantly, to what profound depths.

As if for the sake of politeness, Baldwin agreed with Ms. Giovanni that if they do not give her the world, she should take it; but he forthwith expounded on the corrupting influence of power on white people, who in gaining the world had lost even the capacity to love their own children. If blacks of this generation stress power and lose a sense of themselves, he went on to say, they would create "another kind of instability" and "become just what white people have become." Ms. Giovanni expressed fear that this was happening to the little blacks she was teaching. They are eager for power, eager to become "fascists"; but maybe all they want, after all, she concluded, is to believe in something. She therefore told them to try believing in themselves.

She and Baldwin agreed that there was with them in this discussion only a semantic difficulty; she would call her concern for these children and for others like them "energy"; Baldwin would call it "morality."

Ms. Giovanni was unwilling to posit the black man's lapses and irresponsiblities on moral considerations, as she and Baldwin talked at some length on this subject, which is complemented by Ida Lewis's Foreword and Orde Coombs's Afterword. Having come from a poor but not poverty-stricken family, she was not fully aware of the cost in sheer manhood of the black man's privations and indignities at the hands of the white man in power—of how, for instance, a man, himself mistreated, could come home and mistreat his own family. Baldwin attempted to meet her difficulty with an impassioned plea (recurrent in most of his writings) for an understanding of the price the black man has had to pay for merely being here, and he posed such an understanding as an indispensable condition of the fulfillment of our responsibility to those who will come after us. Her obligation is, in short, to the "kid," Baldwin's emblematic term for the generations to follow. She can do nothing for the kid, for the future, unless she has a clear knowledge of the past. It appeared that only her mind, and not her heart, reluctantly accepted this explanation as good enough reason for a tolerant attitude toward the black man who gives a woman a baby and then deserts her because he is without the price of a crib and is therefore humiliated for not being able to produce that which, according to the standards of this civilization, a man must produce if he is a man.

Ms. Giovanni wanted to know—"to sum things up"—if Baldwin did not "tend to be optimistic." His answer is the latest *published* footnote to his oft-expressed hope for the black man's ultimate self-knowledge and resulting liberation and the eventual reconciliation between black and white. Believing that we must and will fulfill our responsibility to those who are now taking our place, he replied that he is optimistic when he picks up her kid in his arms and when he looks at her. This optimism, which has deep moral and spiritual overtones, is not a facile and romantic optimism; it is born of intense personal anguish and terror. Baldwin relates in that sad and beautiful (but much too scarce) book, *Nothing Personal*[6] (with Richard Avedon), how he slept on rooftops, in basements, and in subways, and how he was often cold and hungry. "But, my God, in that darkness, which was the lot of my ancestors and my own state, what mighty fire burned!"

Baldwin believes that blacks have learned much by relating to this kind of experience, the kind out of which Aretha Franklin's music comes; and he holds that whites will be unable to escape this fire of being a black American. It will, in fact, be the coming ordeal. "Since I am an optimist," he stated in *Rap on Race*,[7] which carries some of his angriest and most pessimistic utterances, "I think this journey, this ordeal, is precisely where the hope of the West lies—that this, in fact, will change, has to change the Western assumptions, and make it a larger civilization than it has ever been before." It is through his "moral center" that Baldwin arrives at this hope. Having left the church before he was twenty years old and subsequently having been given to irreverent remarks about Jesus, this nevertheless profoundly spiritual man wrote, in *Nobody Knows My Name*,[8] that his idea of being with God meant "to be involved with some enormous, overwhelming desire, and joy, and power which controls you." It was, he said, a means of liberation and not an opportunity to control others. He has never advocated power for blacks except as it should lead to control of their own image and of their future.

Baldwin as Scenarist

One Day, When I Was Lost
Baldwin's Unfulfilled Obligation

_____ Patsy Brewington Perry

*B*aldwin explains that he wrote *One Day, When I Was Lost*,[1] his scenario based on Alex Haley's *The Autobiography of Malcolm X*,[2] because

> I didn't want to spend the rest of my life thinking: *It could have been done if you hadn't been chicken.* I felt that Malcolm would never have forgiven me for that. He had trusted me in life and I believed he trusted me in death, and that trust, as far as I was concerned, was my obligation.[3]

Does Baldwin fulfill his obligation, or does "lost" of the title refer more aptly to Baldwin's purpose than to his subject, Malcolm? In his inordinate emphasis on violence in America; in his transformations of important persons and events; and in his undercutting of Malcolm's contributions, achievements, and potential for achievement, Baldwin lost much of the tone of Malcolm's life. Prophetically, as if he anticipated such a rewriting of his story and attempted to forestall it, Malcolm, after signing the contract for *The Autobiography,* looked hard at Alex Haley and said: "A writer is what I want, not an interpreter."[4] While there is evidence in Baldwin's comments about the screenplay that he took his task seriously, there is considerably less evidence that he heeded Malcolm's desire to keep his story safe from "interpreters."

The original plan was to adapt *The Autobiography* for the stage. Baldwin explains that "he [Alex Haley] and Elia Kazan and I had agreed to do it as a play—and I still wish we had."[5] Baldwin's great frustration resulting from the failure to carry out this plan is registered in his rather bizarre actions. On the very day he "realized that a play on *The Autobiography* was not going to be done, that sooner or later [he] would have to say yes or no to the idea of doing a movie," Baldwin flew to Geneva, Switzerland. Upon his arrival, he discovered that he had "no toilet articles" and "virtually no clothes." Baldwin did have *The Autobiography,* which he read and reread "all weekend long." Admitting that he still would have preferred adapting the book as a play, and realizing that he had made no contractual agreement to write a screenplay, Baldwin nonetheless wired Kazan from his next stop, London, that he was doing the movie. Baldwin's own assessment of himself at this point is: "I . . . was very troubled and uncertain in my own mind."[6]

Baldwin *was* sure about the difficulty of the task that he had assigned himself. He writes: "The problems involved in a cinematic translation were clearly going to be formidable, and wisdom very strongly urged that I have nothing to do with it. It could not possibly bring me anything but grief."[7] Citing George Bernard Shaw's advantages in never having known Joan of Arc and in writing about her only after the riddle of her life and death could be read in historical effects, Baldwin focuses on his disadvantage in writing about a contemporary who has been re-created in many different ways by admirers and detractors alike. And, for Baldwin, even more difficult than filtering through the various reconstructions of Malcolm was accepting the fact of his death. The writer comments on this major obstacle: "The imagination . . . which has been assigned the job of recreating and interpreting a life one witnessed and loved simply kicks like a stalled motor, refuses to make contact, and will not get the vehicle to move."[8]

Despite all the obstacles, however, Baldwin completed a scenario of 280 pages in which he presents Malcolm's life in three stages: the misguided youth who was known as Red and, later, Satan; Minister Malcolm X of the Nation of Islam; and, very briefly, Malcolm El-Shabazz, believer in the true Islamic Faith. Except in the opening scene, Baldwin presents each stage of Malcolm's career in order and follows a basic chronological pattern within each stage. Periodically, however, he interrupts the chronology with images from the past.

Baldwin's message—that the history of American Negroes has remained much the same for nearly four hundred years—is carried by three recurring images from Malcolm's past. Immediately following his identification of Malcolm X, Baldwin introduces these three powerful "inexplicable" images: fire, hooded men on horseback riding between a pregnant woman and her home; a voice shouting, "Brothers . . . Our homeland is in Africa!"; and a one-eyed black man on the streetcar tracks watching his own approaching death. These images do not remain inexplicable very long, for the reader is soon given details enough to fill out the Littles' story. Malcolm's father, the Reverend Earl Little, Baptist Minister and organizer for Marcus Garvey's Universal Improvement Association, is the target of Ku Klux Klansmen who terrorize his pregnant wife, Louise Little, and vandalize their home during his absence. Indeed, one rider warns Mrs. Little of the ultimate outcome if her husband "Keep on stirring up the bad niggers. . . ." Midway in the screenplay, Baldwin repeats the images of fire and death, during Malcolm's struggle to bow in prayer and submit to the will of Allah. Picturing Malcolm in feverish agony both day and night, Baldwin characterizes his sleep by using several metaphors of mental anguish—tossing, sweating, and dreaming. Moreover, Malcolm's dream conjures up sounds of a trolley car, a picture of Earl Little's helpless body on the tracks, and the image of fire engulfing the Little home. Then, as if purified by the fire (which Baldwin describes as having filled the screen), a weeping Malcolm rises from his bunk, kneels, and prays for forgiveness. Malcolm's acceptance of his new position takes on a deeper significance when connected with a foregoing scene in which he reads aloud—"Saul—on the road—to Damascus." Baldwin invites the reader's attention to parallels between the life of Saul, an infamous persecutor of Christians, and that of Malcolm, called Satan by other prisoners because of his complete depravity. As with Saul—who saw Christ in a vision, was blinded, refused food and drink for three days, and finally became a new man called Paul—Malcolm refused to eat, saw the will of Allah in a dream, and became a new man called Malcolm X. Through the juxtaposition of Paul's and Malcolm's experiences, Baldwin strongly implies that Malcolm was compelled to continue his earthly father's work in a manner similar to that which convinced Paul to carry on his heavenly Father's work. Though the parallel breaks down at the point of the faith represented by each convert, it is clear that Baldwin drew upon the Holy Bible to suggest the nature of Malcolm's change and to emphasize his new role as a leader aware of reprisals, just as Paul was aware of the "great things he must suffer" for the Lord's sake. (Acts 9:1–31)

Near the end of the screenplay, Baldwin pushes further the idea that there has been no real progress in race relations in the United States since Earl Little's time. There are no Klansmen on horses, but there are men seated in "a dark car, parked across the street" from Malcolm's home. The 1963 vigilantes do not smash the windows of Malcolm's home with gun butts; they smash them with Molotov cocktails. The resulting fire and reactions to it are the same, however. Earl and Louise Little gathered their children, counted them, watched the fire, and watched the firemen watching the fire. Similarly, Malcolm and Betty gather their children, count them, watch the fire, and wonder where the fire engines are. Seeing the burning house and the trolley car bearing down on his father's body, Malcolm moves toward his inevitable and untimely death. Again, though the instrument of death is different, the result is the same. Malcolm, who, like his father, was often accused of "stirring up the bad niggers," is effectively silenced. The fact that both father and son left pregnant wives whose pleas for family security had been largely ignored for the goal of human dignity points up even more poignantly the sad reality of Malcolm's need to continue his father's struggle. It is clear that Baldwin presents Malcolm's life as a sequel to his father's life—that Malcolm's role as a black nationalist leader advocating a spiritual return to Africa and other nonwhite nations was a duplicate of his father's experience as a black nationalist leader advocating a physical return to Africa. Moreover, because these and other leaders are summarily murdered, Baldwin voices an indictment of America which his readers will recognize as the same one he makes in *Notes of a Native Son, The Fire Next Time,* and other essays. In his comment to white reporters at a London press conference held shortly after Malcolm was murdered, Baldwin charged specifically: "You did it . . . whoever did it was formed in the crucible of the Western World, of the American Republic!"[9] In *One Day, When I Was Lost,* Baldwin makes the same accusation through his arrangement of images in clusters at the beginning, middle, and end.[10] Providing a framework, these images of intimidation and destruction summarize Earl Little's life, foreshadow Malcolm's, and expose what can be read as the unchanging history of race relations in America.

Indeed, Baldwin's screenplay might be studied as an extended figure of speech through which the reader is reminded (or informed) of America's legacy of crime against black people. And there is support in *The Autobiography* for Baldwin's view. Malcolm admits, for instance, that he once cherished his "demagogue" role though he was aware that societies often killed those who proclaimed revolutionary changes. He reports, too, that his father was said to have been murdered for advocating the teachings of Marcus Garvey and that he expected his own death to come before the publication of his life's story. A careful reader of *The Autobiography* knows, in fact, that Malcolm makes such admissions throughout the work, but he makes them in the interest of presenting a balanced, truthful account. It is most unlikely that he would have been pleased to see the "demagogue" or any other *one* of his roles used as the shaping idea in a history of his life.

In addition to Baldwin's images of violence, through which he portrays America's historical guilt in the parallel experiences of father and son, he adds a completely extraneous story of a lynching,[11] and refers throughout the scenario to violent deaths of Negroes at the hands of white people. His heavy use of such reports, especially in light of the fact that violence is the controlling metaphor throughout, seems to suggest that the reader invoke Malcolm's early public image, the virulent preacher of black separatism, as the only antidote to such manifestations of racial hatred. For this implication, Baldwin stands guilty with all the others whom Malcolm charged with refusing to allow him to "turn a corner into a new regard by the public, . . ." Explaining that he was angry still about injustices, Malcolm, nonetheless, saw that human vision could be blinded by anger, and insisted that "both races . . . had the obligation, the responsibility, of helping to correct America's human problem."[12]

It is not impossible to draw a lesson of the responsibilities of both races from Baldwin's characterizations of them, even if one must arrive at the obligations of the white race negatively, but the main thrust of the screenplay is a very loud protest—the kind of statement to which Baldwin objected in the writing of Harriet Beecher Stowe and Richard Wright. In his 1955 book of essays, Baldwin denounced specifically "the novels of Negro oppression written in our own, more enlightened day, all of which say only: 'This is perfectly horrible! You ought to be ashamed of yourselves!' " Baldwin denounced further the sentimentality and violence of *Uncle Tom's Cabin* and labeled Mrs. Stowe's determination in presenting such details laudable only "if we pause to ask whether or not her picture is indeed complete; and what constriction or failure of perception forced her to so depend on the description of brutality. . . ."[13] According to his own criteria, then, Baldwin's screenplay is less than satisfactory. By omitting, rearranging, and adding details, he creates a pattern of violent images which says only, "You ought to be ashamed of yourselves." In an attempt to absolve him of this charge, for which he has so readily indicted others, some readers might plead that Baldwin was circumscribed by ready-made materials—by such statements as those which cite "the racist cancer malignant in the body of America"[14] and, therefore, should not be blamed if his portrayal of a racist society led him to transform Malcolm's story into a drama of protest. Such readers might be silenced by being asked whether or not *The Autobiography* places *emphasis* on violence or reduces itself, through a consciously created pattern of violent imagery, to a single, overall statement of protest.

Baldwin's images do not always function explicitly. In fact, he gives a highly impressionistic quality to the screenplay by organizing events according to auditory, visual, and conceptual associations. For example, when the sight of a blond girl reminds Malcolm of Sophia, the blond girlfriend of his

Boston-New York days, the reader is immediately returned to that time in his life. In a similar manner, when Luther, Malcolm's prison mate and teacher, warns his protégé to eat no pork, Malcolm recalls a childhood scene and his mother's directive: ". . . don't let them feed that boy no pig."[15] Another device that Baldwin uses to telescope time and events is the presentation of images in mirrors of all descriptions: the side and rear-view mirrors of Malcolm's car, dressing-room mirrors, and the mirrors of a shoe store and a barbershop. It may be that Baldwin's wide-ranging use of mirrors was suggested by Malcolm's own statement: ". . . all I have been doing is holding up a mirror to reflect, to show, the history of unspeakable crimes that his [the white man's] race has committed against my race."[16] In any event, at crucial points of recognition or reminiscence, Baldwin mirrors his subject's past, thereby adding variety to the flashbacks that he uses throughout the screenplay.

Beginning his account on the day Malcolm was murdered, Baldwin sets the locale in a panoramic Statue of Liberty-to-mid-Manhattan view before focusing on the New York Hilton Hotel garage. He introduces "a man's long, lean silhouette" getting into a car, and, through its rear-view mirror, the driver's "bespectacled eyes." From the radio there is an announcement that Malcolm X will appear at the Audubon Ballroom that evening; then, following several reflections of traffic and people, Baldwin presents Malcolm X, whom he describes as "bearded, harried, and yet, at the same time, calm and proud." Reminding readers of the crucible in which this man's spirit was fired and the heights that he attained, Baldwin introduces the aforementioned images of violation and death from Malcolm's past and has him reflect upon his recent honors by African nations. Thematic unity is gained through use of Earl Little's Back-to-Africa slogans and Malcolm's pronouncement—"I have come back. After many centuries." In addition, Baldwin uses Malcolm's African experience, at which time the leader was given the name Omowale, to introduce the many names and lives that he embraced.

The first of these lives that Baldwin presents is that of Red, admirer and dance partner of Laura, a beautiful, brown-skinned Boston schoolgirl. The love affair between Malcolm and Laura began when she started frequenting the soda shop where he was employed. Though Baldwin changes the setting of their talks to a beach on Cape Cod, he attempts to retain the storybook quality of their relationship by using such sentimental, wooden exchanges as "You're the nicest girl I ever knew" and "You're the nicest boy."[17] He does retain the successful tactics used by Sophia in luring Malcolm away from Laura. No match for an older, more experienced woman of her own race,

Laura is certainly no match for Sophia, for as Malcolm points out, "at that time . . . to have a white woman who wasn't a known, common whore was—for the average black man, at least—a status symbol of the first order."[18] Unfortunately, this admission simply confirms and augments the general reputation of too many Negro men, but it is to Malcolm's credit that he later regretted his treatment of Laura. True to Malcolm's narration in *The Autobiography*, Baldwin curtails attention to Laura when Malcolm, seeing an attractive, blond white woman, is reminded of the real-life Sophia. Their torrid love affair, outlined in the side-view mirror, fades into a prison scene showing Malcolm (now called Satan) in a fist fight. It is only after these experiences of his Massachusetts days that Baldwin picks up what is the opening paragraph in *The Autobiography*, in which Malcolm describes the party of Ku Klux Klan riders who terrorize his pregnant mother during the absence of his father. Baldwin's opening represents his freest use of the chronology established by Malcolm and Alex Haley.

Readers familiar with the balanced arrangement of *The Autobiography* may or may not discern in Baldwin's chronology an order that effectively reveals Malcolm's life. In any case, chronology is not likely to generate the number of questions for such readers as will Baldwin's omissions, substitutions, additions, and modifications of several characters and scenes.

Perhaps one first notices the absence of members of the Little family. After Earl Little's murder and Louise Little's mental collapse, a reader of Baldwin's scenario is led to believe that Malcolm is the sole functioning member of the family. Actually, Malcolm was one of eight children born to the Reverend Earl and Louise Little; in addition, he had two half sisters and one half brother, his father's children by a previous marriage. While it is unlikely that any dramatist would attempt to cast such a great number of siblings, it is reasonable to expect the inclusion of those who were most influential in his subject's life. Ella, Malcolm's half sister, and Reginald, his younger brother just below him, certainly fall within this description. Impressed with Ella from the time of her first visit to the Littles' home in Lansing, Malcolm credits her with having revived in him the meaning of family. He loved hearing her say, "We Littles have to stick together." And when she suggested that they all come with her to visit their mother at the State Mental Hospital, he and the others felt that if anyone could help their mother, it would be Ella.[19] Toward the end of his eighth-grade school year, Malcolm began writing to Ella nearly every other day and finally asked if he could come to Boston to live with her. "No physical move in my life," says Malcolm, "has been more pivotal or profound in its repercussions."[20] When, despite Ella's advice, Malcolm began associating with hustlers and was later imprisoned on charges of burglary, she did not forsake him. She was, in fact, Malcolm's first visitor in prison and, in 1948, succeeded in getting him transferred to the Norfolk, Massachusetts, Prison Colony, an experimental rehabilitation jail. Upon his release from prison, in August, 1952, Ella was the person to whom he turned. And near the end of his life, having received only his expenses and a modest allowance as Minister in the Nation of Islam for nine years, Malcolm still relied upon her. He explains:

> I took a plane to Boston. I was turning again to my sister Ella. Though at times I'd made Ella angry at me, beneath it all, since I had first come to her as a teen-aged hick from Michigan, Ella had never once really wavered from my corner.
> "Ella," I said, "I want to make the pilgrimage to Mecca."
> Ella said, "How much do you need?"[21]

The relationship between Malcolm and Ella was indeed important. He refers to her as his "favorite" sister and describes her as "proud" and "commanding," "a *strong* big, black Georgia-born woman." Finally, he re-emphasizes her importance to him: "She had played a very significant role in my life. No other woman ever was strong enough to point me in directions; I pointed women in directions. . . ."[22] It is regrettable that Ella has no place in Baldwin's screenplay.

Reginald, too, figured very prominently in Malcolm's life. From their early childhood days there was a strong bond between these two brothers, which was strengthened when their mother became ill and, according to Malcolm, "Reginald came under my wing."[23] It was not until after Malcolm's imprisonment, when Reginald became the protector, however, that their mutual love and respect produced the most far-reaching effects: Malcolm's acceptance of Elijah Muhammad's version of Islam. After their oldest brother, Philbert, failed in his attempt to interest Malcolm in the Nation of Islam, the Chicago/Detroit Littles decided that "Reginald, the latest convert, the one to whom [Malcolm] felt closest, would best know how to approach" him. Reginald wrote: "Malcolm, don't eat any more pork, and don't smoke any more cigarettes. I'll show you how to get out of prison."[24] Willing to try anything that would secure his release, Malcolm followed instructions. Moreover, when Reginald visited, Malcolm listened as his younger brother "talked for two solid hours" leaving him "rocking with some of the first serious thoughts [he] had ever had. . . ." Malcolm comments on the reason his brother's plan worked: "Reginald knew how my street-hustler mind operated. That's why his approach was so effective."[25] Indeed, Reginald's plan to convert Malcolm, beginning with small demands that his brother refrain from smoking and eating pork, succeeded to the degree that Malcolm accepted completely and worked unselfishly for the Nation of Islam up to the last year of his life. How could one so very influential in Malcolm's life be omitted?

This question may be answered, in part, by examining the substitutions that Baldwin makes in his scenario. He uses a prisoner named Luther, for instance, to play a part of the role (introducing Malcolm to Islam) that Reginald played in real life. Employing Reginald's basic approach, Baldwin has Luther explain to another inmate the reason that Malcolm is always fighting: "He don't dig being locked up."[26] Later, when Luther and Malcolm are alone, Luther acts on this insight:

LUTHER: ... I can show you how to get out of prison.

....

MALCOLM: How?
       close up: LUTHER, *calculating.*
       close up: MALCOLM, *tense. He shakily lights a cigarette.*
LUTHER: First thing you got to do: you can't eat no more pork.

....[27]

And another thing: when you finish that cigarette—don't smoke any more.[27]

In Baldwin's scenario, it is Luther instead of Reginald who talks for hours about the faith and watches for the doctrines to "take."

In another substitution using Luther, Baldwin, who never names Elijah Muhammad in the screenplay, presents as Luther's many of the words, actions, and relationships that, according to Malcolm, were Elijah Muhammad's. Malcolm describes, for example, his visit to Elijah Muhammad after the publication of a Los Angeles wire-service story concerning paternity suits brought against Mr. Muhammad. He explains that he outlined what was being said and announced that he and Wallace, Mr. Muhammad's son, had found in the Quran and the Bible passages that might be presented to Muslims as fulfillment of prophecy. According to Malcolm, Mr. Muhammad replied:

> "Son, I'm not surprised. . . . You always have such a good understanding of prophecy, and of spiritual things. You recognize that's what all of this is—prophecy. . . .
>
> "I'm David," he said. "When you read about how David took another man's wife, I'm that David. You read about Noah, who got drunk—that's me. You read about Lot, who went and laid up with his own daughters. I have to fulfill all of those things."[28]

In Baldwin's scenario, Luther stands as the accused and presents a similar defense:

LUTHER: ...King David is still King David, even though he slept with Bathsheba and murdered many men. People don't remember that. They remember King David, who wrote the Psalms. People don't remember Noah's drunkenness and nakedness. They remember that he built the ark. People know what you don't know, Malcolm—what's written is written. . . . [29]

Another example of the substitution of Luther in the Elijah Muhammad role can be seen in the ninety-day silencing of Malcolm after his comment concerning the John F. Kennedy assassination. Malcolm, seated in Elijah Muhammad's living room, is being reprimanded:

"That was a very bad statement," he said. "The country loved this man. The whole country is in mourning. That was very ill-timed. A statement like that can make it hard on Muslims in general."

And then, as if Mr. Muhammad's voice came from afar, I heard his words: "I'll have to silence you for the next ninety days—so that Muslims everywhere can be disassociated from the blunder."

I was numb.

But I was a follower of Mr. Muhammad. Many times I had said to my own assistants that anyone in a position to discipline others must be able to take disciplining himself.

I told Mr. Muhammad, "Sir, I agree with you, and I submit, one hundred per cent."[30]

The same episode in Baldwin's scenario is set in Luther's living room:

LUTHER: A statement like that can make it very hard on all Muslims—do you realize that?

MALCOLM: No. I don't really see that. Maybe you ought to spell it out to me a little.

LUTHER: Malcolm, the whole country loved this man. The whole country is in mourning.

....

. . . You were directed to say nothing and you disobeyed. How can you expect to discipline others if you are not disciplined yourself? . . . The Leader—the Honorable Messenger—has instructed me to inform you that you have been silenced for ninety days. That will give us time to dissociate all Muslims from your blunder.

MALCOLM: I will go to the Honorable Messenger myself and tell him that I agree. I agree one hundred per cent.

LUTHER: I have already told him that. [31]

Luther's last line draws attention to the substitution of roles—Baldwin's Luther/Honorable Messenger for that of Malcolm's Elijah Muhammad— almost as forcefully as does his use of the words and situation that here and elsewhere Malcolm presented as Elijah Muhammad's. Moreover, the Honorable Messenger, though referred to, as in the passage above, never actually appears in the scenario. It is likely that Baldwin felt the need to be tactful in his representation of the Messenger of Allah, and one can certainly appreciate the difficulties that would present themselves in casting the role. Perhaps substitution was the answer, but the price of this and other substitutions is very great. Quite clearly, the screenplay becomes a kind of chronicle in which some details of Malcolm's life are preserved while others, possibly some of the most meaningful ones, are either omitted or altered.

Baldwin's omissions and/or substitutions of characters whom Malcolm and Haley pictured as important perhaps necessitated some of his additions of characters and scenes. Three characters who have no counterparts in *The Autobiography* are Daniel, a young man with whom Laura lives in New York; Ada, West Indian Archie's girlfriend; and Lorraine, Luther's wife. These created personages give rise to scenes that, of course, are not in *The Autobiography*. For example, Ada, described as an "ageing, good-natured whore," gives Malcolm information concerning both Laura and Daniel, whom they encounter at a Harlem bar. Happy to see Laura, Malcolm buys drinks "for old times' sake."[32] Aside from the fact that Ada and Daniel are "new" characters, there is no evidence in *The Autobiography* that Malcolm has a New York reunion with Laura. Similarly, Baldwin's addition of Lorraine results in Malcolm's relating to an individual in a setting originating outside *The Autobiography*. The addition of Lorraine is unfortunate in still another way, for never was a female created for so little purpose. Having added Luther, Baldwin felt, I suppose, that Luther must have a family. Lorraine, however, is not even allowed to function fully in the role accorded to women by the Holy Bible, and Baldwin (son of a preacher and child-preacher himself), certainly knows the Bible. Though she is the nominal wife and mother, Lorraine neither converses or interacts appreciably with Luther or her son, Sidney. Relating only to Malcolm, she asks him questions concerning the Movement, sends Sidney to get a piece of cake for their guest, and assures Malcolm that he will make a wonderful husband for Betty. Given the words, a porpoise could have performed as well! The conclusion that Baldwin does not adequately portray women characters, except harlots and others of that kind, forces itself, especially when the reader compares the portrayal of Lorraine with that of Ada, Baldwin's other female addition to the screenplay. Though Ada appears in only one scene, she is indelibly imprinted on the reader's memory. The hustler-type personality breaks through in her opening remarks to Malcolm:

ADA: I just knew my prayers was going to be answered. Because, I got a hole in my
       shoe, you know? And I just did not feel like tempting them nasty elements.

Ain't them elements nasty?—And here you come, with your big handsome self, just like you know how tired and thirsty your Ada was.—Sit down, sugar, and buy me a little sustenance. [34]

Thus, in one scene, Ada wins a higher number of points for vitality, ingenuity, and other human qualities than Lorraine can claim from both her scenes. In his screenplay, as in his fiction, Baldwin demonstrates a weakness in portraying the female in a healthy, normal relationship with the opposite sex, especially in lawful wedlock. It is unfortunate that he added Lorraine, since, in his hands, she is such a mechanical nonentity, exhibiting no distinct personality and serving only to weaken the scenario. (It might be noted also that Baldwin does little better in his portrayal of Malcolm's relationship with his young sweetheart, Laura, or with his wife, Betty.)

Finally, Baldwin's version of Malcolm's *Autobiography* includes the modification of several names, scenes, and relationships. Baldwin uses, for instance, "Flower of Islam"[35] instead of "Fruit of Islam," the name given to young men trained to accept the responsibilities of the Muslim home, community, and nation. Two scenes—Malcolm's first "conk" and his receipt of a conservative outfit from Archie—undergo several changes. Malcolm describes his purchasing ingredients for the "congolene" and taking them to Shorty's room, where his friend processes his hair.[36] In Baldwin's scenario, the same scene takes place in a barbershop.[37] While the barbershop is a natural setting for processing hair, it is highly probable that Baldwin's real reason for relocating this scene was to take advantage of what he himself calls "a kind of hallelujah chorus, or amen corner," of five or six men who are being entertained by a barber's salacious, profanity-riddled monologue. Shorty's entrance with the hair preparations provides new excitement for them, and, in the manner of a Greek chorus, they interpret events, voice approval, and help to relieve the tension with their laughter when Malcolm's ordeal is over. In the second scene mentioned, Malcolm gives an account of Archie's move to "tone down" his wardrobe which emphasizes the subtle, indirect approach used by hustlers aware of the dangers of flamboyance. He explains that Archie measured him, jotted the figures in a notebook, and had waiting for him, on the next day, an expensive, conservatively cut dark blue suit. Baldwin transforms this scene, making it more direct and dramatic:

ARCHIE: ...Get out of them pants, ain't nobody going to take you seriously if you walk around looking like that. You see the way I dress, don't you? Try these, look like your size. . . . [38]

In both these scenes, Baldwin creates a great deal more action (highly desirable, of course, in a screenplay) than is present in *The Autobiography*.

Moreover, he converts Malcolm's descriptions into vivid drama without violating the story. The effectiveness of these and other brief scenes, such as that between Malcolm and Mr. Ostrovski,[39] support the conclusion that Baldwin's forte in the drama is the short, isolated scene that makes a definite point.

A relationship that Baldwin handles with a difference is that between Malcolm and Shorty. Malcolm describes their friendship as having begun in Boston.[40] For no good reason, however, Baldwin pictures them as friends in Lansing, Michigan, before either one had lived in Boston.[41] Unless there is a premium on explicitness in conversation about sex, the topic of Malcolm's and Shorty's only Michigan meeting, Baldwin might have remained faithful to the original, thereby sparing the reader this scene. Still another relationship that Baldwin alters is that between Malcolm and the weekly newspaper that he conceived, established, and named. In describing steps toward the realization of his goal, Malcolm explains that he learned how a newspaper was put together in the office of the Los Angeles *Herald Dispatch* in 1957. Upon his return to New York, he bought a secondhand camera, taught himself to use it, and began writing interesting news about the Nation of Islam. Once each month, he assembled his articles and pictures for the newspaper, which he named *Muhammad Speaks*.[42] In Baldwin's screenplay, Sidney is in charge of the newspaper from the outset. He and Luther explain its purpose after Malcolm has indicated an interest in working on it:

SIDNEY: What it is, Malcolm—it's really a community newspaper—to let black people know what's going on in the black community—what they're doing themselves—
LUTHER: And what they can do. And what they've got to do.[43]

In Betty's subsequent comment that Malcolm and Sidney were the persons who "practically created this paper,"[44] Malcolm still gets only fifty percent of the credit due him. This undercutting of his influence is just one example of his generally shriveled powers that Baldwin represents in the screenplay.

In another example of his reduced status in Baldwin's account, Malcolm, second only to Mr. Muhammad in real life, is relegated to the third place, following the Honorable Messenger and Luther. Despite his lower position, however, Malcolm's qualities as a religious and political leader prove to be far greater than those possessed by Luther. And in Malcolm's comment to Luther, " . . . I know I'm better than you,"[45] it is as if Baldwin, in protest against the hierarchy that he himself established, attempts to reinstate Malcolm to his original position. Whether or not this is the case, Baldwin's presentation of Malcolm as less than he was at any stage is disappointing.

Baldwin undermines Malcolm's complex nature in still another way. In his presentation of Malcolm's last year there is only a brief mention of the new interracial, international, and political perspectives that led to Malcolm's crowning achievement—his work to internationalize the struggle for human rights. This wide-ranging plan, though incomplete at the time of his death, attests to Malcolm's vast potential for initiating programs that might have produced meaningful results for the exploited and oppressed peoples of the world.

Perhaps Baldwin's failure to provide adequate evidence of Malcolm's stature as a man and a leader accounts for the vacuous quality of the scenario as a whole. Though he faithfully preserves in Malcolm's program of self-education both the activism and the mental vitality that led him to become the outstanding religious and political leader that he was, Baldwin does not continue measurably to reveal Malcolm's character through his actions. The reader misses such realistic details as Malcolm's resignation from the Ford Motor Company so that he could work as a full-time minister; his intense training period, during which he learned the worship rituals, organization, and administrative procedures of the Nation of Islam, and the interrelated meanings of the Bible and the Quran; and his establishment of temples in Philadelphia; New York City; Boston and Springfield, Massachusetts; Hartford, Connecticut; and Atlanta, Georgia. The question which comes to mind is whether it is Baldwin's inability to handle the dramatic form or his impatience with details which causes him to substitute comments *about* Malcolm for Malcolm's actions. It is readily apparent to any careful reader that the illumination of Malcolm's character in two action scenes—his handling of a potential riot following Brother Hinton's brutal beating by policemen and his answering charges that Black Muslims represent reverse racism[46]—far outweighs the insight gained from dozens of comments *about* his influence and contributions. Sidney's evaluation, "Malcolm practically made the Movement what it is today," and Betty's observation that "Malcolm's given his life to the Movement"[47] do not convince; they succeed only in making more noticeable the absence of a sufficient number of scenes in which these truths could be revealed.

The double disappointment of finding many aspects of Malcolm's character hastily summarized and others omitted entirely is intensified when the reader realizes that characterization suffers, possibly, because of Baldwin's single-minded efforts toward developing the theme of violence, and that this theme stands naked and practically inviolate. On this point, *One Day* loses completely the positive spirit of *The Autobiography,* which demonstrates that Malcolm's energetic, searching nature was dedicated to ending violence "by any means necessary," including violence, world pressures against America's racist policies, and an appeal to the United Nations to secure rights for all men under international law. For Baldwin to deny his readers the fullness of Malcolm and, at the same time, to use Malcolm's story to make a statement that he has already made time and again in the essays is indefensible. Readers might willingly suspend disbelief in reference to the omission of some of Malcolm's family members, the relocation of scenes, or even the rearrangement and telescoping of events so that a pattern could be established, but they might conclude, as did this reader, that Baldwin asks too much if, in return, he gives just a watered-down version of Malcolm and a message to America which says only, "You ought to be ashamed of your-selves!" While I fully concur with the truth and urgency of Baldwin's mes-sage, I maintain that it does not begin to encompass or even suggest the meaning of Malcolm, who was, first of all, a man of noble proportions. In this respect, Baldwin failed in his obligation to Malcolm, his contemporaries, and his heirs.

Notes

James Baldwin: The Political Anatomy of Space
Donald B. Gibson

[1]This essay is based on earlier explorations of Baldwin's politics, which I undertook in the introduction to *Five Black Writers: Essays on Wright, Ellison, Baldwin, Hughes and LeRoi Jones* (New York: New York University Press, 1970), pp. xix–xxiii; and in "The Politics of Ellison and Baldwin," *The Politics of Twentieth-Century Writers*, ed. George Panichas (New York: Hawthorne Publishing Company, 1971), pp. 307–20.

[2]Arthur Schlesinger, Jr., *A Thousand Days* (Boston: Houghton Mifflin Company, 1963), pp. 962–63.

[3]"Power is the arena in which racism is acted out . . . ." James Baldwin, *No Name in the Street* (New York: Dial Press, 1972), p. 93; "And that battle [school decentralization] is what is really the crucial battle going on now in the world: to get out of the hands of the people who have the means of production and the money, to get it out of their hands and into the hands of the people at various local levels so that they can control their own lives." Margaret Mead and James Baldwin, *A Rap on Race* (Philadelphia: J. B. Lippincott Company, 1971), p. 134.

[4]Baldwin is in a long line of black interpreters of racism who have seen it as a moral problem and whose chief strategy has been to point out the disparity between American ideals and American practices. I think it fair to say that most black critical commentators on the problem from the nineteenth century to the present have so interpreted it.

[5]James Baldwin, *The Fire Next Time* (New York: Dial Press, 1963), pp. 119–20.

[6]Mead and Baldwin, *A Rap on Race*, pp. 174–75.

[7]James Baldwin, *Go Tell It on the Mountain* (New York: Alfred A. Knopf, 1953), p. 274. Subsequent quotations are from this edition.

[8]For an alternative explanation see Colin MacInnes' "The Dark Angel: The Writings of James Baldwin," reprinted in *Five Black Writers*, pp. 127–28. MacInnes believes the characters are white because the story takes place in a predominantly white milieu.

[9]James Baldwin, *Giovanni's Room* (New York: Dial Press, 1956), p. 208. Subsequent quotations are from this edition.

[10]MacInnes agrees in "The Dark Angel," pp. 128–29.

[11]Margaret Mead and James Baldwin argue this point in *A Rap on Race*, pp. 222–26.

[12]Baldwin has discussed the idea of love countless times. In his fictional analysis of human relationships, the capacity to love is *always* central. *Another Country* is fraught with references to characters wanting love, lacking love, capable or incapable of loving. Baldwin discusses the idea of love in *A Rap on Race*, p. 184, where he says, "I think love is the only wisdom."

[13]James Baldwin, *Another Country* (New York: Dial Press, 1962), p. 22. Subsequent quotations are from this edition.

[14]"The only significant realities [in *Another Country*] are individuals and love, and . . . anything which is permitted to interfere with the free operation of this fact is evil and should be done away with." Norman Podhoretz, "In Defense of James Baldwin," *Five Black Writers*, p. 145.

[15]James Baldwin, *Tell Me How Long the Train's Been Gone* (New York: Dial Press, 1968), p. 22. Subsequent quotations are from this edition.

[16]These terms, originally from W. H. Auden's *New Year Letter*, are used as critical terms in the way I have used them here in Nathan Scott's "The Dark and Haunted Tower of Richard Wright," *Five Black Writers*, pp. 17–18.

[17]I would not insist on this point, but frequent instances of self-abnegation on Leo's part, derogation of a racial character referring to blackness, would suggest the relation of race to this cluster of values.

Baldwin and the Problem of Being
George E. Kent

[1]James Baldwin, "As Much Truth As One Can Bear," *New York Times Book Review*, January 14, 1962, p. 1.

[2]James Baldwin, *Notes of a Native Son* (Boston: Beacon Press, 1955), p. 15.

[3]*Ibid.*, p. 23.

[4]"What's the Reason Why: A Symposium by Best Selling Authors," *New York Times Book Review*, December 2, 1962, p. 3.

[5]Ralph Ellison, "The Charlie Christian Story," *Saturday Review*, May 17, 1958, p. 42.

[6]James Baldwin, *The Fire Next Time* (New York: Dial Press, 1963), p. 66.

[7]"James Baldwin: An Interview," *WMFT Perspective*, December, 1961, p. 37.

[8]*Ibid.*

[9]Baldwin, *Notes of a Native Son*, p. 24.

[10] James Baldwin, *Go Tell It on the Mountain* (New York: Alfred A. Knopf, 1953), p. 35.

[11] *Ibid.*, p. 37.

[12] Baldwin, *Notes of a Native Son*, p. 38.

[13] Baldwin, *Go Tell It on the Mountain*, p. 210.

[14] *Ibid.*, pp. 225–26.

[15] *Ibid.*, p. 161.

[16] James Baldwin, "Preservation of Innocence," *Zero*, Summer, 1949, pp. 18–19.

[17] James Baldwin, *Nobody Knows My Name* (New York: Dial Press, 1961), p. 161.

[18] *Ibid.*, p. 162.

[19] James Baldwin, *Giovanni's Room* (New York: Dial Press, 1956), p. 12.

[20] Ralph Ellison, "Society, Morality, and the Novel," in *The Living Novel*, ed. Granville Hicks (New York: Macmillan, 1957), p. 61.

The Ironic Voice in Baldwin's *Go Tell It on the Mountain*
Shirley S. Allen

[1] James Baldwin, *Go Tell It on the Mountain* (New York: Dell Publishing Company, 1953), p. 44. Further references to the novel, given in the text, are to this paperback edition, since the original Dial Press edition is hard to find and differs in pagination from the 1963 Dial edition.

[2] "The Question of Moral Energy in James Baldwin's *Go Tell It on the Mountain*," *CLA Journal* 7 (March, 1964): 219, 221, 223. Much of Graves's argument rests on his contention that the rest of the novel is "absent of this sort of irony." He infers that Baldwin is too deeply involved with these two characters to give them objective life.

[3] A majority argue that the conversion is a trap into which John falls because of "the unsubduable propensity for religious hysteria implanted in him by his nurture," in the words of Nathan A. Scott, "Judgment Marked by a Cellar: The American Negro and the Dialectic of Despair," in *The Shapeless God,* ed. H. J. Mooney and T. F. Staley (Pittsburgh: University of Pittsburgh Press, 1968), p. 160. See also D. E. Foster, " 'Cause my House Fell Down'; the Theme of the Fall in Baldwin's Novels," *Critique: Studies in Modern Fiction* 13, No. 2 (1971): 51; H. M. Harper, *Desperate Faith* (Chapel Hill: University of North Carolina Press, 1967), pp. 144–45; George E. Kent, "Baldwin and the Problem of Being," *CLA Journal* 7 (March, 1964): 204; Robert A. Bone, "The Novels of James Baldwin," *Tri-Quarterly* No. 2 (Winter, 1965):7; Colin MacInnes, "Dark Angel: The Writings of James Baldwin," *Encounter,* August, 1963, pp. 22–23; Marcus Klein, "James Baldwin: A Question of Identity," in *After Alienation: American Novels in Mid-Century* (Cleveland: World Publishing Company, 1962), pp. 180–82.

[4] One of the first reviewers, J. H. Raleigh, *New Republic,* June, 1953, p. 121, complained that "the final impact of the novel is somewhat muffled." Many subsequent critics have shared this view including Michel Fabre, who calls it an "impossible dénouement" in "Pères et Fils dans *Go Tell It on the Mountain* de James Baldwin," *Etudes Anglaises*, 23 (January–March, 1970): 54.

[5]David Noble, *The Eternal Adam and the New World Garden* (New York: George Braziller, 1968), p. 211.

[6]Scott, "Judgment Marked by a Cellar," pp. 160–161.

The Phrase Unbearably Repeated
Eugenia W. Collier

[1]James Baldwin, *Another Country* (New York: Dial Press, 1962), p. 8.

[2]*Ibid.*, pp. 8–9.

[3]James Baldwin, "The Discovery of What It Means to Be an American," in *Nobody Knows My Name* (New York: Dial Press, 1961), p. 5.

[4]"Alas, Poor Richard," *Ibid.*, p. 184.

[5]The Black Boy Looks at the White Boy," *Ibid.*, pp. 230–31.

[6]Baldwin, *Another Country,* p. 49.

[7]*Ibid.*

[8]*Ibid.*

[9]*Ibid.*, p. 49.

[10]*Ibid.*, p. 51.

[11]*Ibid.*, p. 54.

[12]*Ibid.*, pp. 72–73.

[13]*Ibid.*, pp. 81–82.

[14]*Ibid.*, p. 256.

If Baldwin's Train Has Not Gone
William Edward Farrison

[1]Fern Marja Eckman, *The Furious Passage of James Baldwin* (New York: M. Evans and Company, 1966), p. 235. Dan Georgakas. "James Baldwin . . . in Conversation," in *Black Voices: An Anthology of Afro-American Literature,* ed. Abraham Chapman (New York: New American Library, 1968), p. 661.

The Evolution of James Baldwin as Essayist
Nick Aaron Ford

[1]James Baldwin, *Notes of a Native Son* (Boston: Beacon Press, 1955), pp. 6–7. All subsequent references to this work will appear in parentheses in the text.

[2]Eldridge Cleaver, *Soul on Ice* (New York: McGraw-Hill, 1968), p. 105.

[3]James Baldwin, *Nobody Knows My Name* (New York: Dial Press, 1961), p. xiii. All subsequent references to this work will appear in parentheses in the text.

[4]Nick Aaron Ford, "Battle of the Books," *Phylon* 22 (Second Quarter, 1961): 119–20.

[5]Baldwin, "Everybody's Protest Novel," *Notes of a Native Son,* p. 23.

[6]Cleaver, *Soul on Ice,* pp. 97–111.

[7]Robert A. Bone, *The Negro Novel in America*, rev. ed. (New Haven: Yale University Press, 1965), p. 235.

[8]Norman Mailer, "The White Negro," in *Advertisements for Myself* (New York: G. P. Putnam's Sons, Berkley Medallion Editions, 1966), p. 314.

[9]Mailer, "The White Negro," pp. 313–14.

[10]*Ibid.*, p. 329.

[11]James Baldwin, *The Fire Next Time* (New York: Dial Press, 1963), pp. 23–24. All subsequent references to this work will appear in parentheses in the text.

[12]James Baldwin, *No Name in the Street* (New York: Dial Press, 1972), p. 167. All subsequent references to this work will appear in parentheses in the text.

[13]James Baldwin, "As Much Truth as One Can Bear," *New York Times Book Review*, January 14, 1962.

From a Region in *My* Mind: The Essays of James Baldwin
Hobart Jarrett

[1]James Baldwin, *No Name in the Street* (New York: Dial Press, 1972), p. 29.

[2]James Baldwin, *Nobody Knows My Name* (New York: Dell Publishing Company, 1963), p. 187.

[3]James Baldwin, *Notes of a Native Son* (New York: Bantam Books, 1968), p. 6.

[4]Baldwin, *No Name in the Street*, p. 5.

[5]*Ibid.*, p. 3.

[6]Baldwin, *Notes of a Native Son*, p. 73.

[7]James Baldwin, *The Fire Next Time* (London: Penguin Books, 1963), p. 38.

[8]Baldwin, *No Name in the Street*, p. 5.

[9]*Ibid.*

[10]*Ibid.*, p. 9.

[11]Baldwin, *Notes of a Native Son*, p. 74.

[12]*Ibid.*, p. 139.

[13]*Ibid.*, pp. 22–23.

[14]*Ibid.*, p. 16.

[15]*Ibid.*, p. 17.

[16]*Ibid.*, p. 15.

[17]*Ibid.*, p. 54.

[18]Baldwin, *The Fire Next Time*, p. 34.

[19]*Ibid.*, p. 46.

[20]Baldwin, *Notes of a Native Son*, p. 23.

[21]*Ibid.*, p. 15.

[22]Baldwin, *The Fire Next Time*, p. 14.

[23]Baldwin, *Notes of a Native Son*, p. 77.

[24]Baldwin, *Nobody Knows My Name*, p. 65.

[25]*Ibid.*, p. 63.

[26]*Ibid.*

[27]*Ibid.*, p. 17.

[28]*Ibid.*, p. 35.

[29]Baldwin, *The Fire Next Time*, p. 30.
[30]*Ibid.*, p. 31.
[31]*Ibid.*, p. 15.
[32]*Ibid.*, p. 74.
[33]*Ibid.*, p. 54.
[34]*Ibid.*, p. 80.
[35]*Ibid.*, p. 51.
[36]Baldwin, *No Name in the Street*, p. 55.
[37]Baldwin, *The Fire Next Time*, pp. 61–62.
[38]Baldwin, *No Name in the Street*, p. 135.
[39]*Ibid.*, p. 141.
[40]Baldwin, *Notes of a Native Son*, p. 6.
[41]Baldwin, *Nobody Knows My Name*, p. 72.
[42]Baldwin, *No Name in the Street*, p. 123.
[43]Baldwin, *Notes of a Native Son*, p. 6.
[44]Baldwin, *No Name in the Street*, p. 12.
[45]*Ibid.*, p. 10.
[46]*Ibid.*, p. 65.
[47]Baldwin, *Nobody Knows My Name*, p. 69.
[48]Baldwin, *The Fire Next Time*, p. 17.
[49]Baldwin, *Nobody Knows My Name*, p. 92.
[50]*Ibid.* , pp. 93–94.
[51]Baldwin, *Notes of a Native Son*, p. 137.
[52]Baldwin, *The Fire Next Time*, p. 27.
[53]*Ibid.*, p. 74.
[54]*Ibid.*, p. 81.
[55]Baldwin, *Notes of a Native Son*, p. 136.
[56]*Ibid.*, p. 137.
[57]*Ibid.*, p. 138.
[58]*Ibid.*, p. 139.
[59]*Ibid.*
[60]*Ibid.*, p. 140.
[61]*Ibid.*, pp. 142–43.
[62]*Ibid.*, p. 144.
[63]*Ibid.*
[64] *Ibid.*, p. 147.

James Baldwin as Poet-Prophet
A. Russell Brooks

[1]James Baldwin, *Notes of a Native Son* (Boston: Beacon Press, 1955), p. 9.
[2]Margaret Mead and James Baldwin, *A Rap on Race* (Philadelphia: J. B. Lippincott Company, 1971), pp. 200–202.
[3]James Baldwin, *Blues for Mister Charlie* (New York: Dial Press, 1964), p. 42.
[4]Mead and Baldwin, *A Rap on Race*, p. 187.

[5]Baldwin, *Blues for Mister Charlie*, p. 77.

[6]Mead and Baldwin, *A Rap on Race*, pp. 80–81.

[7]Baldwin, *Notes of a Native Son*, p. 169.

[8]*Ibid.*, p. 122.

[9]Mead and Baldwin, *A Rap on Race*, p. 206.

[10]Baldwin, *Notes of a Native Son*, p. 29.

[11]James Baldwin, *Another Country* (New York: Dial Press, 1962), p. 352.

[12]James Baldwin, *Nobody Knows My Name* (New York: Dial Press, 1961), p. 5.

[13]*Ibid.*, p. 98.

[14]*Ibid.*, pp. 3–4.

[15]*Ibid.*, p. 6.

[16]*Ibid.*, pp. 11–12.

[17]James Baldwin, *The Amen Corner* (New York: Dial Press, 1968), pp. 41–42.

[18]James Baldwin, *The Fire Next Time* (New York: Dial Press, 1963), p. 95.

[19]Baldwin, *Notes of a Native Son*, p. 175.

[20]Baldwin, *Nobody Knows My Name*, p. 11.

[21]*Ibid.*, pp. 127–137.

[22]James Baldwin, *No Name in the Street* (New York: Dial Press, 1972), p. 67.

[23]James Baldwin, *Going to Meet the Man* (New York: Dial Press, 1965), pp. 181–82.

[24]Baldwin, *The Fire Next Time*, pp. 23–24.

[25]*Ibid.*, pp. 119–20.

[26]Mead and Baldwin, *A Rap on Race*, p. 96.

[27]Baldwin, *No Name in the Street*, p. 19.

[28]Mead and Baldwin, *A Rap on Race*, pp. 78–79.

[29]Baldwin, *No Name in the Street*, p. 172.

[30]Baldwin, *Nobody Knows My Name*, pp. xiii–xiv.

Thematic Patterns in Baldwin's Essays

Eugenia W. Collier

[1]James Baldwin, *The Fire Next Time* (New York: Dial Press, 1963), pp. 102–103.

[2]*Ibid.*, p. 103.

[3]James Baldwin, *Notes of a Native Son* (Boston: Beacon Press, 1955), p. 19.

[4]James Baldwin, *Nobody Knows My Name* (New York: Dial Press, 1961), p. 61.

[5]*Ibid.*, p. 20.

[6]Baldwin, *Notes of a Native Son*, p. 65.

[7]Baldwin, *The Fire Next Time*, p. 37.

[8]Baldwin, *Notes of a Native Son*, p. 18.

[9]Baldwin, *Nobody Knows My Name*, pp. 63–64.

[10]Baldwin, *Notes of a Native Son*, pp. 24–25.

[11]Baldwin, *The Fire Next Time*, p. 116.

[12]Baldwin, *Notes of a Native Son*, p. 66.

[13]*Ibid.*, p. 14.

[14]*Ibid.*, pp. 6–7.
[15]Baldwin, *Nobody Knows My Name*, p. 203.
[16]Baldwin, *Notes of a Native Son*, p. 26.
[17]*Ibid.*, p. 106.
[18]*Ibid.*, p. 7.
[19]*Ibid.*, p. 59.
[20]Baldwin, *The Fire Next Time*, p. 68.
[21]Baldwin, *Notes of a Native Son*, pp. 113–14.
[22]Baldwin, *The Fire Next Time*, p. 22.
[23]Baldwin, *Nobody Knows My Name*, p. xiv.
[24]Baldwin, *The Fire Next Time*, p. 110.
[25]*Ibid.*, pp. 23–24.
[26]Baldwin, *Nobody Knows My Name*, pp. 136–37.
[27]Baldwin, *The Fire Next Time*, p. 108.
[28]*Ibid.*, pp. 119–20.

Style, Form, and Content in the Short Fiction of James Baldwin
Harry L. Jones

[1]James Baldwin, *Going to Meet the Man* (New York: Dial Press, 1965), p. 133. All page references in the text of this essay are to Baldwin's short stories in this edition.
[2]James Baldwin, *Nobody Know My Name* (New York: Dial Press, 1961), p. 188.
[3]*Ibid.*, p. 142.

James Baldwin's "Previous Condition": A Problem of Identification
Sam Bluefarb

[1]James Baldwin, *Going to Meet the Man* (New York: Dial Press, 1965), p. 83. Citations in the text are from this edition.

"Sonny's Blues": James Baldwin's Image of the Black Community
John M. Reilly

[1]James Baldwin, "Sonny's Blues," *Partisan Review* 24 (Summer, 1957): 327–58. And in *Going to Meet the Man* (New York: Dial Press, 1965), pp. 103–41. Citations in the text are from the latter publication of the story.
[2]Janheinz Jahn, *Neo-African Literature: A History of Black Writing*, trans. Oliver Coburn and Ursula Lehrburger (New York: Grove Press, 1968), p. 166.

Fire as the Symbol of a Leadening Existence in "Going to Meet the Man"
Arthenia Bates Millican

[1]Two of these critics are Joseph Featherstone, "Blues for Mr. Baldwin," *The New Republic*, November 27, 1965, pp. 34–36; and Stanley Kauffman, "Another Baldwin," *New York Times Book Review*, December 12, 1965, p. 5.

[2]Featherstone, "Blues for Mr. Baldwin," p. 35.

[3]David Littlejohn, "Exemplary and Other Baldwins," *Nation*, December 13, 1965, p. 480.

[4]James Baldwin, "Going to Meet the Man," in *Going to Meet the Man* (New York: Dial Press, 1965), p. 243. Other references to the story will be entered by page number in the text.

[5]Littlejohn, "Exemplary and Other Baldwins," p. 480.

[6]James Baldwin, "Notes for Blues," in *Blues for Mister Charlie* (New York: Dial Press, 1964), p. xiv.

[7]*Ibid.*, pp. xiv–xv.

[8]*Ibid.*, p. xv.

[9]James Baldwin, *No Name in the Street* (New York: Dial Press, 1972), p. 189.

[10]James Baldwin, *The Fire Next Time* (New York: Dial Press, 1963), p. 102.

[11]*Ibid.*, p. 57.

[12]*Ibid.*, p. 117.

[13]*Ibid.*, pp. 56–57.

[14]*Ibid.*, p. 57.

[15]Baldwin, "Notes for Blues," p. xiv.

[16]Stanley Kauffmann, review of *Going to Meet the Man* by James Baldwin, *New York Times Review of Books*, December 12, 1965, p. 5.

James Baldwin: Portrait of a Black Exile
Kenneth J. Zahorski

[1]Margaret Mead and James Baldwin, *A Rap on Race* (Philadelphia: J. B. Lippincott Company, 1971).

[2]Editor's Note in *A Rap on Race*.

[3]*Ibid.*, p. 146.

[4]*Ibid.*, pp. 135–36.

[5]*Ibid.*, pp. 67–68.

[6]*Ibid.*, p. 156.

[7]*Ibid.*, p. 69.

[8]*Ibid.*, p. 70.

[9]*Ibid.*, p. 94.

[10]*Ib:d.*, p. 49.

[11]B. A. Bannon, "How Margaret Mead and James Baldwin Got Together for *A Rap on Race*, *Publishers' Weekly* 199 (May 31, 1971): pp. 104–105.

[12]*A Rap on Race*, p. 85.

[13] *Ibid.*

[14] *Ibid.,* pp. 85–86.

[15] *Ibid.,* p. 244.

[16] *Ibid.,* p. 64.

[17] *Ibid.*

[18] *Ibid.,* p. 27.

[19] *Ibid.,* p. 206.

[20] *Ibid.,* p. 244.

[21] *Ibid.,* pp. 220–21.

[22] *Ibid.,* p. 49.

[23] *Ibid.,* p. 86.

[24] *Ibid.,* p. 90.

[25] *Ibid.,* p. 86.

[26] *Ibid.*

[27] *Ibid.,* p. 79.

[28] *Ibid.,* p. 143.

[29] *Ibid.,* p. 256.

[30] Bannon, "How Margaret Mead and James Baldwin Got Together," pp. 104–105.

Power and Morality as Imperatives for Nikki Giovanni and James Baldwin: A View of *A Dialogue*
A. Russell Brooks

[1] James Baldwin and Nikki Giovanni, *A Dialogue.* Foreword by Ida Lewis. Afterword by Orde Coombs (Philadelphia: J. B. Lippincott Company, 1973).

[2] Nikki Giovanni, *Black Feeling, Black Talk/Black Judgment* (New York: William Morrow and Company, 1970).

[3] Nikki Giovanni, *Re: Creation* (Detroit: Broadside Press, 1970).

[4] Nikki Giovanni, *Gemini* (Indianapolis: Bobbs-Merrill Company, 1971).

[5] Nikki Giovanni, *My House* (New York: William Morrow and Company, 1972).

[6] Richard Avedon and James Baldwin, *Nothing Personal.* Photographs by Richard Avedon and text by James Baldwin (New York: Atheneum Publishers, 1964).

[7] Margaret Mead and James Baldwin, *A Rap on Race* (Philadelphia: J. B. Lippincott Company, 1971).

[8] James Baldwin, *Nobody Knows My Name* (New York: Dial Press, 1961).

One Day When I Was Lost: Baldwin's Unfulfilled Obligation
Patsy Brewington Perry

[1] James Baldwin, *One Day, When I Was Lost* (New York: Dial Press, 1973).

[2] Alex Haley, *The Autobiography of Malcolm X* (New York: Grove Press, 1966).

[3] James Baldwin, *No Name in the Street* (New York: Dial Press, 1972), p. 99. In this collection of reminiscences, Baldwin deals mainly with his activities and concerns

during the period 1967–71. The fact that his adaption of *The Autobiography of Malcolm X* was a major concern is supported by his discussions of the project on pages 11, 91–100, 117–20, 122–123, 145–46, 149–52, 157. For comments on the problems that caused Baldwin to give up the screenplay at one time, see pp. 122–23, 150–51.

[4]Haley, *The Autobiography of Malcolm X*, p. 456.

[5]Baldwin, *No Name in the Street*, p. 91.

[6]*Ibid.*, p. 100.

[7]*Ibid.*, p. 99.

[8]*Ibid.*, p. 120.

[9]Haley, Epilogue, *The Autobiography of Malcolm X*, p. 443.

[10]Baldwin, *One Day, When I Was Lost*, pp. 5–25, 47, 157, 271.

[11]*Ibid.*, pp. 148–51.

[12]Haley, *The Autobiography of Malcolm X*, p. 375.

[13]James Baldwin, *Notes of a Native Son* (Boston: Beacon Press, 1955), pp. 9–10.

[14]Haley, *The Autobiography of Malcolm X*, p. 382.

[15]Baldwin, *One Day, When I Was Lost*, p. 139.

[16]Haley, *The Autobiography of Malcolm X*, p. 381.

[17]Baldwin, *One Day, When I Was Lost*, p. 23.

[18]Haley, *The Autobiography of Malcolm X*, pp. 66–67.

[19]*Ibid.*, pp. 32–34.

[20]*Ibid.*, p. 38.

[21]*Ibid.*, p. 317. Baldwin refers to this episode (vaguely, I feel, since he has not mentioned Ella, or any sister, before) in Malcolm's comment "I may never be able to pay my sister back," *One Day, When I Was Lost*, p. 234.

[22]Haley, *The Autobiography of Malcolm X*, pp. 33, 319.

[23]*Ibid.*, p. 11.

[24]*Ibid.*, pp. 155, 157.

[25]*Ibid.*, pp. 158–61.

[26]Baldwin, *One Day, When I Was Lost*, p. 130.

[27]*Ibid.*, pp. 138–139.

[28]Haley, *The Autobiography of Malcolm X*, p. 299.

[29]Baldwin, *One Day, When I Was Lost*, p. 230.

[30]Haley, *The Autobiography of Malcolm X*, pp. 301–02.

[31]Baldwin, *One Day, When I Was Lost*, pp. 220–22.

[32]*Ibid.*, pp. 79–86.

[33]*Ibid.*, pp. 167–70, 197–98.

[34]*Ibid.*, p. 75.

[35]*Ibid.*, p. 203.

[36]Haley, *The Autobiography of Malcolm X*, pp. 52–54.

[37]Baldwin, *One Day, When I Was Lost*, pp. 53–56.

[38]*Ibid.*, p. 73.

[39]*Ibid.*, pp. 42–44.

[40]Haley, *The Autobiography of Malcolm X*, p. 43ff.

[41]Baldwin, *One Day, When I Was Lost*, pp. 35–37.

[42]Haley, *The Autobiography of Malcolm X*, pp. 237–38.

[43]Baldwin, *One Day, When I Was Lost*, p. 171.

[44]*Ibid.*, p. 213.

[45]*Ibid.*, p. 267.
[46]*Ibid.*, pp. 180–87, 202–03.
[47]*Ibid.*, pp. 216–17.

A CLASSIFIED BIBLIOGRAPHY

James Baldwin
A Classified Bibliography

_____Therman B. O'Daniel

I. Books by Baldwin[1]

A. NOVELS

Go Tell It on the Mountain. New York: Alfred A. Knopf, 1953.
Giovanni's Room. New York: Dial Press, 1956.
Another Country. New York: Dial Press, 1962.
Tell Me How Long the Train's Been Gone. New York: Dial Press, 1968.
If Beale Street Could Talk. New York: Dial Press, 1974.

B. ESSAYS

Notes of a Native Son. Boston: Beacon Press, 1955.
Nobody Knows My Name: More Notes of a Native Son. New York: Dial Press, 1961.
The Fire Next Time. New York: Dial Press, 1963.
No Name in the Street. New York: Dial Press, 1972.
The Devil Finds Work: An Essay. New York: Dial Press, 1976.

C. PLAYS

Blues for Mister Charlie. New York: Dial Press, 1964.
The Amen Corner. New York: Dial Press, 1968.

D. SHORT STORIES

Going to Meet the Man. New York: Dial Press, 1965.

[1]Works by Baldwin are listed in chronological order under each classified heading.

E. PHOTO ESSAY

Nothing Personal. Photographs by Richard Avedon and text by James Baldwin. New York: Atheneum Publishers, 1964.

F. DIALOGUES AND RAPS

A Rap on Race. By Margaret Mead and James Baldwin. Philadelphia: J. B. Lippincott Company, 1971.

A Dialogue. By James Baldwin and Nikki Giovanni. Philadelphia: J. B. Lippincott Company, 1973.

G. SCENARIO

One Day, When I was Lost: A Scenario Based on Alex Haley's "The Autobiography of Malcolm X." New York: Dial Press, 1973.

II. Articles and Other Works by James Baldwin

"The Harlem Ghetto: Winter 1948." *Commentary,* February, 1948, p. 165.

"Previous Condition." *Commentary,* October, 1948, pp. 334–42.

"Journey to Atlanta." *The New Leader,* October 9, 1948.

"Everybody's Protest Novel." *Partisan Review* 16 (June, 1949): 578–85.

"Preservation of Innocence." *Zero,* Summer, 1949, pp. 18–19.

"The Negro in Paris." *Reporter,* June 6, 1950, pp. 34–36.

"The Outing." *New Story* (1951).

"Many Thousands Gone." *Partisan Review* 18 (November-December, 1951): 665–80.

"Exodus." *American Mercury,* August, 1952, pp. 97–103.

"Stranger in the Village." *Harper's,* October, 1953, pp. 42–48.

"Paris Letter: A Question of Identity." *Partisan Review* 21 (July-August, 1954): p. 402–10.

"Gide as Husband and Homosexual." *The New Leader,* December 13, 1954, pp. 18–20.

"Life Straight in De Eye." *Commentary,* January, 1955, pp. 74–77.

"Equal in Paris." *Commentary*, March, 1955, pp. 251–59.

"Me and My Home . . . " *Harper's,* November, 1955, pp. 54–61.

"The Crusade of Indignation." *Nation,* July 7, 1956, pp. 18–22.

"Faulkner and Desegregation." *Partisan Review* 23 (Winter, 1956): 568–73.

"Princes and Powers." *Encounter,* January, 1957, pp. 52–60.

"Sonny's Blues." *Partisan Review* 24 (Summer, 1957): 327–58.

"Come Out of the Wilderness." *Mademoiselle,* March, 1958, p. 102.

"The Hard Kind of Courage." *Harper's,* October, 1958, pp. 61–65.

"The Discovery of What It Means to Be an American." *New York Times Book Review,* January 25, 1959, p. 4.

"On Catfish Row: *Porgy and Bess* in the Movies." *Commentary,* September, 1959, pp. 246–48.

"Letter from the South: Nobody Knows My Name." *Partisan Review* 26 (Winter, 1959): 72–82.

"The Precarious Vogue of Ingmar Bergman." *Esquire,* April, 1960, pp. 128–32.

"Fifth Avenue, Uptown." *Esquire,* July, 1960, pp. 70–76.

"They Can't Turn Back." *Mademoiselle,* August, 1960, p. 324.

"This Morning, This Evening, So Soon." *Atlantic Monthly,* September, 1960, pp. 34–52.

"Notes for a Hypothetical Novel." An address delivered at the Third Annual *Esquire* Magazine Symposium on "The Role of the Writer in America" at San Francisco State College, October 22, 1960.

"This Morning, This Evening, So Soon." In *The Best American Short Stories, 1961,* and *the Yearbook of the American Short Story,* ed. Martha Foley and David Burnett, pp. 1–40. Boston: Houghton Mifflin Company, 1961.

"The Dangerous Road Before Martin Luther King." *Harper's,* February, 1961, pp. 33–42.

"The Exile." *Preuve,* February, 1961.

"A Negro Assays the Negro Mood." *New York Times Magazine,* March 12, 1961, p. 25.

"The Survival of Richard Wright." *The Reporter,* March 16, 1961, pp. 52–55.

"Richard Wright." *Encounter,* April, 1961, pp. 58–60.

"The Black Boy Looks at the White Boy Norman Mailer." *Esquire,* May, 1961, pp. 102–06.

"The New Lost Generation." *Esquire,* July, 1961, pp. 113–15.

"An Interview." *WMFT Perspective,* December, 1961, p. 37.

"As Much Truth as One Can Bear." *New York Times Book Review,* January 14, 1962, p. 1.

"Letter From a Region in My Mind." *New Yorker,* November 17, 1962, p. 59.

"A Letter to My Nephew." *Progressive,* December, 1962, pp. 19–20.

"What's the Reason Why: A Symposium by Best Selling Authors." *New York Times Book Review,* December 2, 1962, p. 3.

"Color." *Esquire,* December, 1962, p. 225.

"Letters from a Journey." *Harper's,* May, 1963, pp. 48-52.

Black Man in America. A Recording. Distributed by Credo, Cambridge, Massachusetts. Discussed by John Ciardi in *Saturday Review,* July 6, 1963, p. 13.

"A Talk to Teachers" ["The Negro Child—His Self Image"]. *Saturday Review,* December 21, 1963, p. 42.

"Liberalism and the Negro: A Round-Table Discussion." By James Baldwin, Nathan Glazer, Sidney Hooks, and Gunnar Myrdal. *Commentary,* March, 1964, pp. 25–42.

"The American Dream and the American Negro." By James Baldwin and William F. Buckley, Jr. [Transcript slightly condensed]. *New York Times Magazine,* March 7, 1965, p. 32.

"What Kind of Men Cry?" [Baldwin, Harry Belafonte, Sidney Poitier, and other men give their views on this subject]. *Ebony,* June, 1965, p. 47.

"Race, Hate, Sex, and Colour: A Conversation." By James Baldwin with James Mossman and Colin MacInnes. *Encounter,* July, 1965, pp. 55–60.

"The White Man's Guilt." *Ebony,* August, 1965, pp. 47–48.

"Theatre: The Negro In and Out." *Negro Digest,* April, 1966, pp. 37–44.

"To Whom It May Concern: A Report from Occupied Territory." *Nation,* July 11,

1966, pp. 39–43.

"Negroes Are Anti-Semitic Because They Are Anti-White." *New York Magazine,* April 9, 1967, p. 26.

"Tell Me How Long the Train's Been Gone: Story; Excerpt from Novel." *McCall's,* February, 1967, p. 118.

"*Go Tell It on the Mountain;* Excerpt." *Wilson Library Bulletin* 42 (June, 1968): 984–85.

"How Can We Get the Black People to Cool It? An Interview with James Baldwin." *Esquire,* July, 1968, p. 49.

"Sidney Poitier." *Look,* July 23, 1968, p. 50.

Black Anti-Semitism and Jewish Racism. By James Baldwin and others. Introduction by Nat Hentoff. New York: Richard W. Baron, 1969.

"Sweet Lorraine." *Esquire,* November, 1969, pp. 139–41.

"Why I Left America. Conversation: Ida Lewis and James Baldwin." *Essence,* October, 1970. Reprinted in *New Black Voices,* ed. Abraham Chapman, pp. 409–19. New York: New American Library, 1972.

"A Rap On Race." By Margaret Mead and James Baldwin. [Excerpts]. *McCall's,* June, 1971, p. 84.

"Malcolm and Martin." *Esquire,* April, 1972, p. 94.

" 'Let Me Finish, let me finish . . .': A Television Conversation." By James Baldwin with Peregrine Worsthorne and Bryan Magee (Chairman). *Encounter,* September, 1972, pp. 27–33.

III. Works About Baldwin[2]

Abdul, Raoul. "Negro Artists, Writers Using Talents to Spur the Struggle for Liberation." *Muhammad Speaks,* November 19, 1965, p. 22.

Abramson, Doris E. *Negro Playwrights in the American Theatre, 1925–1959,* pp. 272–79. New York: Columbia University Press, 1969.

Adams, George R. "Black Militant Drama." *American Image,* 28 (Summer, 1971): 107–28.

Adams, J. Donald. "Speaking of Books." *New York Times Book Review,* January 28, 1962, p. 2.

Adelsen, Charles E. "A Love Affair: James Baldwin and Istanbul." *Ebony,* March, 1970, p. 40.

Alexander, Charlotte A. *Baldwin's Go Tell It on the Mountain, Another Country, and Other Works: A Critical Commentary.* New York: Monarch Press, 1968.

Alexander, Charlotte. "The 'Stink of Reality': Mothers and Whores in James Baldwin's Fiction." *Literature and Psychology,* 18 (1968): 9–28.

Alexander, Jean A. "Black Literature for the 'Culturally Deprived' Curriculum." *Negro American Literature Forum* 4 (Fall, 1970): 96–103.

Allen, Shirley S. "Religious Symbolism and Psychic Reality in Baldwin's *Go Tell It on the Mountain." CLA Journal* 19 (December, 1975): 173–99.

[2]Works about Baldwin—books, chapters in books, articles, and any other materials—are all listed together in alphabetical order.

Allen, Walter, *The Modern Novel in Britain and the United States.* New York: E. P. Dutton, 1964.

Alves, Helio O. "James Baldwin: O calabouço impossivel." *Vertice* (Lisbon) 28 (1968): 657–63.

Anonymous. "Three Writers Receive Eugene Saxton Fellowship." *Publishers' Weekly* 149 (January 19, 1946): 308–09.

———. "A Negro Family—*Go Tell It on the Mountain.*" *Nation,* June 6, 1953, p. 488.

———. "Kennedy and Baldwin: The Gulf." *Newsweek,* June 3, 1963, p. 19.

———. "Baldwin: Gray Flannel Muslim?" *Christian Century,* 80 (June 12, 1963): 791.

———. "Baldwin Hits Mallory Case." *Muhammad Speaks,* January 31, 1964, p. 2.

———. "*Blues for Mister Charlie.*" *Time,* May 1, 1964, p. 50.

———. "Anger and Guilt." *Newsweek,* May 4, 1964, p. 46.

———. "Blues for Mr. Charlie." *Ebony,* June, 1964, p. 188.

———. "Sisters Under Their Skin." *Time,* June 5, 1964, p. 96.

———. "Tardy Rainbow." *Time,* April 23, 1965, p. 59.

Auchincloss, Eve, and Nancy Lynch, eds. "Disturber of the Peace: James Baldwin" [A Taped Interview]. *Mademoiselle,* May, 1963, p. 174.

Baker, Houston A., Jr. *Long Black Song: Essays in Black American Literature and Culture,* pp. 40, 54–55, 81–83, 107–08, 129. Charlottesville: The University Press of Virginia, 1972.

Balliett, Whitney, "Wrong Pulpit." *New Yorker,* August 4, 1962, pp. 69–70.

Bannon, Barbara A. "How Margaret Mead and James Baldwin Got Together for *A Rap On Race.*" *Publishers' Weekly,* 199 (May 31, 1971): 104–05.

Banta, Thomas J. "James Baldwin's Discovery of Identity." *Mawazo* (Kampala), 2, i: 33–41.

Bardeen, Constance L. "Love and Hate: Review of *Another Country.*" *Crisis* 69 (November, 1962): 567–68.

Barrett, William. "Weight of the City." *Atlantic Monthly,* July, 1962, pp. 110–11.

Barksdale, Richard K. " 'Temple of the Fire Baptized'." *Phylon* 14 (Third Quarter, 1953): 326–327.

———. "Alienation and the Anti-Hero in Recent American Fiction." *CLA Journal* 10 (September, 1966): 1–10.

Barksdale, Richard, and Keneth Kinnamon, eds. *Black Writers of America: A Comprehensive Anthology,* pp. 722–44. New York: Macmillan Company, 1972.

Beitz, Ursula. "Amerikanische Protestdramen." *Weimarer Meiträge,* 19, No. 7 (1973): 153–160.

Bell, George E. "The Dilemma of Love in *Go Tell it on the Mountain* and *Giovanni's Room.* CLA Journal 17 (March, 1974): 397–406.

Berry, Boyd M. "Another Man Done Gone: Self-Pity in Baldwin's *Another Country.*" *Michigan Quarterly Review* 5 (Fall, 1966): 285–90.

Bhattacharya, Lokenath. "James Baldwin." *Quest,* No. 44 (Winter, 1965), pp. 60–66.

Bigsby, C. W. E. "The Committed Writer: James Baldwin as Dramatist." *Twentieth Century Literature* 13 (April, 1967): 39–48.

———. *Confrontation and Commitment: A Study of Contemporary American*

Drama, 1959–1966. London: Macgibbon & Kee, 1967.

Blaisdel, Gus. "James Baldwin, the Writer." *Negro Digest,* 13 (January, 1964): 61–68.

Bloomfield, Caroline. "Religion and Alienation in James Baldwin, Bernard Malamud, and James F. Powers." *Religious Education* 57 (March-April, 1962): 97–102.

Blount, Trevor. "A Slight Error in Continuity in James Baldwin's *Another Country.*" *Notes and Queries* 13 (March, 1966): 102–03.

Bluefarb, Sam. "James Baldwin's 'Previous Condition': A Problem of Identification." *Negro American Literature Forum* 3 (Spring, 1969): 26–29.

Bone, Robert A. "The Novels of James Baldwin." *TriQuarterly,* No. 2 (Winter, 1965), pp. 3–20.

―――. *The Negro Novel in America,* rev. ed., pp. 215–29. New Haven: Yale University Press, 1966.

Bonosky, Philip. "The Negro Writer and Commitment." *Mainstream* 15 (1962): 16–22.

Boyle, Kay. "Introducing James Baldwin." In *Contemporary American Novelists,* ed. Harry T. Moore, pp. 155–57. Carbondale: Southern Illinois University Press, 1964.

Bradford, Melvin E. "Faulkner, James Baldwin and the South." *Georgia Review* 20 (Winter, 1966): 431–43.

Brathwaite, Edward. "Race and the Divided Self." *Black World* 21 (July, 1972): 54–68.

Breaux, Elwyn E. "Comic Elements in Selected Prose Works by James Baldwin, Ralph Ellison, and Langston Hughes." Dissertation, Oklahoma State University. *Dissertation Abstracts International,* 33 (July-August, 1972): 747-A.

Breit, Harvey. "James Baldwin and Two Footnotes." In *The Creative Present: Notes on Contemporary American Fiction,* ed. Nona Balakian and Charles Simmons. Garden City, N.Y.: Doubleday and Company, 1967.

Britt, David D. "The Image of the White Man in the Fiction of Langston Hughes, Richard Wright, James Baldwin and Ralph Ellison." *Dissertation Abstracts* 29 (November, 1968): 1532-A.

Brooks, A. Russell. "The Comic Spirit and the Negro's New Look." *CLA Journal* 6 (September, 1962): 35–43.

Brooks, Hallie B. "Baldwin in Paperback." *Phylon* 21 (Third Quarter, 1960): 296–97.

Brower, Brock. "Of Nothing But Fact." *American Scholar* 32 (Autumn, 1964): p. 613.

Brown, Lloyd W. "The West Indian as an Ethnic Stereotype in Black American Literature." *Negro American Literature Forum* 5 (Spring, 1971): 8–14.

Brudnoy, David. "Blues for Mr. Baldwin." *National Review,* July 7, 1972, pp. 750–51.

Brustein, Robert. "Everybody's Protest Play." *New Republic,* May 16, 1964, pp. 35–37.

Buckley, William F., Jr. "The Negro and the American Dream." *National Review,* April 6, 1965, p. 273.

―――. "Call to Color Blindness." *National Review,* June 18, 1963, p. 488.

Burgess, Anthony. "The Postwar American Novel: A View from the Periphery." *American Scholar,* 35 (Winter, 1965–66): 150–56.

———. "American Themes." In *The Novel Now: A Guide to Contemporary Fiction,* pp. 198–99. New York: W. W. Norton and Company, 1967.

Burke, William M. "Modern Black Fiction and the Literature of Oppression." Dissertation, University of Oregon. *Dissertation Abstracts International,* 33 (May-June, 1972): 6415-A.

Butcher, Margaret J. *The Negro in American Culture,* pp. 180–181, 275. New York: Alfred A. Knopf, 1956.

Butcher, Philip. "James [Arthur] Baldwin." In *Encyclopedia of World Literature in the 20th Century,* Vol. 1, pp. 91–92. New York: Frederick Ungar Publishing Company, 1967.

Byam, Milton S. "Fiction." *Library Journal* 78 (May 15, 1953): 916.

Cade, Toni. "Black Theater." In *Black Expression,* ed. Addison Gayle, Jr., pp. 134–43. New York: Weybright and Talley, 1969.

Campbell, Finley. "More Notes of a Native Son." *Phylon* 23 (First Quarter, 1962): 92–97.

Cartey, Wilfred. "I've Been Reading: The Realities of Four Negro Writers." *Columbia University Forum* 9 (Summer, 1966): 34–42.

Chapman, Abraham, ed. *Black Voices,* pp. 316–20, 590–604. New York: New American Library, 1968.

———, ed. *New Black Voices,* pp. 409–19. New York: New American Library, 1972.

Charney, Maurice. "James Baldwin's Quarrel with Richard Wright." *American Quarterly,* 15 (Spring, 1963): 65–75.

Ciardi, John. "Manner of Speaking: *Black Man in America.*" *Saturday Review,* July 6, 1963, p. 13.

Clark, Kenneth B. "A Conversation with James Baldwin." *Freedomways* 3 (1963): 367.

———. *The Negro Protest: James Baldwin, Malcolm X, Martin Luther King Talk With Kenneth B. Clark,* pp. 1–14, 49. Boston: Beacon Press, 1963.

Clarke, John Henrik. "The Alienation of James Baldwin." *Journal of Human Relations* 12 (First Quarter, 1964): 30–33.

Cleaver, Eldridge. "Notes on a Native Son." *Ramparts,* June, 1966, pp. 51–56.

Clurman, Harold. *"Blues for Mister Charlie." Nation,* May 1, 1964, pp. 495–96.

———. *"The Amen Corner." Nation,* May 10, 1965, pp. 514–15.

Coles, Robert. "Baldwin's Burden." *Partisan Review* 31 (Summer, 1964): 409–16.

Collier, Eugenia W. "The Phrase Unbearably Repeated." *Phylon* 25 (Fall, 1964): 288–96.

———. "Thematic Patterns in Baldwin's Essays." *Black World* 21 (June, 1972): 28–34.

Corona, Mario. "La saggistica di James Baldwin." *Studi Americani* (Rome), 15 (1969), pp. 433–63.

Cosgrove, William. "Modern Black Writers: The Divided Self." *Negro American Literature Forum* 7 (Winter, 1973): 120–22.

Cox, C. B., and A. R. Jones. "After the Tranquilized Fifties: Notes on Sylvia Plath and James Baldwin." *Critical Quarterly* 6 (Summer, 1964): 107–22.

Curley, Thomas F. "The Quarrel With Time in American Fiction." *American Scholar,* 29 (Autumn, 1960): 552–60.

Dance, Daryl C. "You Can't Go Home Again: James Baldwin and the South." *CLA Journal* 18 (September, 1974): 81–90.

Dane, Peter. "Baldwin's Other Country." *Transition* 5, No. 24 (1966), pp. 38–40.

Davenport, Guy. "Magic Realism in Prose." *National Review,* August 28, 1962, pp. 153–54.

Davis, Arthur P. *From the Dark Tower: Afro-American Writers, 1900 to 1960.* Washington, D.C.: Howard University Press, 1974.

Davis, Arthur P., and Saunders Redding, eds. *Cavalcade: Negro American Writing From 1760 to the Present,* pp. 235, 568, 570, 571–86. Boston: Houghton Mifflin Company, 1971.

Davis, Charles T. "The Heavenly Voice of the Black American." In *Anagogic Qualities of Literature,* ed. Joseph P. Strelka, pp. 107–19. University Park: Pennsylvania State University Press, 1971.

DeMott, Benjamin. "James Baldwin on the Sixties: Acts and Revelations." *Saturday Review,* May 27, 1972, pp. 63–66.

Dickstein, Morris. "Wright, Baldwin, Cleaver." *New Letters* 38 (Winter, 1971): 117–24.

————. "The Black Aesthetic in White America." *Partisan Review* 38 (Winter, 1971–1972): 376–95.

Doumergues, Pierre. "La Négritude Américaine." *Les Langues Modernes* 60 (May-/June, 1966): 94–98.

Downes, Bruce. "On Avedon's Controversial Book." *Popular Photography,* March, 1965, p. 24.

Driver, Tom F. *"Blues for Mr. Charlie:* The Review that Was Too True to Be Published." *Negro Digest,* September, 1964, pp. 34–40.

Dupree, F. W. "James Baldwin and the 'Man'." *New York Review of Books,* 1, No. 1 (February, 1963), pp. 1–2.

Dwyer, Robert J. "I *Know* About Negroes and the Poor." *National Review,* December 17, 1963, p. 517.

Eckman, Fern Marja. *The Furious Passage of James Baldwin.* New York: M. Evans and Company, 1966.

Elkoff, Marvin. "Everybody Knows His Name." *Esquire,* August, 1964, pp. 59–64.

Elliott, George P. "Destroyers, Defilers, and Confusers of Men." *Atlantic Monthly,* December, 1968, pp. 74–80.

Ellison, Ralph. "Ralph Ellison Talks About James Baldwin." *Negro Digest,* September, 1962, p. 61.

Ellison, Ralph. "Society, Morality, and the Novel." In *The Living Novel,* ed. Granville Hicks. New York: Macmillan, 1957.

Emanuel James A., and Theodore L. Gross, eds. *Dark Symphony: Negro Literature in America,* pp. 296–300, 588–89. New York: Free Press, 1968.

English, Charles. "Another Viewpoint." *Jubilee,* September, 1963, pp. 43–46.

Fabre, Michel. "Péres et fils dans *Go Tell It on the Mountain,* de James Baldwin." *Études Anglaises* 23 (January-March, 1970): 47–61.

Farès, Nabile. "James Baldwin: Une interview exclusive." *Jeune Afrique,* September, 1970, pp. 20–24.

Farrell, James T. "Literary Note." *American Book Collector* 17 (May, 1967): 6.

Featherstone, Joseph. "Blues for Mr. Baldwin." *New Republic,* November 27,1965, pp. 34–36.

Fiedler, Leslie. "Caliban or Hamlet: An American Paradox." *Encounter,* April, 1966, pp. 23–27.

Finn, James. "The Identity of James Baldwin." *Commonweal,* October 26, 1962, pp. 172–74.

———. "James Baldwin's Vision." *Commonweal,* July 26, 1963, pp. 447–49.

———. "Reply to John McCudden." *Commonweal,* October 11, 1963, pp. 76–77.

Fishcher, Russell G. "James Baldwin: A Bibliography, 1947–1962." *Bulletin of Bibliography,* 24 (January-April, 1965): 127–30.

Fleming, Robert E. "Contemporary Themes in Johnson's *Autobiography of An Ex-Coloured Man." Negro American Literature Forum* 4 (Winter, 1970): 120–24.

Flint, Robert W. "Not Ideas but Life: Review of *Notes of a Native Son." Commentary,* May, 1956, pp. 494–95.

Foote, Dorothy. "James Baldwin's 'Holler Books'." *CEA Critic* 25 (May, 1963): p. 8.

Foote, F. G. "Therapeutique de la haine." *Preuves,* No. 167, pp. 70–73.

Ford, Nick Aaron. "Search for Identity: A Critical Survey of Significant Belles-Lettres by and About Negroes Published in 1961." *Phylon* 23 (Summer, 1962): 128–38.

———. "Walls Do a Prison Make: A Critical Survey of Significant Belles-Lettres by and About Negroes Published in 1962." *Phylon* 24 (Summer, 1963): 123–34.

———. "The Fire Next Time? A Critical Survey of Belles Lettres By and About Negroes Published in 1963." *Phylon* 25 (Summer, 1964): 123–34.

———. *Black Insights: Significant Literature by Black Americans—1760 to the Present,* pp. 192–219, 300–301. Waltham, Massachusetts, Ginn and Company: 1971.

Foreman, Enid G. *Put Me in Print: A Story of James Baldwin.* Washington: The Associated Publishers, n. d.

Foster, David E. " 'Cause My House Fell Down; the Theme of the Fall in Baldwin's Novels." *Critique: Studies in Modern Fiction* 13, No. 2 (1971): 50–62.

Freese, Peter. "James Baldwin and das Syndrom des Identitatsverlustes: 'Previous Condition' im Lichte des Gesamtwerkes." *Literatur in Wissenschaft und Unterricht* (Kiel), 4, pp. 73–98.

Friedenberg, Edgar Z. "Another Country for an Arkansas Traveler." *New Republic,* August 27, 1962, pp. 23–26.

Friedman, Neil. "James Baldwin and Psychotherapy." *Psychotherapy* 3: 177–83.

Frost, David. *The Americans,* pp. 145–50. New York: Stein and Day Publishers, 1970.

Fuller, Hoyt W. "The Role of the Negro Writer in an Era of Struggle." *Negro Digest,* June, 1964, pp. 62–66.

———. "Contemporary Negro Fiction." *Southwest Review* (1965). Reprinted in *The Black American Writer,* ed. C. W. E. Bigsby. Vol. 1, pp. 229–43. Baltimore: Penguin Books, 1971.

Gayle, Addison, Jr. "A Defense of James Baldwin." *CLA Journal* 10 (March, 1967): 201–08.

———. "The Dialectic of *The Fire Next Time." Negro History Bulletin* 30 (April,

1967): 15–16.

_____. "The Function of Black Literature at the Present Time." In *The Black Aes-thetic,* ed. Addison Gayle, Jr. pp. 383–94. Garden City, N.Y.: Doubleday and Company, 1972.

Geismar, Maxwell. "The American Short Story Today." *Studies on the Left* 4 (Spring, 1964): 21–27.

Georgakas, Dan. "James Baldwin . . . in Conversation." *Arts in Society* (Summer, 1966). Reprinted in *Black Voices,* ed. Abraham Chapman, pp. 660–68. New York: New American Library, 1968.

Gèrard, Albert. "James Baldwin et la Religiositeé Noire." *Revue Nouvelle* 33 (February, 1961): 177–86.

_____. "Humanism and Négritude: Notes on the Contemporary Afro-American Novel, *Diogenes,* No. 37 (Spring, 1962): 115–33.

_____. "The Sons of Ham." *Studies in the Novel* 3 (Summer, 1971): 148–64.

Gibson, Donald B. "Wright's Invisible Native Son." *American Quarterly,* 21, No. 4 (Winter, 1969): 728–738.

Gibson, Donald B., ed. *Five Black Writers: Essays on Wright, Ellison, Baldwin, Hughes, and LeRoi Jones,* pp. xix–xxiii, 119–64. New York: New York University Press, 1970.

_____. "The Politics of Ellison and Baldwin." In *The Politics of Twentieth-Century Writers,* ed. George Panichas, pp. 307–20. New York: Hawthorne Publishing Company, 1971.

Gilman, Richard. "News from the Novel."*New Republic,* August 17, 1968, pp. 27–36.

Gitlin, Todd. "Yet Will I Maintain Mine Own Ways Before Him." *Nation,* April 10, 1972, pp. 469–70.

Glazier, Lyle. "Suffering Doesn't Have a Color." *Litera* 8 (1965): 91–98.

Golden, Harry. "A Comment on James Baldwin's Letter." *Crisis,* LXX (March, 1963): pp 145–146.

Goldstein, Suzy B. "James Baldwin's 'Sonny's Blues': A Message in Music." *Negro American Literature Forum* 8 (Fall, 1974): 231–33.

Goodman, Paul. "Not Enough of a World to Grow In." *New York Times Book Review,* June 24, 1962, p. 5.

Gordon, Caroline. "Letters to a Monk." *Ramparts,* December, 1964, p. 4.

Graves, Wallace. "The Question of Moral Energy in James Baldwin's *Go Tell It on the Mountain." CLA Journal* 7 (March, 1964): 215–23.

Gray, Simon. "Whose Little Boy." *Delta* (Cambridge, England), No. 35 (Spring, 1965): pp. 2–8.

Green, Martin. "The Need for a New Liberalism" (Review-Article of Fern Marja Eckman, *The Furious Passage of James Baldwin;* and of William Styron, *The Confessions of Nat Turner*), *Month* 226 (September, 1968): pp. 141–47.

Gresset, Michel. "Sur James Baldwin." *Mercure de France* 350: 653–55.

Gross, Barry. "The 'Uninhabitable Darkness' of Baldwin's *Another Country:* Image and Theme." *Negro American Literature Forum* 6 (Winter, 1972): 113–21.

Gross, John. "Day of Wrath." *New Statesman,* July 19, 1963, pp. 79–80.

Gross, Seymour L., and John Edward Hardy, eds. *Images of the Negro in American Literature,* pp. 19–20, 265–88. Chicago: University of Chicago Press, 1966.

Gross, Theodore L. "The World of James Baldwin." *Critique* (Minnesota) 7 (Winter, 1964–65): 139–49.

———."The Idealism of Negro Literature in America." *Phylon* 30 (Spring, 1969): 5–10.

Hagopian, John V. "James Baldwin: The Black and the Red-White-and-Blue." *CLA Journal* 7 (December, 1963): 133–40.

Hall, John. "Interview with Baldwin." *Transatlantic Review,* 37 and 38 (Autumn-Winter, 1970–1971): 5–14.

Handlin, Oscar. *"Going to Meet the Man." Atlantic Monthly,* November, 1965, p. 191.

Harper, Howard M., Jr. *Desperate Faith: A Study of Bellow, Salinger, Mailer, Baldwin, and Updike,* pp. 137–61. Chapel Hill: University of North Carolina Press, 1967.

Haslam, Gerald W. "Two Traditions in Afro-American Literature." *Research Studies* 37 (September, 1969): 183–93.

———, ed. *Forgotten Pages of American Literature,* pp. 96, 250, 332–41. Boston: Houghton Mifflin Company, 1970.

Hassan, Ihab. *Radical Innocence: Studies in the Contemporary American Novel.* Princeton: Princeton University Press, 1961.

———. "The Novel of Outrage: A Minority Voice in Postwar American Fiction." *American Scholar* 34 (Spring, 1965): 239–53.

Heermance, J. Noel. "The Modern Negro Novel." *Negro Digest,* May, 1964, pp. 66–76.

Heiberg, Inger. "James Baldwin—negerforfatter og dikter." *Samtiden* 73 (May, 1965): 280–87.

Hemenway, Robert, ed. *The Black Novelist,* pp. 111–33, 218–26. Columbus: Charles E. Merrill Publishing Company, 1970.

Hentoff, Nat. "Uninventing the Negro." *Evergreen Review* 7 (Winter, 1964–65): 34.

Hernton, Calvin C. "Blood of the Lamb: The Ordeal of James Baldwin" and "A Fiery Baptism." *Amistad: Writings on Black History and Culture* 1: pp. 183–225.

Hewes, Henry. "The Gospel Untruth." *Saturday Review,* May 1, 1965, p. 49.

———. "Change of Tune." *Saturday Review,* May 9, 1964, p. 36.

Hicks, Granville. "Commitment Without Compromise." *Saturday Review,* July 1, 1961, p. 9.

———. "A Gun in the Hand of a Hater." *Saturday Review,* May 2, 1964, pp. 27–28.

Hill, Herbert, ed. *Anger, and Beyond: The Negro Writer in the United States,* pp. xx, 2–3 *passim.* New York: Harper & Row, 1966.

Hobson, Susan, comp. "New Creative Writers: 42 Novelists Whose First Work Appears This Season." *Library Journal* 78 (February 15, 1953): 364.

Hoffman, Frederick J. *The Modern Novel in America,* rev. ed., p. 250. Chicago: Henry Regnery Company, 1963.

Hoffman, Stanton. "The Cities of Night: John Rechy's *City of Night* and the American Literature of Homosexuality." *Chicago Review* 17: 2 and 3, Double Issue (1964): 195–206.

Howe, Irving. "Black Boys and Native Sons." *Dissent,* No. 4 (Autumn, 1963): pp.

353–368.

Howe, Irving. "James Baldwin: At Ease in Apocalypse." *Harper's,* September, 1968, p. 92.

Hughes, Langston. "From Harlem to Paris." *New York Times,* February 26, 1956, p. 26.

Ickstadt, Heinz. "Gesichter Babylons: Zum Bild der Grossstadt im modernen amerikanischen Roman." *Jahrbuch für Amerikastudien* 16 (1971): pp. 60–76.

Inge, M. Thomas. "James Baldwin's Blues." *Notes on Contemporary Literature,* 2, IV (1972): 8–11.

Isaacs, Harold R. "Five Writers and Their African Ancestors." *Phylon* 21 (Winter, 1960): 322–29.

Ivy, James W. "The Fairie Queen: Review of *Giovanni's Room." Crisis* 64 (February, 1957): 123.

————. "Review of *Nobody Knows My Name." Crisis* 68 (October, 1961): 522.

Jackson, Blyden. "The Continuing Strain: Résumé of Negro Literature in 1955." *Phylon* 17 (First Quarter, 1956): 35–40.

Jacobson, Dan. "James Baldwin as Spokesman." *Commentary,* December, 1961, pp. 497–502.

Jarrett, Thomas D. "Search for Identity." *Phylon* 17 (First Quarter, 1956): 87–88.

Jones, B. B. "James Baldwin: The Struggle for Identity." *British Journal of Sociology,* XVII (June, 1966): 107–121.

Jones, Mary E. "CAAS Bibliography No. 5: James Baldwin," pp. 1–20. Mimeographed, Atlanta: Atlanta University's Center for African and African-American Studies, n. d.

Jordan, Jennifer. "Cleaver vs. Baldwin: Icing the White Negro." *Black Books Bulletin.* Chicago: Institute of Positive Education, 1:2 (Winter, 1972): 12–15.

Karp, David. "A Squalid World." *Saturday Review,* December 1, 1956, p. 34.

Kattan, Naim. "Deux écrivains americains." [Malamud and Baldwin] *Ecrits du Canada Francais* 17 (1964): 87–135.

————. "L'éclatement du mythe." *Quinzaine Litteraire* 126 (October, 1971): 12.

Kauffman, Stanley. "Another Baldwin." *New York Times Book Review,* December 12, 1965, p. 5.

Kazin, Alfred. "Close to Us." *Reporter,* August 17, 1961, pp. 58–60.

————. "The Essays of James Baldwin." In *Contemporaries,* pp. 254–58. Boston: Little, Brown and Company, 1962.

————. "Bothers Crying Out for More Access to Life." *Saturday Review,* October 2, 1971, pp. 33–35.

Keller, Joseph. "Black Writing and the White Critic." *Negro American Literature Forum,* 3 (Winter, 1970): 103–10.

Kent, George E. "Baldwin and the Problem of Being." *CLA Journal* 7 (March, 1964): 202–14.

————. "Struggle for the Image: Selected Books By or About Blacks During 1971." *Phylon* 33 (Winter, 1972): 304–23.

Killens, John Oliver. "Broadway in Black and White." *African Forum* 1 (Winter, 1966): 66–76.

Kim, Kichung. "Wright, the Protest Novel, and Baldwin's Faith." *CLA Journal* 17 (March, 1974): 387–96.

Kindt, Kathleen A. "James Baldwin: A Checklist, 1947–1962." *Bulletin of Bibliography* 24 (January-April, 1965): 123–26.

Klein, Marcus. "James Baldwin: A Question of Identity." In *After Alienation: American Novels in Mid-Century,* pp. 147–95. New York: World Publishing Company, 1962.

Langer, Johannes. "James Baldwin." *Ry Højskoles julehilsen* (1968), pp. 25–31.

Langer, Lawrence. "To Make Freedom Real: James Baldwin and the Conscience of America." *Americana-Austriaca* 58: 217–28.

Larry 5X. "Baldwin 'Baptised' in Fire This Time." *Muhammad Speaks,* February 23, 1973, p. 25.

Lash, John. "A Long, Hard Look at the Ghetto: A Critical Summary of Literature By and About Negroes in 1956." Phylon 18 (First Quarter, 1957): 7–24.

_____. "Baldwin Beside Himself: A Study in Modern Phallicism." *CLA Journal* 8 (December, 1964): 132–40.

Leaks, Sylvester. "James Baldwin—I Know His Name." *Freedomways,* III (Winter, 1963): 102–105.

Lee, Brian. "James Baldwin: Caliban to Prospero." In *The Black American Writer,* ed. C. W. E. Bigsby. Vol. 1, pp. 169–79. Baltimore: Penguin Books, 1971.

Lee, Robert A. "James Baldwin and Matthew Arnold: Thoughts on 'Relevance'." *CLA Journal* 14 (March, 1971): 324–30.

Levant, Howard. "Aspiring We Should Go." *Midcontinent American Studies Journal* 4 (Fall, 1963): 3–20.

Levin David. "James Baldwin's Autobiographical Essays: The Problem of Negro Identity." *Massachusetts Review* 5 (Winter, 1964): 239–47.

Lewis, Theophilus. "Blues for Mr. Charlie." *America* 110 (May 30, 1964): 776–77.

_____. *"The Amen Corner." America* 112 (May 8, 1965): 690.

Littlejohn, David. "Exemplary and Other Baldwins." *Nation,* December 13, 1965, pp. 478–80.

_____. *Black on White: A Critical Survey of Writing by American Negroes,* pp. 72–74, 119–37. New York: Grossman, 1966.

Llorens, David. "Books Noted" *[Tell Me How Long the Train's Been Gone]. Black World,* August, 1968, p. 51.

Long, Richard A., Eugenia W. Collier, eds. *Afro-American Writing: An Anthology of Prose and Poetry.* Vol. 2, pp. 619–31. New York: New York University Press, 1972.

Long, Robert Emmet. "From Elegant to Hip." *Nation,* June 10, 1968, pp. 769–70.

_____. "The Vogue of Gatsby's Guest List." *Fitzgerald-Hemingway Annual* (1969), pp. 23–25.

_____. "Love and Wrath in the Fiction of James Baldwin." *English Record* 19, iii: 50–57.

Lottman, Herbert R. "It's Hard to Be James Baldwin: An Interview." *Intellectual Digest,* July, 1972, pp. 67–68.

Lucas, Lawrence E. *"The Amen Corner." Catholic World,* June, 1965, pp. 215–16.

Macauley, Robie. "The Pre-empted Domain." *Saturday Review,* June 4, 1966, pp. 20–21.

McCarten, John. "Grim Stuff." *New Yorker,* May 9, 1964, p. 143.

_____. "Tabernacle Blues." *New Yorker,* April 24, 1965, p. 85.

McCudden, John. "James Baldwin's Vision" [Reply to James Finn]. *Commonweal*, October 11, 1963, pp. 75–76.

Macdonald, Dwight. "The Bright Young Man in the Arts." *Esquire*, September, 1958, pp. 38–40.

McDonnell, Thomas. "The Emergence of the Negro in Literature." *Critic* 20 (December, 1961–January, 1962): 31–34.

Macebuh, Stanley. *James Baldwin: A Critical Study*. New York: The Third Press. Joseph Okpaku Publishing Company, Inc., 1973.

MacInnes, Colin. "Dark Angel: The Writings of James Baldwin." *Encounter*, August, 1963, pp. 22–33.

McWhirt, William A. "After Years of Futility Baldwin Explodes Again." *Life*, July 30, 1971, p. 63.

Madden, David. "The Fallacy of The Subject-Dominated Novel." *English Record* 18 (April, 1968): 11–19.

Mailer, Norman. *Advertisement for Myself*, pp. 471–72. New York: G. P. Putnam's Sons, 1959.

———. "Norman Mailer vs. Nine Writers." *Esquire*, July, 1963, p. 63.

Malcolm, Donald. "The Author in Search of Himself." *New Yorker*, November 25, 1961, pp. 233–34.

Marcus, Steven. "The American Negro in Search of Identity." *Commentary*, November, 1953, pp. 456–63.

Margolies, Edward. "The Negro Church: James Baldwin and the Christian Vision." In *Native Sons*, pp. 102–26. Philadelphia: J. B. Lippincott Company, 1968.

Markholt, Ottilie. "White Critic, Black Playwright: Water and Fire." *Negro Digest*, April, 1967, pp. 54–60.

Materassi, Mario. "James Baldwin, un profeta del nostro temp (con un breve inedito)." *Ponte* 22: 359–69.

May, John R. "Images of Apocalypse in the Black Novel." *Renascence*, 23, No. 1 (Autumn, 1970): 31–45.

Mayfield, Julian. "A Love Affair with the United States." *New Republic*, August 7, 1961, p. 25.

———. "And Then Came Baldwin." *Freedomways* 3 (1963): 143–55.

Mead, Margaret. *"A Rap on Race:* How James Baldwin and I Talked a Book." *Redbook*, September, 1971, pp. 70–72.

Mellard, James M. "Racism, Formula, and Popular Fiction." *Journal of Popular Culture*, 5, No. 1 (Summer, 1971): 10–37.

Mergen, Bernard. "James Baldwin and the American Conundrum." *Moderna Sprak* 57, 4 (1963): 397–405.

Merideth, Robert. "The Revival of *Uncle Tom's Cabin"* (Review-Article). *Phylon* 24 (Fall, 1963): 300–302.

Meriwether, L. M. "James Baldwin: Fiery Voice of the Negro Revolt." *Negro Digest*, August, 1963, pp. 3–7.

———. *"The Amen Corner."* *Negro Digest*, January, 1965, pp. 40–47.

Merton, Thomas. "The Negro Revolt." *Jubilee*, September, 1963, pp. 39–43.

———. "La Revolution Noire." *Revue Nouvelle* 39 (February, 1964).

Meserve, Walter. "James Baldwin's 'Agony Way'." In *The Black American Writer*, ed. C. W. E. Bigsby. Vol. 2, pp. 171–86. Baltimore: Penguin Books, 1971.

Mitchell, Lofton. *Black Drama: The Story of the American Negro in the Theatre.* New York: Hawthorne Books, 1967.

Mitra, B. K. "The Wright-Baldwin Controversy." *Indian Journal of American Studies* 1 (1969): pp. 101–05.

Moore, John Rees. "An Embarrassment of Riches: Baldwin's *Going to Meet the Man.*" *Hollins Critic* 2 (December, 1965): pp. 1–12.

Morrison, Allan. "The Angriest Young Man." *Ebony,* October, 1961, pp. 23–30.

_____. "James Baldwin, Protest Fiction, and the Blues Tradition." In *The Omni-Americans,* by Albert Murray, pp. 142–68. New York: Outerbridge and Dienstfrey, 1970.

Morsberger, Robert E. "Segregated Surveys: American Literature." *Negro American Literature Forum* 4 (March, 1970): 3–8.

Moten, Etta. *"Another Country:* Review." *Muhammad Speaks,* July 15, 1962, p. 23.

Mowe, Gregory, and W. Scott Nobles. "James Baldwin's Message for White America." *Quarterly Journal of Speech, 58,* No. 2 (April, 1972): 142–51.

Murray, Albert. "Something Different, Something More." In *Anger, and Beyond,* ed. Herbert Hill, pp. 112–37. New York: Harper & Row, 1966.

Neal, Lawrence P. "The Black Writers' Role: James Baldwin." *Liberator,* April, 1966, pp. 10–11, 18.

Newman, Charles. "The Lesson of the Master: Henry James and James Baldwin." *Yale Review* 56 (October, 1966): 45–59.

Nichols, Charles H. "New Calvinism." *Commentary,* January, 1957, pp. 94–96.

_____. "Color, Conscience and Crucifixion: A Study of Racial Attitudes in American Literature and Criticism." *Jahbuch ·fur Amerikastudien* 6 (1961): pp. 37–47.

_____. "James Baldwin: A Skillful Executioner" (Review-Article). *Studies on the Left* 2 (Winter, 1963): 74–79.

Noble, David. *The Eternal Adam and the New World Garden.* New York: George Braziller, 1968.

Nower, Joyce. "The Traditions of Negro Literature in the United States." *Negro American Literature Forum* 3 (Spring, 1969): 5–12.

_____. "Cleaver's Vision of America and the New White Radical: A Legacy of Malcolm X." *Negro American Literature Forum* 4 (March, 1970): 12–21.

Nyren, Dorothy. "Baldwin, James." In *A Library of Literary Criticism,* ed. Dorothy Nyren, pp. 32–34. New York: Frederick Unger Publishing Company, 1961.

O'Brien, Conor Cruise. "White Gods and Black Americans." *New Statesman,* 67 (May 1, 1964): 681–682.

O'Daniel, Therman B. "James Baldwin: An Interpretive Study." *CLA Journal* 7 (September, 1963): 37–47.

Ognibene, Elain R. "Black Literature Revisited: 'Sonny's Blues'." *English Journal* 60 (January, 1971): 36–37.

Palosaari, Ronald G. "The Image of the Black Minister in the Black Novel from Dunbar to Baldwin." *Dissertation Abstracts International* (University of Minnesota) 32 (1970): 394A–395A.

Patterson, H. Orlando. "The Essays of James Baldwin." *New Left Review* 26, (Summer, 1964), pp. 31–38.

Petersen, Fred. "James Baldwin and Eduardo Mallea: Two Essayists' Search for

Identity." *Discourse* 10: 97–107.

Phillips, Louis. "The Novelist as Playwright: Baldwin, McCullers, and Bellow." In *Modern American Drama: Essays in Criticism.* Deland, Florida: Everett/Edwards, 1968.

Pickrel, Paul. "Outstanding Novels." *Yale Review,* n. s., 42 (Summer, 1953): X.

Plessner, Monika. "James Baldwin und das land der Verheissung: Zwischen Farbsymbolik und Farbindifferenz." *Merkur* 20: 515–33.

Plummer, Wayne. "Baldwin's Burden." *The Christian Century,* 80 (1963): 1057.

Podhoretz, Norman. "The Article as Art." In *Doings and Undoings,* pp. 126–42. New York: Farrar, Straus & Company, 1964.

————. "In Defense of Baldwin." In *Doings and Undoings,* pp. 244–50. New York: Farrar, Straus & Company, 1964.

Poore, Charles. "Books of the Times." *New York Times,* July 15, 1961, p. 17.

————. "Books of the Times." *New York Times,* June 26, 1962, p. 13.

Popkin, Henry. *"Blues for Mister Charlie,* "dramatic journalism." *Vogue,* July, 1964, p. 32.

Potter, Vilma. "Baldwin and Odets: The High Cost of 'Crossing'." *CES* 1, iii (1965): 17–41.

Pratt, Louis H. "James Baldwin and 'The Literary Ghetto.' " *CLA Journal* 20 (December, 1976): 262–72.

Prescott, Orville. "Books of the Times." *New York Times,* May 19, 1953, p. 17.

Preston, Malcolm, ed. "The Image: Three Views." *Opera News,* December 8, 1962, pp. 8–12.

Raddatz, Fritz J. "Schwarz ist die Farbe der Einsamkeit: Skizze zu einer Porträt James Baldwin." *Frankfurter Hefte* 20: 44–52.

Raleigh, J. H. "Messages and Sagas." *New Republic,* June 22, 1953, p. 21.

Ranier, D. "Rage Into Order." *Commonweal,* January 13, 1956, pp. 384–86.

Redding, Saunders. "Sensitive Portrait of a Lonely Boy." *New York Herald Tribune Book Review,* May 17, 1953, p. 5

————. "James Baldwin Miscellany." *New York Herald Tribune Book Review,* February 26, 1956, p. 4.

————. "In His Native Land." *New York Herald Tribune Lively Arts,* June 25, 1961, p. 36.

————. "The Problems of the Negro Writer." *Massachusetts Review* 6 (Autumn-Winter, 1964–1965): 57–70.

Reid, Kenneth R. "James Baldwin's Fiction: Literary Artistry in Special Pleading." Dissertation, Kansas State University. *Dissertation Abstracts International,* 33 (November-December, 1972): 2392-A.

Reilly, John M. " 'Sonny's Blues' : James Baldwin's Image of Black Community." *Negro American Literature Forum* 4 (July, 1970): 56–60.

Rolo, Charles. "Other Voices, Other Rooms." *Atlantic Monthly,* December, 1956, p. 98.

————. "Questions of Color." *Atlantic Monthly,* July, 1961, pp. 126–28.

Root, Robert. "It's a Wasteland." *Christian Century* 79 (1962): 1354–55.

Roth, Phillip. "Channel X: Two Plays on the Race Conflict." *New York Review of Books,* May 28, 1964, pp. 10–13.

Sayre, Robert. "James Baldwin's Other Country." In *Contemporary American*

Novelists, ed. Harry T. Moore, pp. 158–69. Carbondale: Southern Illinois University Press, 1964.

Schatt, Stanley. "You Must Go Home Again: Today's Afro-American Expatriate Writers." *Negro American Literature Forum* 7 (Fall, 1973): 80–82.

Scheller, Bernhard. "Die Gestalt des Farbigen bei Williams, Albee und Baldwin und ihre szenische Realisierung in DDR-Aufführungen." *Zeitschrift für Anglistick und Amerikanistik* (East Berlin).

Schlesinger, Arthur M., Jr. *A Thousand Days: John F. Kennedy in the White House,* pp. 956–62. Boston: Houghton Mifflin Company, 1965.

Schraufnagel, Noel. *From Apology to Protest: The Black American Novel.* Deland, Florida: Everett/Edwards, Inc., 1973.

Schrero, Elliot M. *"Another Country* and the Sense of Self." *Black Academy Review* 2, 1–2 (Spring-Summer, 1971): 91–100.

Schroth, Raymond A. "James Baldwin's Search." *Catholic World,* February, 1964, pp. 288–94.

Scott, Nathan A., Jr. "Judgment Marked by a Cellar: The American Negro Writer and the Dialectic of Despair." *Denver Quarterly* 2 (Summer, 1967): 5–35.

Scott, Robert L. "Rhetoric, Black Power, and Baldwin's *Another Country." Journal of Black Studies* 1 (September, 1970): 21–34.

Shayon, R. L. "T. V. and Radio." *Saturday Review,* February 24, 1962, p. 35.

Sheed, Wilfred. "Amen, Amen." *Commonweal,* May 7, 1965, pp. 221–22.

_____. "James Baldwin: *Tell Me How Long the Train's Been Gone."* In *The Morning After: Selected Essays and Reviews,* pp. 76–78. New York: Farrar, Straus & Giroux, 1971.

Silvera, Frank. "Toward a Theater of Understanding." *Negro Digest,* April, 1969, pp. 33–35.

Simmons, Harvey G. "James Baldwin and the Negro Conundrum." *Antioch Review* 23 (Summer, 1963): 250–55.

Singh, Raman K. "The Black Novel and Its Tradition." *Colorado Quarterly* 20 (Summer, 1971): 23–29.

Southern, Terry. "When Film Gets Good . . . " *Nation,* November 17, 1962, pp. 331–32.

Southwick, Albert B. "James Baldwin's Jeremiad." *Christian Century* 82 (March 24, 1965): 362–64.

Spector, Robert D. "Everybody Knows His Name." *New York Herald Tribune Book Review,* June 17, 1962, p. 3.

Spender, Stephen. "James Baldwin: Voice of a Revolution." *Partisan Review* 30 (Summer, 1963): 256–60.

Spingarn, Arthur B. "Notes of a Native Son." *Crisis* 63 (February, 1956): 87.

Standley, Fred L. "James Baldwin: The Crucial Situation." *South Atlantic Quarterly* 65 (Summer, 1966): 371–81.

_____. "James Baldwin: A Checklist, 1963–1967." *Bulletin of Bibliography* 25 (1968): 135.

_____. "James Baldwin: The Artist as Incorrigible Disturber of the Peace." *Southern Humanities Review* 4 (Winter, 1970): 18–30.

_____. *"Another Country,* Another Time." *Studies in the Novel* 4 (Fall, 1972): 504–12.

Stanton, Robert. "Outrageous Fiction: *Crime and Punishment,* and *Native Son.*" *Pacific Coast Philology* 4 (April, 1969): 52–58.

Starke, Catherine Juanita. *Black Portraiture in American Fiction,* pp. 121, 204–07, 222–25. New York: Basic Books, 1971.

Steinem, Gloria. "James Baldwin, An Original." *Vogue,* July, 1964, p. 78.

Stephens, Martha. "Richard Wright's Fiction: A Reassessment." *Georgia Review* 25 (Winter, 1971): 450–70.

Stevenson, David L. "The Activists." *Daedalus* 92 (Spring, 1963): 238–49.

Stone, Edward. "The Two Faces of America." *Ohio Review,* 13, No. 2 (1972): pp. 5–11.

Strong, Augusta. "Notes on James Baldwin." *Freedomways* 2 (Spring, 1962): 167–71.

Strout, Cushing. *"Uncle Tom's Cabin* and the Portent of Millenium." *Yale Review* 57 (Spring, 1968): 375–85.

Sullivan, J. F. "Fatal Ambiguity," *Commonweal,* 1956, p. 318.

Taubmann, Robert. "Early Sartre." *New Statesman,* July 13, 1962, p. 53.

Thelwell, Mike. *"Another Country:* Baldwin's New York Novel." In *The Black American Writer,* ed. C. W. E. Bigsby, Vol. 1, pp. 181–98. Baltimore: Penguin Books, 1971.

Thompson, John. "Baldwin: The Prophet as Artist." *Commentary,* June, 1968, pp. 67–69.

Thompson, Thomas. "Magical 11th-Hour Save: *The Amen Corner.*" *Life,* May 14, 1965, p. 16.

Trout, Lawana. "The Teaching of Protest and Propaganda Literature." *Negro American Literature Forum* 2 (Fall, 1968): 46–52.

Turner, Darwin T. *"The Negro Novel in America:* In Rebuttal." *CLA Journal* 10 (December, 1966): 122–34.

————. *Black American Literature: Essays, Poetry, Fiction, Drama,* pp. 113–19, 393–09. Columbus: Charles E. Merrill, Publishing Company, 1970.

Turpin, Waters. "The Contemporary American Negro Playwright." *CLA Journal* 9 (September, 1965): 12–24.

Tuttleton, James W. "The Negro Writer as Spokesman." In *The Black American Writer,* ed. C. W. E. Bigsby, Baltimore: Penguin Books, Inc., 1971. Two Volumes: Vol. I: pp. 245–259. Deland, Florida: Everett/Edwards, 1969.

Ulman, Ruth. "James Baldwin: Biographical Sketch." *Wilson Library Bulletin* 33 (February, 1959): 392.

Utley, Francis Lee. "The Morality of Rhetoric." *CEA Critic* 32 (March, 1970): 11–14.

Van Sickle, Milton. "James Baldwin, in Black and White." *Trace,* 54 (Autumn, 1964): 222–25.

Wade, Melvin, and Margaret Wade. "The Black Aesthetic in the Black Novel." *Journal of Black Studies* 2 (June, 1972): 391–408.

Walters, Raymond. "The Critics Separate the Wheat from Chaff." *Saturday Review,* June 20, 1953, p. 13.

Watkins, Mel. "The Fire Next Time This Time." *New York Times Book Review,* May 28, 1972.

Watson, Edward A. "The Novels of James Baldwin: Case-Book of a 'Lover's War' with the United States." *Queen's Quarterly* 72: 385–402.

Webster, H. C. "Community of Pride." *Saturday Review,* May 16, 1953, p. 14.

West, Anthony. "Sorry Lives." *New Yorker,* June 20, 1953, p. 85.

Whalen, Marcella. "Dear James Baldwin." *National Review,* August 13, 1963, p. 120.

Williams, Sherley Anne. "The Black Muscian: The Black Hero as Light Bearer." In *Give Birth to Brightness.* pp. 145–166. New York: Dial Press, 1972.

Wills, Gary. "What Color is God?" *National Review,* May 21, 1963, pp. 408–14.

Winslow, Henry F. "Church Sermon." *Crisis* 60 (1953): 637–38.

_____. "They Speak of Brotherhood." *Crisis* 63 (1956): 375–77.

Wolff, Geoffrey. "Muffled Voices." *Newsweek,* May 24, 1971, p. 100.

Wüstenhagen, Heinz. "James Baldwin's Essays und Romane: Versuch einer ersten Einschatzung." *Zeitschrift für Anglistik und Amerikanistik* 13, 2 (1965): 117–57.

Zeitlow, Edward R. "Wright to Hansberry: The Evolution of Outlook in Four Negro Writers." *Dissertation Abstracts International* 28: 701.

Notes on Contributors

SHIRLEY S. ALLEN, Associate Professor of English at the Hartford branch of the University of Connecticut, is a graduate of Carleton College with a B.A. degree, and holds M.A. and Ph.D. degrees from Bryn Mawr College. She is the author of a book on Shakespearean stage history entitled *Samuel Phelps and Sadler's Wells Theatre,* published, in 1971, by the Wesleyan University Press.

A. RUSSELL BROOKS is the retired Chairman of the English Department at Kentucky State University. He is a graduate of Morehouse College, and holds M.A. and Ph.D. degrees from the University of Wisconsin. In addition, he attended Extra-mural Lectures at Cambridge University during one summer, and studied for a year at the University of Edinburgh. The author of many articles, he is also author of *James Boswell* in the Twayne's English Authors series.

SAM BLUEFARB is Associate Professor of English at the Los Angeles Harbor College, and author of *The Escape Motif in the American Novel: Mark Twain to Richard Wright.* He holds a bachelor's degree from UCLA, an M.S. in Library Science from the University of Southern California, and a Ph.D. degree in English from the University of New Mexico. His articles have appeared in the *English Journal, Accent, Trace, The Realist, College English,* the *CLA Journal, Drama Survey, Studies in Short Fiction, Negro American Literature Forum, Conradiana,* and other publications.

EUGENIA W. COLLIER, a graduate of Howard and Columbia universities, teaches English at the Community College of Baltimore, where, in collaboration with four colleagues, she authored *A Bridge to Saying It Well,* a freshman textbook. More recently, she has co-edited, with Professor Richard A. Long of Atlanta University,

Afro-American Writing: An Anthology of Prose and Poetry. Her research articles have appeared in *Phylon,* the *CLA Journal,* and *Black World,* and her fiction and poetry in *Negro Digest* and *Black World.* Her 1969 *Negro Digest* short story "Marigolds" won the fiction prize in the first Gwendolyn Brooks Literary Awards.

WILLIAM EDWARD FARRISON, Professor Emeritus, North Carolina Central University, is author of the definitive biography *William Wells Brown: Author and Reformer,* and editor of the Citadel Press editions of Brown's *Clotel or, The President's Daughter,* and Brown's *The Negro in the American Rebellion.* A *magna cum laude* graduate of Lincoln University in Pennsylvania, he holds an M.A. degree from the University of Pennsylvania and a Ph.D. degree from Ohio State University. A frequent contributor of articles and book reviews to scholarly publications, Professor Farrison is also co-editor, with Hugh M. Gloster and the late Nathaniel P. Tillman, of *My Life, My Country, My World: College Readings for Modern Living.*

NICK AARON FORD, Emeritus Professor of English at Morgan State University, is a former president of the College Language Association, a former department head, and a charter member of the NCTE Commission on the Profession. A graduate of Benedict College, he holds M.A. and Ph.D. degrees from the University of Iowa. He is the author of four books, the editor of another one, and the co-author of three others, including *Basic Skills for Better Writing* and *Extending Horizons.* His articles have appeared in *College English, The English Journal, Teachers College Record, New England Quarterly,* the *CLA Journal,* and other scholarly publications. His two latest books are *Black Insights,* an anthology, and *Black Studies: Threat or Challenge?*

DONALD B. GIBSON, Professor of English at Rutgers University, is author of *The Fiction of Stephen Crane* and editor of *Five Black Writers: Essays on Wright, Ellison, Baldwin, Hughes, and LeRoi Jones.* After earning two degrees at the University of Kansas City and a Ph.D. at Brown University, Professor Gibson was a Fulbright Lecturer in American Literature at Jagiellonian University, in Cracow, Poland, for two years, and a summer lecturer, in 1965, at the American Studies Seminar in Falkenstein, Germany. His latest book is *Modern Black Poets: A Collection of Critical Essays.*

JOHN V. HAGOPIAN is Professor of English at Harpur College, Binghamton, New York. He is a graduate of Wayne University with B.A. and M.A. degrees, and holds a Ph.D. degree from Western Reserve University, where he wrote a dissertation on "The Morphology of John Donne." Before joining the faculty at Harpur, he was a Visiting Professor and Fulbright Lecturer at several European universities, and was a member of the English Department at the University of the Saar, in Saarbruecken, Germany. Professor Hagopian is the author of more than thirty scholarly articles, which have appeared in American and foreign journals.

HOBART JARRETT, Professor of English at Brooklyn College, is a graduate of Wiley College, and holds M.A. and Ph.D. degrees in English from Syracuse University. A humanities specialist in the fields of Shakespeare and seventeenth-century literature, he has written and lectured extensively in these fields. During 1973 Professor Jarrett was named a recipient of one of the twenty City University Awards for Excellence in Teaching.

HARRY L. JONES, Professor of English at Morgan State University and Lecturer at the University of Pennsylvania, holds B.A. and M.A. degrees from Howard University and a Ph.D. degree from Catholic University of America, where he wrote his dissertation on Jones Very. He is a former lecturer in world literature at the International Peoples' College, in Elsinore, Denmark. A frequent contributor to the *CLA Journal,* Professor Jones' articles and book reviews have appeared in *Satire Newsletter* and other periodicals.

GEORGE E. KENT, Professor of English at the University of Chicago, is a graduate of Savannah State College and holds M.A. and Ph.D. degrees from Boston University. The author of poems, essays, and fiction, Professor Kent's byline appears regularly in *Black World* and the *CLA Journal.* Having published his book of critical essays, *Blackness and the Adventure of Western Culture,* in 1972, he is now completing a book on William Faulkner.

JOHN S. LASH, Professor of English and Director of Special Projects at Texas Southern University, is a graduate of Livingstone College and holds M.A. and Ph.D. degrees from the University of Michigan. He is the author of many articles and studies in American literature, which have appeared in *College English, Journal of Negro Education, Social Forces, Phylon,* the *Bulletin of Bibliography, Negro History Bulletin,* the *CLA Journal,* and other publications.

ARTHENIA BATES MILLICAN, Professor of English at Norfolk State College, is a graduate of Morris College with a B.A. degree, of Atlanta University with an M.A. degree, and of Louisiana State University with a Ph.D. degree. Talented as a creative writer as well as a teacher and research scholar, she has won awards for her poems and short stories, and is the author of *Seeds Beneath the Snow,* a volume of short stories and sketches. Recently, *The Deity Nodded,* her first novel, has appeared.

CARLTON W. MOLETTE, playwright and drama scholar, is Professor of Speech and Drama and Director of Play Production at Spelman College, Atlanta, Georgia. A graduate of Morehouse College with a B.A. degree, he holds an M.A. degree from the State University of Iowa, and a Ph.D. degree from Florida State University.

THERMAN B. O'DANIEL, editor of this volume, is Professor of English at Morgan State University. One of the founders of the *CLA Journal,* he has been its only editor. A graduate of Lincoln University in Pennsylvania, he holds an M.A. degree from the University of Pennsylvania, and a Ph.D. degree from the University of Ottawa (Canada). He has studied also at Harvard University and Pennsylvania State University, and has been a General Education Board Fellow at the University of Chicago, and a Ford Foundation Fellow at the University of Ottawa. His articles on

Cooper, Melville, Emerson, Hughes, Baldwin, Ellison, and other writers have appeared in *Phylon,* the *CLA Journal,* and other publications. In 1970, he wrote the introduction to Collier Books' reprint of Wallace Thurman's *The Blacker the Berry;* and, in 1971, he edited for the College Language Association and for William Morrow and Company, *Langston Hughes, Black Genius: A Critical Evaluation.*

JACQUELINE E. ORSAGH is a *cum laude* graduate of Cornell University, where she completed her work not only with honors in English but with distinction in all subjects. She holds an M.A. degree from Michigan State University, where she is now a candidate for the Ph.D. degree, and where she also teaches— conducting a writing workshop for students on the sophomore, junior, and senior levels.

PATSY BREWINGTON PERRY is an Associate Professor of English at North Carolina Central University, where she received her B.A. and M.A. degrees. Her Ph.D. degree was earned at the University of North Carolina, at Chapel Hill, where she wrote a dissertation covering the editorial and journalistic career of Federick Douglass. She is currently engaged in research and writing on several aspects of Douglass' career, and one of her articles, "The Literary Content of *Frederick Douglass' Paper Through 1860,"* recently appeared in the *CLA Journal.*

JOHN M. REILLY, a former Woodrow Wilson Fellow and the recipient of a Danforth Teaching Grant, is an Associate Professor of English at the State University of New York at Albany. He is a graduate of West Virginia University, and holds a Ph.D. degree from Washington University, in St. Louis. The author of critical studies of several modern Afro-American authors, he is also the editor of *Twentieth-Century Interpretations of Invisible Man: A Collection of Critical Essays.*

DARWIN T. TURNER, Professor of English and Director of the Institute of Afro-American Culture at the University of Iowa, has published critical studies on Afro-American literature, drama, American literature, and literary criticism in the *CLA Journal, Southern Humanities Review, Massachusetts Review, Mississippi Quarterly, Black World,* and other publications. A Phi Beta Kappa graduate of the University of Cincinnati, he received his M.A. degree there, and a Ph.D. degree from the University of Chicago. He is co-editor of *Images of the Negro,* author of study guides to *The Scarlet Letter* and *Huckleberry Finn,* compiler of *Afro-American Writers,* a bibliography, and author of *Katharsis,* a volume of verse. Also, he is the editor of three companion volumes for black studies: *Black American Literature: Essay, Black American Literature: Fiction,* and *Black American Literature: Poetry;* the editor of *Black Drama in America: An Anthology;* and the author of *In a Minor Chord: Three Afro-American Writers and Their Search for Identity.*

WATERS E. TURPIN, before his death, in 1968, was Professor of English and Associate Director of Drama at Morgan State University, his alma mater. He also held M.A. and Ed.D. degrees from Columbia University, where, among studies in literary history and drama, he did special work in the educational theater. A talented and industrious scholar and creative writer, the late Professor Turpin was the author of numerous research articles and book reviews, of plays, a folk opera, and three novels: *These Low Grounds, O Canaan,* and *The Rootless.*

KENNETH J. ZAHORSKI   is an Associate Professor of English at St. Norbert College, De Pere, Wisconsin. A graduate of Wisconsin State University, River Falls, he holds an M.A. degree from Arizona State University, and a Ph.D. degree from the University of Wisconsin, and has studied, on a National Endowment for the Humanities Grant, in the Institute for Afro-American Culture at the University of Iowa. An active member and office holder in the Wisconsin Council of Teachers of English, he has chaired section meetings and delivered papers at recent conventions. As a consultant for *Choice,* he has submitted numerous reviews and has also contributed critical reviews to the *CLA Journal.*

Index